The Cambridge Companion to Henry David Thoreau is an accessible guide to reading and understanding the works of Thoreau. Presenting essays by a distinguished array of contributors, the *Companion* is a valuable resource for historical and contextual material, whether on early writings such as *A Week on the Concord and Merrimack Rivers,* on the monumental *Walden,* or on his Journal and later writings. It also serves as a biographical guide, offering insights into his publishing career and his brief but extraordinarily original life.

In short, the *Companion* helps the reader to approach Thoreau's writings, as he would say, "deliberately and reservedly," by suggesting how Thoreau uses language, how his biography informs his writing, how personal and historical influences shaped his career, and how his writings function as literary works.

HENRY DAVID THOREAU

Cambridge Companions to Literature

Continued on page following Index

THE CAMBRIDGE
COMPANION TO
HENRY DAVID
THOREAU

EDITED BY

JOEL MYERSON

University of South Carolina

CAMBRIDGE
UNIVERSITY PRESS

PUBLISHED BY THE PRESS SYNDICATE OF THE UNIVERSITY OF CAMBRIDGE
The Pitt Building, Trumpington Street, Cambridge, United Kingdom

CAMBRIDGE UNIVERSITY PRESS
The Edinburgh Building, Cambridge CB2 2RU, UK   http: //www.cup.cam.ac.uk
40 West 20th Street, New York, NY 10011-4211, USA   http: //www.cup.org
10 Stamford Road, Oakleigh, Melbourne 3166, Australia

First published 1995
Reprinted 1996, 1998, 1999

Typeset in Sabon

A catalogue record for this book is available from the British Library

Library of Congress Cataloguing-in-Publication Data is available

ISBN 0-521-44037-8 hardback
ISBN 0-521-44594-9 paperback

Transferred to digital printing 2004

CONTENTS

CONTENTS

CONTRIBUTORS

LAWRENCE BUELL is Professor of English at Harvard University. His publications include *Literary Transcendentalism: Style and Vision in the American Renaissance* and *New England Literary Culture: From Revolution Through Renaissance.*

STEVEN FINK is Associate Professor of English at The Ohio State University. He is the author of several articles on Thoreau and *Prophet in the Marketplace: Thoreau's Development as a Professional Writer.*

LEN GOUGEON is Professor of American Literature at the University of Scranton. He is the author of *Virtue's Hero: Emerson, Antislavery, and Reform* and co-editor, with Joel Myerson, of *Emerson's Anti-Slavery Writings.* He is currently at work on a study of relationships between New England and British authors as they were affected by the Civil War.

PHILIP F. GURA is Professor of English and Adjunct Professor of American Studies and of Religious Studies at the University of North Carolina at Chapel Hill. His publications include *The Wisdom of Words: Language, Theology, and Literature in the New England Renaissance, A Glimpse of Sion's Glory: Puritan Radicalism in New England, 1620–1660,* and, with Joel Myerson, *Critical Essays on American Transcendentalism.* He is a member of the editorial board of the forthcoming *A History of the Book in America.*

WALTER HARDING is Distinguished University Professor of American Literature Emeritus at the State University of New York, College at Geneseo. For fifty years he was Secretary of the Thoreau Society and editor of its publications. He is the author, among numerous other books, of *The Days of Henry Thoreau, A Thoreau Handbook,* and *The Variorum Walden.*

RONALD WESLEY HOAG is Associate Professor of English at East Carolina University. He has published on Thoreau and other American writers in such places as *ESQ: A Journal of the American Renaissance, Texas Studies in Literature and Language, Studies in the Novel, Modern Fiction Studies, Studies in American Fiction, Southern Literary Journal, Southern Review, Georgia Review*, and *Paris Review*. Editor of the Thoreau Society's *Concord Saunterer*, he is currently writing a book on Thoreau.

LINCK C. JOHNSON is Professor of English at Colgate University. He is the author of *Thoreau's Complex Weave: The Writing of "A Week on the Concord and Merrimack Rivers," with the Text of the First Draft*, the "Historical Introduction" to *A Week* in the Princeton edition of *The Writings of Henry D. Thoreau*, and numerous essays and reviews. He is currently writing a book on Emerson and Thoreau in relation to antebellum reform.

JOSEPH J. MOLDENHAUER holds the Mody C. Boatright Regents Professorship in American and English Literature at the University of Texas in Austin. He has published widely on Thoreau, Poe, and other American writers, and has edited *The Maine Woods, Early Essays and Miscellanies*, and *Cape Cod* in the Princeton edition of *The Writings of Henry D. Thoreau*. His edition of Thoreau's Canadian narrative will appear in *Excursions*.

JOEL MYERSON, Carolina Research Professor of American Literature at the University of South Carolina, is President of the Thoreau Society. The editor of the annual *Studies in the American Renaissance*, his most recent books include *Emerson and Thoreau: The Contemporary Reviews* (editor), *Walt Whitman: A Descriptive Bibliography*, and *Emerson's Anti-Slavery Writings* (co-editor, with Len Gougeon).

LEONARD N. NEUFELDT is Professor of English and Chair of American Studies at Purdue University. His recent publications include *The Economist: Henry Thoreau and Enterprise*, the fourth volume of the Journal in *The Writings of Henry D. Thoreau*, and three volumes of poems: *Raspberrying, Yarrow*, and *Car Failure North of Nimes*.

ROBERT D. RICHARDSON, JR., is the author of *Henry Thoreau: A Life of the Mind*, as well as *Myth and Literature in the American Renaissance* and a forthcoming biography of Emerson. He teaches at Wesleyan University's College of Letters.

ROBERT SATTELMEYER is Professor of English at Georgia State University. He is the author of *Thoreau's Reading* and General Editor of the Journal in *The Writings of Henry D. Thoreau.*

RICHARD J. SCHNEIDER is Professor of English at Wartburg College. He is the author of *Henry David Thoreau* in the Twayne United States Authors Series. He is also the editor of the forthcoming *Approaches to Teaching Thoreau's "Walden" and Other Works.*

ELIZABETH HALL WITHERELL is Editor-in-Chief of *The Writings of Henry D. Thoreau* and Curator of Manuscripts in the Department of Special Collections at the Davidson Library of the University of California at Santa Barbara.

INTRODUCTION

It may seem odd to publish a book of essays whose purpose is to provide strategies for reading the works of Henry David Thoreau. After all, judging from the many editions of Thoreau's works in many languages, Henry has done quite well for himself all these years without needing anyone's help. The question, then, is not whether it is necessary to have help in reading Thoreau – millions have done so on their own – but whether, with help, we can read him better. That is the goal of this book: to help readers read Thoreau better.

Thoreau himself gives us cautionary words about the subject in his chapter on "Reading" in *Walden*, where he warns that "It is not all books that are as dull as their readers" (107). "To read well," he states, "that is, to read true books in a true spirit, is a noble exercise." Moreover, "Books must be read as deliberately and reservedly as they were written" (100–1).

The Cambridge Companion to Henry David Thoreau helps the reader to come to Thoreau's writings "deliberately and reservedly" by suggesting how Thoreau uses language, how his biography informs his writing, how personal and historical influences shaped his career, and how his writings function as literary works.

In the first essay, Walter Harding surveys the development of Thoreau's reputation – from how he was perceived by his contemporaries to the views of more recent academic critics – and in doing so gives the proof to Thoreau's own statement in *Walden* that he had "several more lives to live" (323).

Robert D. Richardson, Jr., sets the background for us by discussing the impact that Concord, Massachusetts, had on Thoreau, who was, of all the famous writers who lived in the town, the only one actually born there. One cannot underestimate the importance of Concord for Thoreau: his masterwork, *Walden*, is set there, and his non-Concord works use the town as a reference point.

Equally important to Thoreau was Concord's leading citizen, Ralph

Waldo Emerson. As editor of the journal the *Dial*, Emerson championed Thoreau, and he was also instrumental in helping him to publish his books. After Thoreau's death in 1862, Emerson published a eulogy of him that has (somewhat negatively) affected our view of Thoreau up to the present. Robert Sattelmeyer shows how the friendship of the two men developed warmly, then splintered, then reformed on a different basis.

Thoreau's "least familiar book," *A Week on the Concord and Merrimack Rivers,* is the subject of Linck C. Johnson's essay, which asks the question, "What kind of book is it?" This question has stumped many readers, who are frustrated with *A Week* because it does not fit neatly into a preexisting literary category. Johnson shows how Thoreau wrote the book and what literary genres it appropriates.

Elizabeth Hall Witherell discusses the small body of poetry that Thoreau left behind – primarily in his Journal, in the *Dial,* and in *A Week* – and how that poetry figured into Thoreau's attempt to develop an "original voice."

Like all published authors, Thoreau wrote for an audience, and Steven Fink helps us to understand it better. Fink defines Thoreau's audience and explains how Thoreau attempted to obtain readers and to influence them; he also shows what Thoreau's expectations of his editors were. These things are important to know, for Thoreau did not write only for himself, but in the context of the marketplace.

Richard J. Schneider takes on the herculean task of helping us to better understand *Walden*. First, he illuminates Thoreau's aims in writing the book. Then, concentrating on Thoreau's skills at organization and his artful use of language, Schneider takes us through the book and suggests strategies for reading it.

Thoreau's longest work – in length of pages and in time spent on it – is his Journal. Leonard N. Neufeldt discusses the general concepts of journals and journal-keeping before taking us on a tour of the "voices" Thoreau employed in his Journal. This is an especially relevant chapter because Thoreau's Journal is now being reedited, and this edition will bring to it a new generation of readers.

Thoreau's two travel books show that his gifts for natural observation were not restricted to Concord. Joseph J. Moldenhauer, in discussing *The Maine Woods,* shows the literary and personal backgrounds to the book, including how Thoreau derived lectures from it, as well as information about its publication. Using a different approach to *Cape Cod,* Philip F. Gura connects this work to Thoreau's other writings, especially *Walden*.

Ronald Wesley Hoag deals with Thoreau's later natural history essays: "Walking," "Autumnal Tints," "Wild Apples," "Huckleberries," "The

Dispersion of Seeds," "Wild Fruits," "A Yankee in Canada," and "The Succession of Forest Trees." Hoag finds that in all of these, there is more to nature than meets our eye and that Thoreau encourages us to see better, "more naturally," than we do.

In discussing Thoreau and the natural environment, Lawrence Buell takes on one of the most salient and contemporary thrusts of Thoreau's writings. Buell shows how Thoreau gradually introduced ecological concerns into his works and how he used nature both as a naturalist and as an artist. Although he concentrates on *Walden*, Buell also gives space to Thoreau's later field biology and scientific study of nature.

Finally, in his chapter on Thoreau and reform, Len Gougeon deals with some of Thoreau's most powerful essays – "The Service," "Paradise (to be) Regained," "Reform and the Reformers," "Herald of Freedom," "Wendell Phillips," "Resistance to Civil Government," "Slavery in Massachusetts," "Life Without Principle," and "A Plea for Captain John Brown" – as he traces Thoreau's evolution from a passive to an active role in the events of his time.

Returning again to the "Reading" chapter of *Walden*, we find Thoreau's interesting definition of literacy: "I confess I do not make any very broad distinction between the illiterateness of my townsman who cannot read at all, and the illiterateness of him who has learned to read only what is for children and feeble intellects" (107). *The Cambridge Companion to Henry David Thoreau* hopes to make its readers more literate by showing the ways in which Thoreau's writings can be approached. We hope we are successful.

1817   July 12: born in Concord, Massachusetts
1818   Family moves to Chelmsford, Massachusetts
1821   Family moves to Boston, Massachusetts
1823   Family returns to Concord, Massachusetts
1827   Writes "The Seasons," his earliest known work
1833   Enters Harvard College
1835   Teaches school in Canton, Massachusetts, between terms
1837   Graduates from Harvard; begins Journal; teaches a short time in Concord public schools; November 25: first publication, an obituary, appears in a Concord paper
1838   Opens private school, where he teaches with his brother, John; delivers first lecture at Concord Lyceum; makes first trip to Maine
1839   Makes trip on Concord and Merrimack rivers with John
1840   July: publishes his first essay, "Aulus Persius Flaccus," and his first poem, "Sympathy," in the *Dial*
1841   Moves in with Ralph Waldo Emerson and his family
1842   January 11: John Thoreau dies
1843   Helps Emerson edit the *Dial*; contributes to *Boston Miscellany* and *Democratic Review*; moves to Staten Island, New York, to tutor William Emerson's children
1844   Accidentally sets fire to Concord Woods
1845   March: begins work on cabin at Walden Pond; July 4: moves into Walden cabin
1846   Arrested for nonpayment of poll tax; makes trip to Maine woods
1847   September: leaves Walden cabin; moves into Emerson's house; contributes to *Graham's Magazine*
1848   January 26: delivers lecture before Concord Lyceum on "The Rights and Duties of the Individual in Relation to Government" ("Resistance to Civil Government"); returns to family home; contributes to *Union Magazine*

1849	May 26: publishes *A Week on the Concord and Merrimack Rivers*; June 14: sister, Helen, dies; publishes "Resistance to Civil Government" in *Aesthetic Papers*; makes first trip to Cape Cod
1850	Makes second trip to Cape Cod; makes trip to Canada
1852	Contributes to *Sartain's Union Magazine*
1853	Makes second trip to Maine Woods; contributes to *Putnam's Monthly Magazine*
1854	August 9: publishes *Walden*
1855	Visits Cape Cod; contributes to *Putnam's Monthly Magazine*
1856	Meets Walt Whitman in Brooklyn
1857	Travels to Cape Cod and Maine Woods; meets Captain John Brown
1858	Visits the White Mountains and Mount Monadnock; contributes to *Atlantic Monthly*
1859	February 3: his father dies
1860	Contracts the cold that leads to his fatal illness
1861	Visits Minnesota
1862	May 6: dies in Concord
1863	*Excursions*, edited by his sister Sophia and Ralph Waldo Emerson, is published
1864	*The Maine Woods*, edited by Sophia Thoreau and Ellery Channing, is published
1865	*Cape Cod*, edited by Sophia Thoreau and Channing, and *Letters to Various Persons*, edited by Emerson, are published
1866	*A Yankee in Canada, with Anti-Slavery and Reform Papers*, edited by Channing and Sophia Thoreau, is published
1873	The first book-length biography, Ellery Channing's *Thoreau: The Poet-Naturalist*, is published
1881	*Early Spring in Massachusetts*, edited by H. G. O. Blake, is published
1884	*Summer*, edited by Blake, is published; *Walden* is first published in England
1888	*Winter*, edited by Blake, is published
1889	*A Week on the Concord and Merrimack Rivers* is first published in England
1892	*Autumn*, edited by Blake, is published
1894	Eleven-volume Riverside edition, the first collected edition of Thoreau's writings, is published
1906	Twenty-volume Walden edition of Thoreau's writings is published, including fourteen volumes of the Journal

ABBREVIATIONS

CC	*Cape Cod*
Corr	*Correspondence*
EEM	*Early Essays and Miscellanies*
J	*Journal* (in 1906 Walden edition)
MW	*The Maine Woods*
PJ	*Journal* (in the Princeton edition)
RP	*Reform Papers*
Reading	Sattelmeyer, *Thoreau's Reading*
W	*Walden*
Week	*A Week on the Concord and Merrimack Rivers*

Full bibliographical citations may be found in the "Further reading" section.

THE CAMBRIDGE
COMPANION TO
HENRY DAVID THOREAU

I

WALTER HARDING

Thoreau's reputation

Thoreau's reputation is unique. It has a pattern all its own, filled with paradoxes and contradictions, and widely vacillating from decade to decade. In his own day he was generally dismissed as a minor writer who would soon be forgotten; yet in our day he is universally recognized as one of the few American writers of the nineteenth century who deserve the appellation "great." But the progress of his reputation has not been steady.

Aside from a bit piece that he published anonymously in a local Concord newspaper in 1837, just after graduating from Harvard, he broke into print in the pages of the Transcendentalist *Dial* in 1840, where his neighbor and mentor Ralph Waldo Emerson pressured the editor, Margaret Fuller, to print some of his early essays and poems. Later, after Emerson himself took over the editorship of the *Dial,* he included more of Thoreau's short works. Other than an occasional bit of praise in some newspaper reviews, they achieved little notice and were generally dismissed as just another effusion of another of Emerson's many minor disciples. One of the earliest published evaluations of Thoreau's writing, James Russell Lowell's *A Fable for Critics* (1848), dismissed him as one who had "stolen all his apples from Emerson's orchard" and urged him to strike out on his own. This was a charge that would haunt Thoreau's literary career not only throughout his lifetime, but well into the twentieth century, even though it would be difficult to think of an author more ruggedly independent, or one who more fiercely prided himself on his distinct individualism than Henry Thoreau. Ironically, although Emerson's intentions were of the best, it has been suggested that in the long run he probably hindered the development of Thoreau's literary career rather than enhanced it, for he encouraged Thoreau in his early works to follow the styles and philosophy of the Transcendentalists, and it was only when Thoreau began to break out of that mold that he began to attract attention on his own.[1]

By 1843 Thoreau was able to place essays in the *Boston Miscellany* and the *Democratic Review,* but it was through his becoming acquainted with

Horace Greeley, the editor of the *New York Tribune,* late that year that he began achieving wider recognition. Greeley encouraged him to write on more popular subjects and then, acting as his agent, placed these works in such magazines of national circulation as *Graham's, Sartain's,* and *Putnam's.* What is more, Greeley went out of his way to praise these essays in the pages of his *Tribune* to be sure they were noticed.

When, while at Walden Pond, Thoreau wrote his first book, *A Week on the Concord and Merrimack Rivers,* Emerson urged him to rush it into print. It might have been a much more successful book had Thoreau taken more time to polish it, as he did later with *Walden.* As it was, it was an unmitigated commercial disaster. Of the thousand copies printed by James Munroe of Boston in 1849, only 219 copies were sold, and Thoreau was forced to pay Munroe $290 for printing costs. Although the book received more than twenty reviews, most of them were brief and many were generally unfavorable. The religious journals in particular were offended by Thoreau's "paganism" and the literary critics by the structural problems of the book.[2] Although Munroe had promised and had even advertised in the back pages of *A Week* his plan to publish Thoreau's *Walden* "soon," the failure of *A Week* caused Munroe to withdraw his offer, and it was another five years before Thoreau could persuade another publisher to issue *Walden.* By then it was a vastly different and improved book.

Thoreau was early active in the antislavery movement, but that fact did not endear him to many of his neighbors, who already dismissed him as a ne'er-do-well who wasted his time and Harvard education by living in a "hut" in the woods and wandering daily in the woods and fields of Concord. After he had spent a night in jail for refusing to pay taxes, rather than support a government that condoned slavery, he delivered a lecture before the Concord Lyceum on "The Relation of the Individual to the State." It caught the eye of that Transcendentalist enthusiast Elizabeth Peabody, and she published it under the title "Resistance to Civil Government" in the one and only issue of her *Aesthetic Papers,* in the spring of 1849. Neither the periodical nor Thoreau's essay attracted much attention, and most of the few who did notice it dismissed it as the work of a crank. In a later reincarnation, when it became known as "Civil Disobedience," it was to become one of the most influential political tracts in American history, but in Thoreau's lifetime it was ignored.

The lyceum movement, founded by Josiah Holbrook in the mid-1820s, had become rapidly widely popular in New England, sponsoring lectures to enliven the long winter evenings. Thoreau joined the Concord Lyceum as a child and, soon after returning to Concord from college, began speaking regularly before it. His early attempts were not particularly successful, being too abstract and Transcendental for his audience. But when at his audience's suggestion he began to report on his life at Walden Pond, things changed for the better. He livened up his delivery, and his audiences found his lectures filled with good humor – though a few who missed his wit thought him churlish and grumpy. Nonetheless his good reputation spread, and he began to receive invitations from lyceums outside of Concord, eventually going as far as Portland, Maine, and Philadelphia to lecture. Yet he was never able to arrange the long lecture tours with which some of his friends, such as Emerson, were to earn their livelihood.

To try to stir up more interest in Thoreau's lectures, Horace Greeley in the spring of 1849 editorialized about him in the *Tribune* and followed it up with some concocted correspondence in the "letters to the editor" column, but it apparently had little effect. However, it was just about this time that H. G. O. Blake, a Worcester, Massachusetts, schoolteacher and former Unitarian minister, came across one of Thoreau's early essays in the *Dial* and overnight became Thoreau's first and most ardent disciple. They immediately began a long friendship and correspondence. Whenever Blake received a letter from Thoreau, he would call in a group of his friends and read the letter to them. Soon he began arranging regularly to have Thoreau lecture in Worcester and developed there a circle of friends who did much to boost Thoreau's reputation.

With the postponement of the publication of *Walden*, Thoreau went to work to improve the manuscript, eventually rewriting the text seven times, dramatically strengthening and improving it.[3] The rising firm of Ticknor & Fields in Boston accepted it for publication in 1854 and printed two thousand copies. Although there has grown up a legend that *Walden*, like *A Week*, was ignored on its publication, it actually received nearly one hundred reviews and notices, most of them highly favorable, and it sold all but 256 copies in its first year.

As we have seen, Thoreau was early active in the abolitionist movement, not only speaking out as he had with his "Civil Disobedience," but participating actively in the Underground Railroad aiding runaway slaves in escaping to freedom in Canada. His cabin at Walden Pond, despite tradition, was not a station on the railroad – it was too small to use as a hiding place. But he did make regular use of his parents' home in Concord to hide the fugitives overnight, then steered them on to Canada. When William Lloyd Garrison, the editor of the *Liberator*, called a protest meeting against the Fugitive Slave Law, in Framingham, Massachusetts, on July 4, 1854, Thoreau read a stirring paper, "Slavery in Massachusetts," protesting the shipping of captured slaves back to the South. It was published in both Garrison's *Liberator* and Greeley's *Tribune*.

Thoreau was introduced to Captain John Brown of Osawatomie when Brown toured New England in the winter of 1857 to raise funds for his antislavery activities in Kansas. Then, after Brown struck against Harpers Ferry, in October 1859, in an effort to incite slaves to open rebellion, Thoreau was one of the first in the entire country to speak out in Brown's defense, even though most abolitionists were denouncing Brown as demented. Thoreau called a meeting in Concord's Town Hall to deliver his fiery "Plea for Captain John Brown" and succeeded in winning many to his side; later he repeated the lecture in both Boston and Worcester. He also called a memorial meeting in Concord on the day of Brown's hanging and later wrote a third piece for delivery at Brown's burial. The former two received wide circulation when printed in James Redpath's popular *Echoes of Harper's Ferry* (1860).

While Thoreau had been at Walden in 1846, he took time out for a trip to the Maine Woods with his cousin George Thatcher, paddling the rivers and climbing Mount Katahdin (Ktaadn). Writing up his "excursion," as he liked to call it, he gave it first as a lecture in Concord and then published it in five installments in *Sartain's Union Magazine*. It set a new pattern for him, and he followed it up later with accounts of excursions to Cape Cod, Quebec, and twice more to Maine. Unfortunately, he more than once quarreled with his editors over their editing of his papers, and none of these essays were printed in book form before his death.

Because Thoreau thus published little in his last years of life, the impression has arisen that he had early written himself out. As a matter of fact he was busily engaged in writing right up through his final illness, but, as Emerson said in his eulogy of Thoreau, his writings were on so large a scale that he simply could not complete them. He became particularly involved in botanical studies, both in constructing a phenological chart of the Concord area, or, as he called it, a calendar of the seasons – a project that was never completed nor published – and a study of tree growth, which he delivered as a lecture at the local cattle show in 1860. The latter was published in both the county and the state agricultural reports for the year and also in the pages of the *New York Tribune*. It was Thoreau's one major contribution to scientific literature and is still accepted by botanists today. Subsidiary studies of his in the field have only recently started reaching print, among the most notable a gemlike essay on "Huckleberries" (1970) and "The Dispersion of Seeds" and other late natural history essays now available in *Faith in a Seed* (1993).

When in 1861 Thoreau realized he was dying of tuberculosis, he began a herculean effort to gather, edit, and publish as many as possible of his uncollected and unpublished works in order, as he said, to leave an estate for his widowed mother and unmarried sister. As a result, just after his death, in 1862, a number of his shorter essays, among them some of his now best-known – such as "Walking," "Wild Apples," Autumnal Tints," and "Life Without Principle" – first appeared in the pages of the *Atlantic Monthly,* sponsored by his publisher, Ticknor & Fields. What is more, they brought both *A Week* and *Walden* back into print within weeks of Thoreau's death, and they have never been out of print since.

Thoreau's death inspired astonishingly wide notice for an author who was supposedly so obscure and little-known in his lifetime. Ralph Waldo Emerson preached the eulogy at his funeral, and an expanded version was soon published in the pages of the *Atlantic Monthly;* it has been reprinted regularly ever since and was long the best-known piece ever written about Thoreau. Unfortunately, Emerson believed that Thoreau's greatest claim to fame was as a Stoic, and he tended to overemphasize the cold and the negative in his portrait; indeed, he so overdid it that he inadvertently turned many people away from Thoreau. Several years later when he came to edit Thoreau's *Letters to Various Persons* (1865), he did the same thing again, editing out of the letters anything that showed warmth and human kindness. Basically derogatory essays by James Russell Lowell and Robert Louis Stevenson, both of which attained wide circulation and reprinting, did much to spread a negative picture of Thoreau, even though Stevenson later recanted his position.

Meanwhile, however, Thoreau's family and friends were able to persuade Ticknor & Fields that there would be a demand if more of Thoreau's unpublished and uncollected works were brought into print. Sophia Thoreau and her brother's closest friend and later biographer Ellery Channing set to work editing them. *Excursions,* a collection of his shorter travel and natural history essays, appeared in 1863, with Emerson's eulogy as an introduction; *The Maine Woods,* in 1864; *Cape Cod* and Emerson's edition of the *Letters* in 1865; a grab-bag miscellany entitled *A Yankee in Canada, with Anti-Slavery and Reform Papers* in 1866; and a newly reset edition of *A Week* in 1868, correcting the hundreds of typographical errors of the first edition. Although their sales were not large, they did serve to keep interest in Thoreau alive.

It was Emerson who, in 1837, persuaded Thoreau to start keeping a daily journal, primarily as a source and practice book for his more formal writings. Both *A Week* and *Walden* were culled and polished largely from this journal. By the early 1850s the Journal began gradually to become for Thoreau an end in itself. Its daily entries expanded greatly and became much more polished and finished. Soon after Thoreau's death his friends began efforts to get at least some of the Journal into print. Bronson Alcott proposed a volume of selections, but his project never got off the ground. Thomas Wentworth Higginson tried to persuade Sophia Thoreau to release the manuscript for publication, but she was convinced it was too personal and private to publish. When Higginson attempted to enlist Judge Rockwood Hoar, one of Concord's leading citizens, Hoar could only ask who would ever read it if it were printed.

Sophia Thoreau willed the manuscript volumes of the Journal to his Worcester disciple H. G. O. Blake. Blake soon developed the habit of gathering all the entries of a certain date together and on that date reading them to a gathering of Thoreau's friends. In the spring of 1878 Blake published in the pages of the *Atlantic* some of these gatherings of selections. It was just at the point when there was a great surge of interest in nature writings and it was nature writing that Blake had emphasized in his selections. Houghton Mifflin, the heirs of Ticknor & Fields, issued *Early Spring in Massachusetts,* a gathering of these spring pieces. They were soon followed by similar volumes: *Summer* in 1884, *Winter* in 1887, and *Autumn* in 1892. Thoreau rose to new heights of popularity.

Houghton Mifflin had been remarkably astute about Thoreau's writings even with little earlier encouragement. It was not until after 1880 that any of Thoreau's works achieved an average annual sale of more than two hundred copies. But in the 1870s Houghton Mifflin bought up all the available Thoreau copyrights from the heirs, and in the 1890s they issued in eleven volumes the first collected edition of Thoreau's works, the Riverside edition – though it sold only 310 sets in that decade.[4]

When Blake died, in 1898, the Thoreau manuscripts were willed to his friend E. Harlow Russell, the principal of the State Normal School in Worcester, Massachusetts. Russell apparently had little other than a monetary interest in them, for he first successfully sued the Thoreau family heirs for their copyrights to the unpublished works and in turn sold those rights to Houghton Mifflin for three thousand dollars. He sold the manuscripts themselves to J. Pierpont Morgan for his New York City library. (Ironically, Morgan cared not one jot for Thoreau, but George Hellman, Russell's agent, insisted Morgan buy the Thoreau manuscripts if he were to obtain the manuscript of Henry Wadsworth Longfellow's "Children's Hour," which he did want and which Hellman owned. Nowadays the Thoreau manuscripts are looked upon as one of the greatest treasures of the Morgan Library.)

Houghton Mifflin, like many other publishers of the time, had been issuing limited "manuscript editions" of their major authors, so called because a leaf of the author's manuscript was included in the first volume.

Professor Bliss Perry of Harvard, a Houghton Mifflin consultant, and Francis H. Allen, a young member of the company's staff who happened to be a Thoreau enthusiast, persuaded the firm to add Thoreau to their list. The Manuscript edition of *The Writings of Henry David Thoreau* came out in 1906 in twenty volumes, fourteen of them the nearly complete Journal, scrupulously edited by Allen (though it was to the then-popular nature writer Bradford Torrey that the credit for editing was assigned). It was limited to six hundred numbered copies, supplemented by the unnumbered Walden edition printed from the same plates but in a less luxurious binding. Although Houghton Mifflin was skeptical of its sales potential, it was sold out before publication. It has been reprinted in its entirety four different times since then, though Houghton Mifflin strangely never bothered to renew the copyright when it expired in 1934.

Although a few copies of the first editions of *A Week* and *Walden* had been shipped to England, neither volume was printed in England until *Walden* was issued by Walter Scott in 1886, and *A Week* in 1889. A. H. Japp, writing under the pseudonym "H. A. Page," had published a rather skimpy Thoreau biography in London in 1878, but it was followed in 1890 by the first good solid life, by Henry Salt, a British Fabian. In the United States, Ellery Channing's biography had been published in 1873, and Franklin B. Sanborn's in 1882, but both were so eccentrically written that they added little to Thoreau's fame or stature. Salt's biography, on the other hand, aroused much interest, particularly among British socialists, for Salt was the first to emphasize that side of Thoreau. Members of the British Labour Party became so interested that they often named their local chapters "Walden Clubs." Indeed, at the turn of the century, there was probably more interest in Thoreau in England than in his own country.

It was Salt who personally introduced Thoreau's works to Mohandas K. Gandhi. Gandhi had come to England to study law and met Salt through their mutual interest in vegetarianism. When Gandhi later settled in South Africa to give legal aid to Indian laborers suffering under segregation laws, he adopted Thoreau's "Civil Disobedience" as a manual of arms in his nonviolent fight for freedom. So great was his success that he was invited back to his native India to lead its campaign for independence from the British throne. Although his progress there was slow, he won international stature and, immediately after World War II, complete freedom for his country. Meanwhile, Count Leo Tolstoi in Russia had discovered the same Thoreau essay and did much to spread its fame among European intellectuals.

In Denmark, in the early days of World War II, "Civil Disobedience" was adopted by the anti-Nazi resistance movement, and Thoreau became a national folk hero. In the 1950s Dr. Martin Luther King, Jr. used the techniques of Thoreau's essay in his battle for equality for African-Americans and made more progress in his fight in a few years than others had in the previous century. King won the Nobel Peace Prize in 1964 for his efforts. Ironically, he, like Gandhi, fell victim to an assassin's violence in the end.

In the late years of the nineteenth century, Franklin Benjamin Sanborn, a Concord resident and acquaintance of Thoreau, set himself up as self-appointed protector of Thoreau's reputation and turned out a vast number of books and articles about Thoreau and his contemporaries. Not only was he extremely careless in recording facts, he also fancied himself superior to Thoreau as a writer and insisted on rewriting much of Thoreau's work that he edited. Fortunately, a small coterie of ardent Thoreau scholars and enthusiasts led by Dr. Samuel Arthur Jones and E. B. Hill of Michigan and Fred Hosmer of Concord worked together to correct some of Sanborn's worst effusions and to establish more accurate facts and editions.[5]

For a period during and after World War I interest in Thoreau went into an eclipse of sorts, but with the coming of the Depression of the 1930s suddenly his philosophy of the simple life became usefully appealing and a revival was on. As early as 1913, John Macy, in his popular *Spirit of American Literature,* had emphasized Thoreau's political and economic theories, and in 1927 Vernon Louis Parrington, in his widely influential *Main Currents in American Thought,* furthered that interest in Thoreau.[6]

Although Houghton Mifflin around the turn of the century had helped to popularize Thoreau in the public schools of the country through their Riverside Literature Series of pamphlets, professors of literature on the college and university level showed strikingly little interest in Thoreau. The first doctoral dissertation on Thoreau (unfortunately now lost) had been done at the University of Michigan in 1899 by Ella Knapp, under the direction of Samuel Arthur Jones. Oddly enough, the second, by Helen A. Snyder, appeared in Germany in 1913. The third, Raymond Adams's *Henry Thoreau's Literary Theories and Criticism,* did not appear until 1928. Adams, by issuing an occasional mimeographed "Thoreau Newsletter" in the late 1930s, did much to arouse academic interest and new dissertations began appearing regularly. F. O. Matthiessen's seminal book, *American Renaissance* (1941), for the first time taking Thoreau seriously as a literary artist, launched a whole series of studies of Thoreau's artistry. Outstanding among them was Sherman Paul's *The Shores of America* (1953), still by far the best serious study of Thoreau's ideas. While Thoreau dissertations still continue to flow steadily from the universities, many unfortunately have become so pedantic and picayune that they have had little impact on the general public.

In 1941, I initiated a gathering together of a small group of Thoreau scholars and enthusiasts to organize the Thoreau Society and established the quarterly *Thoreau Society Bulletin*. The society has gradually grown into an international membership of fifteen hundred, and its annual meetings held in Concord, Massachusetts, at the time of Thoreau's birthday in July, are a regular event for Thoreauvians. It is the largest and longest-lived organization of its kind devoted to an American author.

Because so large a portion of Thoreau's writings was not published under his personal supervision during his lifetime, there have long been major problems with the accuracy of his texts. Finally, in the late 1960s, the Modern Language Association, the National Endowment for the Humanities, and Princeton University Press joined efforts and brought together a group of scholars to start work on a new edition of all of Thoreau's works, with texts established by the latest scholarly methods. Eleven volumes have appeared so far, and a total of approximately twenty-five are planned.

Thoreau was slow to be translated into other modern languages, and even today *Walden* and "Civil Disobedience" are the only works of his that have been widely translated.[7] *Walden* appeared in German in 1897, Dutch in 1907, Russian in 1910, Japanese in 1911, French in 1922, Czechoslovakian in 1924, and Italian in 1928. After World War II, interest in Thoreau burgeoned around the world and *Walden* began appearing in virtually every major modern language. Some of the editions were sponsored by the American government. The Indian government, as a tribute to Mahatma Gandhi, sponsored the translation of *Walden* into at least fifteen of the country's major languages.

There has been a particular interest in Thoreau in Japan. *Walden* has been translated into Japanese a great many times. English editions with Japanese footnotes are standard texts in Japanese high schools. Editions of *Walden* are more generally available in Japanese bookstores than in American. A Japanese Thoreau Society was established in 1965, meets regularly twice a year, and publishes its own bulletin. And a great flood of books and articles on Thoreau comes from the Japanese universities.

Interest in Thoreau both in this country and abroad particularly flourished with the growth of student dissent during the Vietnam War. "Civil Disobedience" was translated into many of the major modern languages and became readily available on newsstands not only in the United States but also around Europe and Asia. The United States even issued a commemorative postage stamp in Thoreau's honor in 1967, and "listening to a different drummer" became the mode of the day. The Beat Generation of Jack Kerouac and Allen Ginsberg had idolized Thoreau in the 1950s, and now so did the hippies of the 1960s. As Lawrence Buell has so well pointed out, Thoreau's popularity took on many of the aspects of a cult.[8] Jerome Lawrence and Robert Lee's *The Night Thoreau Spent in Jail* became one of the most widely performed plays of all time.

With the rise of the environmental movement in the 1970s and 1980s, Thoreau became its patron saint. "In wildness is the preservation of the world" became the slogan of the influential Sierra Club, and other slogans from Thoreau became popular bumper-sticker copy. The popular-music star Don Henley, who had discovered *Walden* in high school, started a fund to protect Walden Pond and Walden Woods when he learned that real estate developers were planning to build condominiums and office buildings near the pond; through a series of rock concerts Henley and other performers succeeded in raising many millions of dollars. With the revival of interest in American nature writers, Thoreau became the most quoted of them all.

Thus has been the course of Thoreau's reputation over the years. Ignored at first, he gradually gained recognition in a series of advances based on widely differing appeals – as a nature writer, an economist, a literary artist, an exponent of the simple life, a philosophical anarchist, and an environmentalist. That perhaps is his greatest achievement – his multifaceted appeal. Once nearly forgotten, he is now a household name.

NOTES

1 Steven Fink, *Prophet in the Marketplace* (Princeton: Princeton University Press, 1992), p. 61.
2 Gary Scharnhorst, *Henry David Thoreau: An Annotated Bibliography of Comment and Criticism Before 1900* (New York: Garland, 1992), pp. 13–19. With more than two thousand annotated entries, this volume is an astoundingly comprehensive guide to Thoreau's reputation in the nineteenth century.
3 J. Lyndon Shanley, *The Making of Walden* (Chicago: University of Chicago Press, 1957). Fascinating as a detective story, this volume traces the development of *Walden* through all its various stages and gives the text of the first draft to compare with the final version.
4 Lawrence Buell, "Henry Thoreau Enters the Literary Canon," in *New Essays on "Walden"*, ed. Robert F. Sayre (New York: Cambridge University Press, 1992), p. 36. This article prints many new details on Thoreau's publisher's part in enhancing his reputation.
5 *Toward the Making of Thoreau's Modern Reputation*, ed. Fritz Oehlshlaeger and George Hendrick (Urbana: University of Illinois Press, 1979), passim.
6 Michael Meyer, *Several More Lives to Live: Thoreau's Political Reputation in America* (Westport, Conn.: Greenwood, 1977), passim.

7 *Thoreau Abroad: Twelve Bibliographical Essays,* ed. Eugene F. Timpe (Hamden, Conn.: Shoestring, 1971), studies Thoreau's impact in various foreign countries.
8 Lawrence Buell, "The Thoreauvian Pilgrimage: The Structure of an American Cult," *American Literature* 61 (1989): 175–99, is a fascinating pioneering study of the beginnings of Thoreau worship.

2

ROBERT D. RICHARDSON, JR.

Thoreau and Concord

Thoreau dedicated his genius with such entire love to the fields, hills, and
waters of his native town, that he made them known and interesting to all
reading Americans, and to people over the sea.

Emerson, "Thoreau"

In the entire range of American literature there is no stronger tie between
a writer and a place than the tie between Henry Thoreau and Concord,
Massachusetts. He was born there, on July 12, 1817. He grew up in Concord, returned there after college and, except for the brief time he boarded
on Staten Island, New York, lived in Concord all his life. Concord was his
only home; it provided him with much of his education and most of his
literary subjects. Concord was his world, the pivot of his emotional, intellectual, and physical life. His attachment to Concord gave his writing a
sense of place unsurpassed in American writing. Even Thoreau's characteristic form, the excursion, derives in part from the powerful centripetal pull
of Concord on Thoreau, on his need to return home after every outing.
Almost every important aspect of his life and work is bound up, in one
way or another, with Concord.

I. HIS NATIVE CONCORD

I have never got over my surprise that I should have been born into the
most estimable place in all the world, and in the very nick of time, too.

Thoreau, *Journal*, December 5, 1856

Of the writers who have made Concord, Massachusetts, a special precinct
of the American imagination, only Henry Thoreau was born there. His
paternal grandfather, Jean Thoreau, was a privateersman – not quite a

pirate – born at St. Helier on the Isle of Jersey. Jean came to America involuntarily when he was nineteen, after being shipwrecked and rescued. Jean became John, married Jane Burns, the daughter of old Boston Quakers, and moved to Concord in 1800, where he bought what is now the north end of the Colonial Inn. He died in 1801, aged forty-seven, of tuberculosis aggravated by a cold caught while patrolling the streets of Boston against an anti-Catholic riot. A Mrs. Munroe of Concord told Thoreau she remembered his grandfather "calling one day and inquiring where blue vervain grew, which he wanted to make a syrup for his cough." The same tuberculosis would later kill Jean's grandson. Jean's son, John, was thirteen when the family moved to Concord. He became a storekeeper, a trader, a pencil-maker, and the father of Henry.

Thoreau's maternal grandmother, Mary Jones of Weston, Massachusetts, the only grandparent Henry knew, was a Tory who had helped her brothers break out of the Concord jail when they were locked up there by patriots during the Revolution. She smuggled files in with their food and had horses ready. She married the Reverend Asa Dunbar; when he died, she married Captain Jonas Minott and moved to Concord in 1798. Her daughter Cynthia Dunbar married John Thoreau in 1812. They had four children: Helen, born October 22, 1812; John, born 1815; David Henry (he later reversed his first two names), on July 12, 1817; and Sophia, on June 24, 1819. Cynthia Thoreau was a lively, talkative, hospitable person, active in all the town charities and in the antislavery society. When the First Parish in Concord went Unitarian, in 1826, she was one of those who left to found a Trinitarian Congregational church. Later in life she returned to the First Parish. She had a strong personality – unlike her husband – and spoke her mind freely. She never willingly accepted anything of second quality from the Concord merchants.

Thoreau was born in his maternal grandmother's house on Virginia Road. The next year the family moved into the village; John Thoreau moved his family to Chelmsford, to Boston, and back to Concord. By the time Henry was twenty, they had relocated ten times. Of the approximately 250 houses in the Concord of 1830, Thoreau lived in nine, eight of which are still standing. Other writers might be *in* Concord; Thoreau was *of* it.

II. EMERSON'S CONCORD

When Mr. Carlyle comes to America, I expect to introduce Thoreau to
him, as *the* man of Concord.

Emerson.'

The Concord that Thoreau left in 1833, to go to college at Harvard, was
different from the Concord that he returned to after graduation, in 1837,
in one important respect. Ralph Waldo Emerson had moved to Concord
in 1835. Emerson was thirty-two; he was popular, outgoing, and hospitable. The Emerson home became at once the intellectual center of the town,
attracting a steady stream of visitors. Thoreau's most important friendship
was with Emerson; from 1837 on, Thoreau was always involved with
Emerson's Concord. Thoreau walked and talked with Emerson. He read
the books in Emerson's library, built his cabin at Walden Pond on Emerson's land, made friends and professional acquaintances with Emerson's
friends, grew fond of Emerson's family, and became a virtual member of
that family. All in all, Thoreau lived at Emerson's for about as long as he
lived at Walden Pond. Thoreau's association with Emerson's circle gave
him access to an even larger intellectual world than Harvard had. The
Harvard of Thoreau's time had a president, eleven professors, and seven
instructors. An average meeting of the Transcendental club of which Emerson was a leader drew eleven members; on occasion it could draw as
many as seventeen. The intellectual and literary candle-power of the club
easily exceeded that of the college. If Thoreau came to regard Concord as
a microcosm of the intellectual world of his time, it was Emerson who
provided the foundation for the metaphor.

III. THOREAU AS A CITIZEN OF CONCORD

I have never declined paying the highway tax, because I am as desirous of
being a good neighbor as I am of being a bad subject.

Thoreau, "Resistance to Civil Government"

Thoreau made a great show of living a private life. He says in *Walden*
(1854) that he wrote for a local journal "of no very wide circulation, whose
editor has never yet seen fit to print the bulk of my contributions." (This
state of affairs has now been remedied; the local journal was Thoreau's
two-million-word Journal, and it has since been printed in two editions.)
Instead of holding elected office, he tells us, "for many years I was self-

appointed inspector of snowstorms and rainstorms, and did my duty faithfully: surveyor if not of highways, then of forest paths and all across-lot routes." He did not fight in the Civil War; he served, as Emerson noted, as captain of the local huckleberry parties.

There was nevertheless a public side to Thoreau. He gave public lectures, he served on the Lyceum committee for inviting visiting speakers, and he was active in antislavery work. He was a regular conductor on the Underground Railroad between Concord and North Fitchburg, and he risked jail to help one of John Brown's men escape to Canada after the attack on Harpers Ferry.

"Resistance to Civil Government," more popularly known as "Civil Disobedience," is one of the world's great statements of how social justice is based on individual conscience. "It is not desirable to cultivate a respect for the law, so much as for the right," Thoreau says. "This people must cease to hold slaves, and to make war on Mexico, though it cost them their existence as a people." This tract, which has influenced history, sprang directly from Thoreau's experiences as a Concord citizen and taxpayer. Thoreau refused to pay his locally collected poll tax because the money would go to a federal government that was supporting slavery and making war on Mexico. When Thoreau was jailed in 1846 for nonpayment, the result was the essay on civil disobedience.

Despite his accidentally burning off a large tract of Concord woods (by foolishly making a fire to fry fish in an old stump, full of what he ought to have known was fat-wood), Thoreau was a good neighbor, loved by the town children and admired even by Sam Staples, whose duty it had been to arrest and jail Thoreau. Concord has maintained a running quarrel with Thoreau from that day to this, but it has never repudiated him. Practically no one, however, thinks of him as Citizen Thoreau.

IV. CONCORD RIVERS

The Musketaquid . . . will be Grass-ground River as long as grass grows and water runs here; it will be Concord River only while men lead peaceable lives on its banks.

Thoreau, *A Week*

Concord was the first town above tide water to be established by the English settlers in Massachusetts in the seventeenth century. It lies fifteen miles west of Boston at the confluence of the Sudbury River (also known as the Musketaquid, as Concord River, as Great River, and as South River), and

the Assabet (or North) River. These broad, slow-moving rivers, together
with five major brooks and the low-lying meadows along them, were the
heart of old Concord. The topography favored farming; there were few
dam sites and therefore little water-power for mills.

Thoreau was as much a man of the rivers as of the fields and woods. He
walked their banks, waded in them, measured them, swam and rowed
them, alone and with friends and family. As the huge town – at one time
comprising all of Lincoln, Acton, Carlisle, and part of Bedford – was held
together by streams, so Thoreau's first book was organized around a river
trip that started and ended in Concord. Emerson pointed out that "they
who made England, Italy, or Greece venerable in the imagination, did so
by sticking fast where they were, like an axis of the earth." Thoreau never
saw the Thames, the Amazon, the Rhine, or the Nile. Instead he made the
most of his sleepy local streams. One can see his strategy in the opening
sentence of *A Week on the Concord and Merrimack Rivers* (1849): "The
Musketaquid, or Grass-ground River, though probably as old as the Nile
or Euphrates, did not begin to have a place in civilized history, until the
fame of its grassy meadows and its fish attracted settlers out of England in
1635...." Thoreau knew the history of the rivers, but his focus was the
rivers themselves. "It is easier," he says at the end of the book, "to discover
another such a new world as Columbus did, than to go within one fold of
this which we appear to know so well; the land is lost sight of, the compass
varies, and mankind mutiny; and still history accumulates like rubbish before the portals of nature."

V. WALKING IN CONCORD

I have travelled a good deal in Concord.

Thoreau, *Walden*

Thoreau was familiar with every sight in Concord; he was himself a familiar sight there. Of medium height, he had large features. He had a prominent nose, and his strong, serious eyes were blue in some lights, gray in
others. He walked with a long ungainly stride that reminded people of an
Indian's. His eyes rarely left the ground. He wore old corduroys, stout
shoes, and a straw hat. Emerson described Thoreau's field equipment: "under his arm he carried an old music-book to press plants; in his pocket, his
diary and pencil, a spy-glass for birds, microscope, jack-knife and twine."
He drifted into surveying and was much in demand because of the accuracy
of his work. Surveying Concord was his life's work.

He taught himself how to see things, how to give to every leaf and twig a separate intention of the eye. His Concord was a very real, very concrete place. He tramped the Old Marlborough Road and the Old Carlisle Road; he rambled and sauntered to Nine-Acre-Corner and Great Meadows, to Fair Haven Hill, Punkatasset Hill, and Emerson's Cliff, to Nut-Meadow Brook, Goose Pond, and Ministerial Swamp. He saw things precisely. He identified trees and flowers and grasses. He noted when each bird returned in spring. He measured river levels, tree rings, seedling roots. We can delight in his delight in detail and nuance: his respect for unbudging fact gives his writing heft and edge. But the details of the Concord land and landscape also gave Thoreau access to a larger world.

Thoreau once said that he needed a walk of at least four hours a day to preserve his health and spirits. His walks did more than ward off melancholy. Emerson had observed that the mind common to the universe is revealed to each individual through his own mind. Similarly, Thoreau understood that the larger world is revealed to each of us through the particular place in which each of us finds himself or herself.

Thoreau discovered that, from a certain point of view, he had access, in Concord, to the same raw material for art and life that had been enjoyed by the greatest persons of earlier times. "I walk out," Thoreau wrote in "Walking," "into a nature such as the old prophets and poets, Menu, Moses, Chaucer, walked in. You may name it America, but it is not America." The insight is important, and Thoreau returned to it often. In "Walking," he tells how he went to see a panorama of the Rhine River, complete with its Roman bridges and Crusaders' castles. It seemed to recall the heroic ages of chivalry. Then he went to see a panorama of the raw Mississippi, unbridged and without castles, full only of snags, floodwater, and steamboats loading wood. "I saw that this was a Rhine stream of a different kind; that the foundations of the castles were yet to be laid, and the famous bridges were yet to be thrown over the river, and I felt that *this was the heroic age itself* [Thoreau's italics], though we know it not, for the hero is commonly the simplest and obscurest of men."

Concord is Everyplace, finally, just as the Transcendentalist "I" is Everyperson. From his expressed preference for walking westward rather than eastward in Concord, Thoreau throws a bridge out to a larger West and then leaps to what that West might mean. "The West of which I speak is but another name for the Wild, and what I have been preparing to say is that in Wildness is the preservation of the world." As Concord gave him the West and Wildness, so also it provided him with a religion. "I believe," he wrote, "in the forest, and in the meadow, and in the night in which the corn grows."

VI. BEAUTY: THE MATERIAL OF A MILLION CONCORDS

The victorious beauty of the rose, as compared with other flowers, depends wholly on the delicacy and quantity of its color gradations, all other flowers being either less rich in gradations, not having so many folds of leaf; or less tender, being patched and veined instead of flushed.

Ruskin, *The Elements of Drawing*

Emerson had argued in *Nature* (1836) that since "Nature is a sea of forms," and since what these forms have in common is beauty, the standard of beauty must therefore be "the entire circuit of natural forms, the totality of nature." Thoreau found that entire circuit of forms in Concord. "Be native to the universe," he wrote in his Journal. "I, too, love Concord best but am glad when I discover, in oceans and wildernesses far away, the material out of which a million Concords can be made." It worked both ways; as everything in his reading and travels could be applied back to Concord, so his experience of Concord colored his experience elsewhere. "Concord is still a cynosure of my eyes," he wrote his mother from Staten Island in 1843; "and I find it hard to attach it, even in imagination, to the rest of the globe, and tell where the seam is." Thoreau was acutely aware of "how little appreciation of the beauty of the landscape there is among us. We have to be told that the Greeks called the world *kosmos,* beauty, or order, but we do not see clearly why they did so." But Thoreau saw more than most of us, and, for him, Concord was the cosmos. He described it over and over in his painterly prose: "We had a wonderful sunset one day last November," he wrote in "Walking"; "I was walking in a meadow; the source of a small brook, when the sun at last, just before setting, after a cold, gray day, reached a clear stratum in the horizon, and the softest brightest morning sunlight fell on the dry grass and on the stems of the trees in the opposite horizon and in the leaves of the shrub oaks on the hillside, while our shadows stretched long over the meadow eastward, as if we were the only motes in its beams. It was such a light as we could not have imagined a moment before, and the air also was so warm and serene that nothing was wanting to make a paradise of that meadow."

VII. CONCORD, THE LABORATORY
OF CREATION

The coming in of Spring is like the creation of Cosmos out of Chaos and
the realization of the Golden Age.

Thoreau, *Walden*

The older Thoreau got, the more interested he became in science. He collected specimens in Concord for Louis Agassiz, the great opponent of Darwin. He belonged to the Boston Natural History Society, he read
extensively in science, and served on the Harvard Examining Committee
in Natural Science. He read Darwin's *Voyage of the Beagle* and *The Origin
of Species*, agreed with Darwin about how species originate, and wrote an
early work on ecology, called "The Succession of Forest Trees." Transcendentalism insisted that science, religion, and literature were not separate
enterprises with different standards of value. Emerson spent much of his
life trying to demonstrate that these fields are linked by the concept of self-
evidence – that when an equation, an insight, or a poem is found to be
true, it is not because of authority or precedent but because it is its own
best evidence.

Thoreau did not believe, as *Genesis* has it, that the world was created
once for all in the beginning. He believed that creation is continuous, going
on all around us all the time. Thoreau tried to live according to what he
called "a newer testament – the gospel according to this moment." In "The
Dispersion of Seeds," he says: "we find ourselves in a world that is already
planted, but is also still being planted as at first." Concord was, to Thoreau,
the laboratory of creation. In the chapter of *Walden* called "Spring," as
Thoreau details the little streams of sand and water flowing in intricate
leaflike patterns down the side of a fresh railroad cut, he declares that "this
one hillside illustrated the principle of all the operations of nature." The
strangely moving phenomenon of the flowing sand-foliage leads him to
conclude that "there is nothing inorganic. . . . The earth is not a mere frag-
ment of dead history, stratum upon stratum like the leaves of a book, to
be studied by geologists and antiquaries chiefly, but living poetry like the
leaves of a tree, which precede flowers and fruit, – not a fossil earth, but
a living earth."

VIII. TAHATAWAN'S CONCORD

Henry D. Thoreau ... knows Indian also – not the language quite as well
as John Eliot – but the history, monuments, and genius of the sachems.

Emerson, letter of August 7, 1847

Thoreau's Concord, like Schliemann's Troy, had many layers. One of the
oldest and most important to Thoreau was its Native American layer. Before the white man came to Musketaquid and renamed the place and the
river, it was a principal village of the Mattacusets tribe, ruled over by
Nanepashemet, a "great king or sachem" who lived in what is now Med-
ford. The local chief of Musketaquid was Tahatawan, who, together with
Nanepashemet's widow, called by the English "Squaw Sachem," consented
to the sale of Concord to the newcomers. The Indians were soon concentrated in the reserved townships of Natick and Nashoba, the latter some
six miles west of Concord. Over the years, these reservations were abandoned as their inhabitants scattered, died, or were relocated on Deer Island,
in Boston Harbor, after King Philip's War (1675).

Two hundred years later, there remained a few Indians to be seen in
Thoreau's Concord. "Still here and there an Indian squaw with her dog,
her only companion, lives in some lone house, insulted by schoolchildren,
making baskets and picking berries her employment ... a daughter of the
soil; one of the nobility of the land." Occasionally, a small party of Penobscot Indians would camp in their tents along the Concord River. Once,
in 1850, Thoreau visited such an encampment and admired the Indians'
collapsible moose-hide canoe, their salmon spears with barbs and retainers,
their log traps, and their snowshoes. Even as a young man, Thoreau identified strongly with these earlier Americans, and his interest may be traced
from his first book, *A Week on the Concord and Merrimack Rivers,* to the
posthumous *The Maine Woods* (1864), to his unpublished "Indian Notebooks," and to a never-fulfilled plan to write a pre-Columbian history of
North America. Nothing symbolizes Thoreau's affinity with the Indians
better than his uncanny knack for finding arrowheads. His friends thought
he could find them virtually at will. Once, when he was twenty, he was
out near the mouth of Swamp-bridge Brook with his brother John. Thoreau
launched into an extravagant eulogy. "Here," he exclaimed, "stood Tahatawan; and there (to complete the period) is Tahatawan's arrowhead."
Thoreau reached for the first stone he saw in order to carry out his little
drama. To his surprise, it "proved a perfect arrowhead, as sharp as if just
from the hands of the Indian fabricator." Some people would call this luck,
but with Thoreau it was not luck but a gift of unremitting intent.

IX. AFRICAN-AMERICAN CONCORD

For human society I was obliged to conjure up the former occupants of these woods.

Thoreau, *Walden*

The part of Concord in which Walden Pond lies, and in which Thoreau built his cabin, near the present Lincoln line, had been a modest African-American community in earlier times. Thoreau was aware that for about a hundred years, African-Americans had made up between one and two percent of Concord's population. In 1830, there were twenty-eight free blacks in a population of 2,021 or just under 1.4 percent. But the area around Walden Pond was an abandoned black community, and there is an elegiac tinge to Thoreau's accounts of Cato Ingraham, who had lived just east of Thoreau's bean-field; of Zilpha, who had spun linen for the townsfolk in a little house by the very corner of the same field; and of Brister Freeman, once a slave of Squire Cummings and later an orchard keeper whose trees still bore fruit down the road from Thoreau's hut. He inquired into their personal histories (as the town historian, Lemuel Shattuck, had not), but discovered little. "All I can learn of their conclusions amounts to just this, that 'Cato and Brister pulled wool:' which is about as edifying as the history of more famous schools of philosophy." Thoreau also took an active role in the abolition movement, in supporting John Brown, and in helping slaves escape to Canada. Years later, one of Thoreau's neighbors, Mrs. Bigelow, remembered that "nearly every week some fugitive would be forwarded with the utmost secrecy to Concord." She added that "sometimes they went by [railroad] cars from Concord, and then Henry Thoreau went on escort, probably more often than any other man."

X. THE PONDS OF CONCORD

And when shall I show you a pretty pasture and woodlot which I bought last week on the borders of a lake which is the chief ornament of this town, called Walden Pond?

Emerson, letter of September 30, 1844

The first thing one notices about Walden Pond, the spiritual center of Thoreau's and Emerson's Concord, is that it is much larger than one expected, being in fact a good-sized lake. Thoreau described it as "a clear and deep green well, half a mile long and a mile and three quarters in circumference, and [containing] about sixty-one and a half acres: a perennial spring in the midst of pine and oak woods, without any visible inlet or outlet except by the clouds and evaporation." Concord has several ponds; besides Walden there is White Pond, Flints' or Sandy Pond, and Goose Pond. Walden will always occupy a special place in the American imagination because Thoreau lived there, but even Thoreau conceded that "since the woodcutters, and the railroad, and I myself have profaned Walden, perhaps the most attractive, if not the most beautiful, of all our lakes, the gem of the woods, is White Pond." White Pond is now accessible only to members of a private swimming association; it is a reminder of a fate that might have overtaken Walden. Thoreau includes White Pond with Walden in the wonderful last paragraph of his chapter on the ponds, where he calls them "great crystals on the surface of the earth, Lakes of Light."

If Walden was not as pretty as White Pond, still it was sufficient for Thoreau's purposes; it became his symbol for purity and for perception. As Emerson wrote about being a transparent eyeball, so Thoreau said that a lake was "earth's eye, looking into which the beholder measures the depth of his own nature." Through the strenuous efforts of many people, Walden Pond remains a beautiful place, and a place open to the public. If you get up early and walk out along its shores at dawn before the crowd arrives, it is still possible to experience it as Thoreau did. The water washes the shore just as it did in his day. "For the first week," he noted carefully, "whenever I looked out on the pond, it impressed me like a tarn high up on the side of a mountain."

XI. THE LITERARY FORMS OF CONCORD

I think I could write a poem to be called Concord.

Thoreau, *Journal*, September 4, 1841

Concord provided Thoreau with much of his subject matter. The journal entry just cited goes on: "for argument I should have the River, the Woods, the Ponds, the Hills, the Fields, the Swamps and Meadows, the Streets and Buildings, and the Villagers. Then Morning, Noon, and Evening, Spring, Summer, Autumn, and Winter, Night, Indian Summer, and The Mountains in the Horizon." So strong was the pull of Concord on Thoreau that it even influenced the form of his writings. His favorite literary form, the excursion, evolved as a sort of literary analogue of his daily walk. *Walden* is formally organized as a single year, beginning with summer and ending with spring. It is also organized as a celebration of place.

Concord gave shape to Thoreau's work in other ways. Thoreau considered his huge Journal a sort of Book of Concord, and there is reason to think that the vast uncompleted manuscript projects he left behind were intended to coalesce into a grand Calendar of a Concord Year. What is certain is that from early on, from 1841 at least, Thoreau completely understood what John Ruskin once said was "the guiding principle of all right practical labors, and source of all healthful life energy," the principle "that your art is to be the praise of something that you love."

XII. THE SUFFICIENCY OF CONCORD

I expect to leave Concord, which is my Rome, and its people, who are my Romans, in May, and go to New York.

Thoreau, letter of April 2, 1843

It is perfectly true that travel is broadening, yet it can be, as with a river, at the expense of depth. What good does it do to end up like the upper Missouri or the Platte, a mile wide and an inch deep? Thoreau wrote several books on his North American travels (*The Maine Woods, Cape Cod* [1865], *A Yankee in Canada* [1866]), but he successfully resisted travel abroad. He was a homebody; he adhered to Concord, to what Emerson called its "sit-fast acres." Thoreau saw the day as an epitome of the year, and Concord as an epitome of the world. We each have our own Concord somewhere. This need not be a provincial attitude, especially for a person who read as much as Thoreau did. Provincialism, as Matthew Arnold remarked, is ignorance of the standards by which your work will be judged. It has nothing to do with where you live.

In the "Spring" chapter of *Walden,* Thoreau describes a hawk, alternately soaring and tumbling high in the air over the Concord River. "It was not lonely, but made all the earth lonely beneath it." Place is not what matters; *caring* about a place is what matters. Concord was sufficient for Thoreau. His work guarantees that any direct personal experience, no matter how humble or local, is preferable to any secondhand experience, no matter how grand. This is also the teaching of Emerson's "Self-Reliance," and of ancient Stoic philosophy from Zeno and Marcus Aurelius to Montaigne. "Do what you love," he wrote a friend; "know your own bone; gnaw it, bury it, unearth it and gnaw it still." Thoreau did what he loved, and he knew what he loved. "The sight of a marsh hawk in Concord meadows," he wrote, "is worth more to me than the entry of the allies into Paris."

NOTES

1 David Greene Haskins, *Ralph Waldo Emerson: His Maternal Ancestors* (Boston: Cupples, Upham, 1887), p. 119.

3

ROBERT SATTELMEYER

Thoreau and Emerson

When Henry Thoreau began to keep a journal, in October 1837, he almost certainly did so in response to the prompting of Ralph Waldo Emerson: " 'What are you doing now?' he asked, 'Do you keep a journal?' – So I make my first entry to-day" (*PJ* 1:5). Eventually the Journal became the major work of Thoreau's imaginative life, providing the raw material for his published writings and filling nearly fifty notebooks by the time of his death in May 1862. When Thoreau died, Emerson arranged for the funeral service to be held at Concord's First Parish Church, and he delivered the eulogy. Emerson expanded his address for the *Atlantic Monthly*, in August, and reprinted it as the introduction to the volume of Thoreau's *Excursions*, which he helped to edit in 1863. Eventually, Emerson's "Thoreau" came to stand as the introduction to the twenty-volume Houghton Mifflin "Walden Edition" (1906) that has been the standard text of Thoreau's writings for most of the twentieth century.

Thus, Emerson not only called Thoreau into being as a writer but also launched him toward posterity with the first extended account of his life and career. As we shall see, Emerson's "Thoreau" was hardly the typical laudatory summing-up of a departed friend's life and achievements. Enormously influential in defining the terms of Thoreau's reception and of the critical discourse about him in the following century, Emerson's memorial was also the last word in a long personal struggle between the two men: a struggle to be heard, to be understood, to prevail philosophically, and to realize the high and noble friendship that each aspired to but despaired of ever achieving. During the early years of Thoreau's literary career, Emerson played a central role as mentor and adviser, giving their relationship a professional, as well as a personal, dimension that further complicated it.

Moreover, the relationship of the two men has acquired an almost mythical status in American culture that renders any attempt to describe it even more difficult.[1] Take, for example, the famous but probably apocryphal anecdote about Thoreau's night in jail for refusing to pay his poll tax in protest against slavery. In an exchange that appears in the *Oxford Dictionary of Quotations,* but for which there is no reliable authority, Emerson is supposed to have visited Thoreau in jail and asked him, "Why are you here?" Thoreau is supposed to have shot back, "Why are you not here?" In this scene Thoreau plays the radical, committed activist, while Emerson appears as conventional and conservative – a myth that starkly oversimplifies both men and their roles in the abolitionist movement.

Nevertheless, some general observations about their relationship may be advanced to ground the discussion, if only provisionally: Overall, it was important and productive for both men. At various times they assisted one another in literary work, and at other times their disagreements forced each to a sharper articulation of his own position, so that an implicit dialectic may be traced in their work. While each man looked to the other for true and deep friendship as well as cooperation and association, each was somewhat disabled from maintaining intimacy with others. Emerson suffered from what he called the "trick" of his solitariness, an aloofness that held him apart from those he was most closely connected to; and Thoreau's prickly personality, disregard of convention, and inflexibly severe standards of judgment made him difficult to deal with. Additionally, both men shared a basic Transcendental belief that nowadays, in this age of talk-show confessionals, may seem to make actual friendship impossible: true friendship operated on so high a plane that no discussion of it – especially of any problems that might exist with it – could take place.

Finally, the relationship was more important to Thoreau than to Emerson, and he suffered more from its ruptures than Emerson did, for the simple reason that Emerson was *the* inspiration of his early years, his mentor, and the one person on whom he staked his hopes for an ideal friendship. Thoreau, on the other hand, was only one of several, mostly younger friends whom Emerson valued and cultivated at various times, including Ellery Channing, Jones Very, Charles King Newcomb, Samuel Gray Ward, Bronson Alcott, and Margaret Fuller. Unlike Thoreau, Emerson also had a conventional social life and a wife and children.

In the beginning, their friendship was based on the roles of mentor and protégé. After resigning his pastorate in 1832 and traveling abroad, Emerson began his career as a lecturer. He moved to Concord in 1834. He married his second wife, Lidian, the next year, and in 1836 – at age thirty-three – confirmed his position as the leading spokesman for the "new views," called (sometimes disparagingly) Transcendentalism, by publishing *Nature.*

Meanwhile, Thoreau was working his way through Harvard. In his senior year he read *Nature* and was sufficiently moved by it to give it as a graduation present to a classmate. More important, Emersonian thought began to infuse his college writing (*Reading* 22–3). It must have seemed a great good fortune to him that Emerson had recently moved to his native village. Exactly when they met is unknown, but by the time Thoreau was a senior, Emerson knew him well enough to write to the president of Harvard on his behalf for a scholarship. Emerson also gave the Phi Beta Kappa oration at Thoreau's graduation, in 1837. Later entitled "The American Scholar," it was a call to the youth of America to free themselves from dependency on European cultural models and to devote themselves to the life of the mind through nature, books, and action – an injunction that clearly spoke to Thoreau, the bent of whose genius already lay in those directions.

By virtue of Emerson's presence, the Concord that Thoreau returned to after graduation had become the center of radical thought in New England. Thoreau quickly became a fixture among the idealists who were gathering around Emerson with ambitious plans for reforming the arts, religion, and society itself. As "The American Scholar" suggests, Emerson was deeply interested in attracting to his views young people who would have some transformative influence on American culture. He saw almost immediately in his young townsman not only a guide to the woods and rivers he was learning to love but also an original voice that might be enlisted in the cause:

> 17 February [1838]. My good Henry Thoreau made this else solitary afternoon sunny with his simplicity & clear perception. How comic is simplicity in this doubledealing quacking world. Every thing that boy says makes merry with society though nothing can be graver than his meaning. I told him he should write out the history of his College life as Carlyle has his tutoring.[1]

Emerson's suggestion that Thoreau "write out the history of his College life" indicates (along with his prompting Thoreau to keep a journal) that he sought from the beginning to steer the young man toward a literary career. It would be easy to overlook Emerson's use of the possessive pronoun in this passage – "My good Henry Thoreau" – were it not so persistent a feature of his references to Thoreau: he rarely mentions him during these years without that "my," as though he viewed Thoreau in some sense as his own creation, the embodiment of his ideology set at large in the world to change it.

Some fundamental disequilibrium in their relationship was of course inevitable, for Emerson was fourteen years Thoreau's senior, the acknowledged leader of the Transcendentalist circle, and well connected to Boston society by virtue of his family and clerical ties. Thoreau was a recent college graduate with unfocused literary aspirations, marking time as a village schoolteacher. Over the next several years, Emerson used his advantages for Thoreau not only by giving him advice and encouragement but also by lobbying publishers and editors on behalf of his literary projects, advancing him money, and providing him a place to live and leisure to write.

Not surprisingly, as a patron Emerson also patronized. He formed notions of Thoreau's proper course that Thoreau was either unwilling or unable to fulfill. Having provided him with means and opportunities for a career, Emerson also – though probably unconsciously – scripted that career. And however much Thoreau may have exceeded expectations in some areas, he was also perennially a puzzle and a disappointment to Emerson. At the same time, Emerson himself changed in ways that caused him to decline in Thoreau's estimation, so that about a decade after their friendship began, a serious rift had developed between them. By 1850, each was writing about the estrangement as accomplished, and looking at the other with a mixture of disappointment, anger, and resignation.

Their period of closest association and greatest intimacy was from 1841 to 1848, a period bracketed by Thoreau's two stints of living in Emerson's house: from the spring of 1841 to the spring of 1843, in the capacity of a general handyman who also assisted Emerson in editing the magazine of Transcendentalism, the *Dial;* and from 1847 to 1848, when he returned to help manage the household during Emerson's extended European visit and lecture tour. In between these stays he remained tied to Emerson as well, living on Emerson's land at Walden Pond from 1845 to 1847, and living with Emerson's brother William on Staten Island, New York, while he tried to write for the magazines there in 1843.

Initially, Emerson's confidence in Thoreau's literary promise seemed justified. In 1839, a year after he noted Thoreau's penchant for "making merry" with society, he announced to Margaret Fuller that "My Henry Thoreau has broke out into good poetry & better prose; he, my protester." Then, a few months later, as the *Dial* was in its planning stage, Emerson predicted to his brother that "My Henry Thoreau will be a great poet for such a company, & one of these days for all companies."[3]

However, Thoreau's early offerings to the *Dial* were not well received by its tough-minded editor, Margaret Fuller, though Emerson continued to plead for his protégé. But when Fuller resigned and Emerson reluctantly agreed to take over the editorship in 1842, he was able to give Thoreau – then living in his house – more exposure in the magazine and employ him, as he put it, "as private secretary to the President of the Dial" (*Letters* 3: 47). Particularly important at this time was Emerson's suggestion that Thoreau write an essay reviewing recently published surveys of the flora and fauna of Massachusetts.

This suggestion resulted in Thoreau's first natural history essay, "Natural History of Massachusetts," in the July 1842 issue of the *Dial*. Up to this point Thoreau had thought of himself as a conventional man of letters, writing poetry, literary criticism, and familiar essays. His interest in nature had always been profound, but apparently he had not thought of writing about it for publication. For him to do so required not just Emerson's suggestion but in a sense his authorization, so closely had Thoreau identified himself with the older man's literary program.

When Thoreau sought, the following year, to expand his horizons and try the New York literary marketplace, Emerson smoothed his way by securing him a position as tutor to William Emerson's son. The experiment was not a success. Thoreau found he had no "bait" that would tempt the "rats" of the New York publishing world, but he continued to write for the *Dial* while he was in New York and to look back on his stay in the Emerson household with affection, especially for Lidian Emerson. It was she to whom he wrote his warmest and most ardent letters and who began to represent to him, even more than her husband, the ideal friend that he sought, someone whose virtues he could admire and aspire to in order to ennoble himself, but who possessed an emotional warmth as well (*Corr* 103–4, 119–20).

Nevertheless, it was her husband who continued to guide Thoreau's tenuous literary career, even after the *Dial* ceased publication in 1844, and to help him secure freedom to write. Emerson gave Thoreau permission to build a cabin on land he had recently purchased on Walden Pond, and Thoreau took up residence there in the summer of 1845. The "private business" he alludes to in *Walden* as his reason for going to live by the pond was the writing of his first book, *A Week on the Concord and Merrimack Rivers*. *A Week* was intended as a memorial to his brother John, who had died of tetanus in 1842, but it was also a testimonial to Emerson's influence, a summing-up of Thoreau's efforts to fulfill the duties of the American Scholar that Emerson had outlined in 1837. That first year at the pond, working on his book, Thoreau wrote in his Journal his strongest and most direct acknowledgment of the veneration he felt for Emerson: "His personal influence on young persons greater than any man's In his world every man would be a poet – Love would reign – Beauty would take place – Man & nature would harmonize" (*PJ* 2:224).

As this suggests, there was a powerful element of idealization in Thoreau's concept of Emerson. This was orthodox in the ideology of Transcendentalism, which held that one should love the *spirit* of the person more than his or her worldly self, and that friendship itself is an idealizing force that causes us to be aware of our highest potential (through our friend's love of what is best in us) and to love in turn only the noblest part of our friend's nature. The affinity between true friends has nothing to do with ordinary affection, mutual assistance, and mere companionship. As Thoreau said, a Newfoundland dog could perform those functions. Again, the noblest friendship takes place on a level that makes discussing it impossible: if you have to speak of it you've already lowered it. "It is an exercise of the purest imagination and the rarest faith," Thoreau wrote in his essay on friendship in *A Week.* But he also warned that "The constitutional differences which always exist, and are obstacles to a perfect Friendship, are forever a forbidden theme to the lips of Friends" (*Week* 272, 283). The severity of this ideal, of course, made sustained actual friendship virtually impossible.

Emerson's influence at this time also extended to the very mundane problems of helping Thoreau find a publisher for *A Week.* This was a role Emerson was used to, for he had frequently acted as agent or editor for writers whose work he was interested in promoting, most notably Thomas Carlyle and the young poets Jones Very and Ellery Channing. So he advised Thoreau and wrote letters on his behalf to publishers and other persons with influence in the book trade. Negotiations were protracted and generally unsatisfactory, for Thoreau was naturally interested in gaining as wide an audience for his book as possible, while at the same time limiting his own risk. Given the prevailing conditions in the American publishing industry, this was difficult for a relatively unknown author.

The absence of an international copyright agreement meant that American publishers could reprint popular British books without paying authors' royalties. So they had little incentive to publish at their own risk books by obscure young American writers, and they generally agreed to publish them only if the author underwrote the costs of production. After that, the author and the publisher would share the profits. Several publishers offered to put out *A Week* on these terms. Even had he been willing, such an arrangement would have been difficult if not impossible for Thoreau to carry out. It would have cost him about $400, more than a year's wages for a working person. While writing *A Week,* Thoreau had lived at Walden Pond without any regular income.

Emerson, however, encouraged him to follow this path, offering assurance that the book would find readers and that he would incur little risk (*Corr* 195).[4] Eventually, Thoreau contracted with James Munroe, Emerson's publisher in Boston, who was willing to let him pay the costs of production out of sales. As it turned out, however, it was a bad bargain all the way around, for Munroe did little to promote or distribute the book, and it only sold about two hundred of the thousand copies that were printed, leaving Thoreau a debt that took him several years to pay off.

The commercial fiasco of *A Week* prompted what was probably a beneficial change in Thoreau's professional relations with Emerson, for it forced Thoreau to strike out more independently and reassess his possibilities in the literary marketplace. Emerson's advice had been well meaning and sound from his own experience, but it was inappropriate for Thoreau. Emerson *preferred* to underwrite the production of his books because it gave him a greater share of their profits and greater control over the production. He could afford to capitalize his own books because he had an independent income from the estate of his first wife and regular income from his lecturing. He liked using Munroe and could depend on a predictable sale in the Boston area because his name was well established. But changes in the industry were making this arrangement for book publishing obsolete, and if Thoreau was to have any success he would have to accommodate himself to the new realities of the book trade.

He got concrete instruction in these new realities from Horace Greeley, the publisher of the *New York Tribune*. Greeley, who was a supporter of the Transcendentalists generally, had met Thoreau when he was in New York in 1843 and began to act as a sort of unofficial literary agent for him in the late 1840s. Greeley gave him advice about writing for magazines (which Thoreau often disregarded), urged him to put off writing books until he was better known, and worked diligently to get Thoreau's articles placed and paid for. Significantly, when Thoreau was finally ready to publish *Walden* in 1854, he was able to negotiate a contract with Ticknor and Fields to publish it at their risk, he published extracts from it in magazines in advance, and he had no help from Emerson.

But the publication of *A Week* was a symptom of more than a shift in the economics of authorship, for it led to an open acknowledgment by both men of a deep rift between them, one that had in fact been building for several years.[5] Shortly after May 1849, when *A Week* was published, Thoreau confided to his Journal that the breach had already occurred:

> I had a friend, I wrote a book, I asked my friend's criticism, I never got but praise for what was good in it – my friend became estranged from me and then I got blame for all that was bad, – & so I got at last the criticism which I wanted.
>
> While my friend was my friend he flattered me, and I never heard the truth from him, but when he became my enemy he shot it to me on a poisoned arrow. (*PJ* 3:26)

It needs to be emphasized that Emerson and Thoreau did not have their initial falling out over *A Week;* rather, as Thoreau's Journal entry makes clear, there was an estrangement and then the "truth" could come out about the book in a wounding way. But what had led to this prior, unspoken estrangement during the period of their closest association?

Looking back, it seems clear that Emerson had begun to be frustrated with Thoreau in the early 1840s, when it seemed to him that Thoreau failed to live up to his early promise. As early as July 1842, when Thoreau published "Natural History of Massachusetts" in the *Dial,* Emerson had been disappointed. He confessed to Margaret Fuller:

> I am sorry that you, & the world after you, do not like my brave Henry any better. I do not like his piece very well, but admire this perennial threatening attitude.... But I have now seen so many threats incarnated which "delayed to strike" & finally never struck at all, that I begin to think our American subsoil must be lead or chalk or whatever represents in geology the phlegmatic. (*Letters* 3:75)

What is crucial here is not so much Emerson's disappointment with this early essay, but his seeing Thoreau's failure to measure up to his expectations as symptomatic of a wider failing on the part of Thoreau's generation, especially those ardent spirits who had been attracted to Emerson himself. Their failure to seize commanding positions in American culture was an indictment of Emerson himself and contributed to the crisis of spirit that Emerson underwent during the early 1840s, particularly after the death of his son Waldo, in 1842. This crisis is dramatized and analyzed in Emerson's great essay "Experience," in which he makes the representativeness of Thoreau clear: A remark applied to Thoreau in Emerson's Journal (*JMN* 8: 375) is now generalized: "We see young men who owe us a new world, so readily and lavishly they promise, but they never acquit the debt; they die young and dodge the account: or if they live, they lose themselves in the crowd."[6]

Emerson's response to this perceived failure of his literary sons (and to the death of his actual son) was to position himself in what he called in the essay the "mid-world" and to accept into his world of high idealization the reality of limiting circumstances. No longer did he confidently assert, as he had in *Nature,* "Build therefore your own world." Instead he ventured that "We live amid surfaces, and the true art of life is to skate well upon them" ("Experience," 35). Although he ended the essay by reinvoking what he hoped for from Thoreau and his contemporaries – "the transformation of genius into practical power" – he was resigned not to expect it anytime soon.

This drift away from his early idealism and toward an increased respect for material accomplishment accelerated during Emerson's second European sojourn in 1847–8, while Thoreau was living in his home again. "It is a pity," he wrote to Henry, "that you should not see this England, with its indiscribable material superiorities of every kind" (*Corr* 212). Unless it was a veiled reproach, this was a curious remark for Emerson to direct to Thoreau, for he knew very well that his friend scorned "material superiorities" of every kind and had just finished living in a one-room cabin in the woods for two years.

The Emerson who returned from Europe with the image of British material success vividly before him found Thoreau still practicing his renunciations and leading his solitary life. Emerson's feelings of disappointment finally came to the surface and, sometime shortly after his return, he finally spoke to Thoreau about their differences, with no very happy results:

> I spoke of friendship, but my friends & I are fishes in their habit. As for taking T.'s arm, I should as soon take the arm of an elm tree. . . . Henry Thoreau is like the woodgod who solicits the wandering poet & draws him into antres vast & desarts idle, & bereaves him of his memory, & leaves him naked, plaiting vines & with twigs in his hand. Very seductive are the first steps from the town to the woods, but the End is want & madness. (*JMN* 10:343–5)

In his quest for wildness and in his single-minded pursuit of natural history studies (which began in earnest about this time), Thoreau had settled upon a path which seemed to border on madness to Emerson, especially at a time when he himself was turning more to society and "the town." In turn, it was this conversation, or one very similar to it, that prompted Thoreau to realize that their friendship had passed a point of no return. For him, as we know, the very act of speaking of one's friendship constituted a fatal blow to it. Just previous to his bitter complaint about Emerson's "poison arrow" critique of *A Week*, sometime during the summer of 1849, he acknowledged that this had happened:

> I had tenderly cherished the flower of our friendship till one day my friend treated it as a weed. It (did not survive the shock but) drooped & withered from that hour. – A Friend avoids the subject of friendship – in conversation. – It is a very sacred relation which is not liable to a vulgar difference. (*PJ* 3: 20)

The break was especially disturbing for Thoreau because he had venerated Emerson for so long. Unlike Emerson's record of gradual disenchantment with him, Thoreau's Journal provides no evidence of moderating esteem over the years. Compounding the injury was his sense, reinforced by his recent stay in the Emerson house, that the worshipful friendship he had sought was in fact possible. His affection for Lidian Emerson, who had suffered patiently her husband's absence and a number of illnesses during Thoreau's residence in the household, was stronger than ever; and at the same time that his Journal records his anguish at the rupture with Emerson, it records a moving and passionate tribute to "A Sister" – almost certainly Lidian Emerson (*PJ* 3:17–18).

The difficulty in his friendship with Emerson would of course affect his closeness to Lidian, and so there was a double loss, one that disturbed Thoreau deeply and probably played a role in his increasing absorption in natural history studies beginning in 1849. The remark in *Walden* about turning "to the woods, where I was better known" is on one level a typical Thoreauvian paradox; but it may also be read as a lament for failed human relationships.

One further twist of the knife that ought to be mentioned is the ironic fact that in October 1848, at just the point of their estrangement and acknowledgment of diverging paths, Thoreau was parodied as an imitator of Emerson in James Russell Lowell's popular satiric poem "A Fable for Critics." Friends and detractors alike had commented privately on Thoreau's resemblance to his mentor, but this public ridicule as a second-rate imitator of the apostle of self-reliance must have been a bitter humiliation to the proud and sensitive Thoreau.

For his part, Emerson acknowledged their estrangement but tried in 1850 to patch things up and engage Thoreau on their old terms of intimacy, recording in his Journal the outline of a "Rambling talk with H. T. . . . in accordance with my proposal to hold a session, the first for a long time, with malice prepense, & take the bull by the horns" (*JMN* 11:283). But the talk ended up reverting to their old disagreement about the relative merits of England and America, Emerson's position being a thinly disguised substitution for his old complaint about the lack of American (and Thoreauvian) accomplishment. Emerson concludes, sadly and somewhat cryptically: "Yes, we have infinite powers, but cannot use them. When shall we attain our majority, & come to our estate? Henry admitted, of course, the solstice" (*JMN* 11:286).

Thereafter their friendship, though close, lacked the sine qua non of high expectations and aspirations. It degenerated, as they both would have thought, to the level of ordinary friendship, where people do not make the highest demands of one another. And each came to represent to the other a problem in American society, raising their quarrel to the level of cultural criticism. After Emerson's return from England and his increased involvement in social activities like the Town and Country Club, he came to represent to Thoreau the conventional man of the world who observed proprieties and etiquette rather than essentials. In fact, Thoreau thought that Emerson's manners had become his essence:

> But when I consider what my friends relations & acquaintances are – what his tastes & habits – then the difference between us gets named. I see that all these friends & acquaintances & tastes & habits are indeed my friend's self.
> (*PJ* 4:137 [October 10, 1851])

Emerson, in turn, continued to think that Thoreau's intense, solitary nature study was a tragic waste of his talents, even though Emerson could see the attraction of his friend's pursuits. In early 1858, for example, he found Thoreau walking in his (Emerson's) woods, studying as usual the evidence of minute seasonal change in plants. "How divine these studies!" he was prompted to exclaim. "Here there is no taint of mortality. How aristocratic, & of how defiant a beauty! This is the garden of Edelweisen" (*JMN* 14:195–6).

Though Emerson would later use this image of the rare and beautiful alpine flower Edelweiss in the conclusion of his funeral address to represent the purity of Thoreau's life, he could not keep up his admiration for long. A few pages later in Emerson's Journal, again responding to an outing with Thoreau, he confesses that he listened to Thoreau's account of a man living a hermit's life in the Maine wilderness "with despair," and he wonders if the hermit "has found it foolish & wasteful to spend a tenth or a twentieth of his active life with a muskrat & fried fishes" (*JMN* 14:203). As if to emphasize their disagreement, Emerson writes on the next page a mock letter to Thoreau summarizing his exasperation:

> My dear Henry,
>   A frog was made to live in a swamp, but a man was not made to live in a swamp. Yours ever,
>   R.

This withdrawal from the world of society to the world of nature is doubtless what Emerson had in mind when he noted, going through Thoreau's letters and Journal after his death, "I see the Thoreau poison working today in many valuable lives, in some for good, in some for harm" (*JMN* 15:487). In the final analysis, there is an irreducible contradiction in Emerson's encouragement and admiration of Thoreau's nature study and nature writing and his belief that this life path involved a tragic waste of his friend's talents and a loss to American civilization. Somehow, he managed both to see and not to see what Thoreau was about; or, at the least, his early and fixed belief that Thoreau should play a more active role in American society and culture prevented him from seeing that Thoreau's study and writing had lasting value.

Thus, when he came to write his friend's eulogy and then expand it as the biographical memoir "Thoreau," he perhaps not surprisingly fashioned a portrait of Thoreau that is narrowly faceted. Emerson softened many of his critical and disapproving remarks in revision,[7] but the finished essay still displays an ambivalence toward its subject that is rather remarkable for the genre. Though one senses Emerson's genuine admiration and even love for Thoreau throughout, there is also a persistent thread of disapproval running through the essay. It was not that New Englanders were simply more honest and plain-spoken a hundred and thirty years ago: Louisa May Alcott, who was in attendance, wrote to a friend that Emerson's address was "not appropriate to the time or place."[8] Had its influence stopped with the local audience, little harm would have been done, for those who heard Emerson doubtless knew something of his long quarrel with Thoreau and could make allowances. But his criticisms became canonical, as it were, in that his essay came to serve as the introduction to the two major editions of Thoreau's writings that appeared in the century following his death – and it continues to be widely reprinted and anthologized.

To appreciate the slant of Emerson's memoir, we need look only at a portion of the second paragraph, describing Thoreau's early adulthood:

> His father was a manufacturer of lead pencils, and Henry applied himself for a time to this craft, believing he could make a better pencil than was then in use. After completing his experiments, he exhibited his work to chemists and artists in Boston, and having obtained their certificates to its excellence and to its equality with the best London manufacture, he returned home contented. His friends congratulated him that he had now opened his way to fortune. But he replied, that he should never make another pencil. "Why should I? I would not do again what I have done once." He resumed his endless walks, and miscellaneous studies, making every day some new acquaintance with Nature, though as yet never speaking of zoology or botany, since, though very studious of natural facts, he was incurious of technical and textual science. ("Thoreau," 35)

This passage leads a reader to two distinctly misleading conclusions. The first is that Thoreau gave up making pencils after having invented a better one. He did help improve the product, but that did not bring him to stop making pencils. His improvements became part of the manufacturing process.[9] In fact, he continued to work off and on at the family business all his life. After his father died, in 1859, he took over its management, though by that time it largely consisted of supplying graphite not for pencils but for electrotyping. Ironically in view of Emerson's statement, making pencils was one of the ways Thoreau worked off his debt for *A Week on the Concord and Merrimack Rivers*.[10]

Second, Thoreau did not begin his "endless walks" until about 1849, at which time he began systematically to study biology, especially botany. To say that he was "incurious of technical and textual science" is simply not true. Emerson, who frequently walked with Thoreau even after their falling out, had ample opportunity to observe his taxonomic expertise. And Thoreau was well read in the theoretical as well as the practical side of contemporary natural science, and Emerson knew this, too, for he had recorded in his Journal Thoreau's comments on Darwin's *Origin of Species* and on the theories of Louis Agassiz, America's foremost natural scientist.

The point here is not so much to catch Emerson in factual errors as to demonstrate that his Thoreau is essentially a character of his devising, complete with invented dialogue. All biography (and autobiography, for that matter) is fictional to a degree, and we should always bear in mind that it is the biographer's version of the subject that we are receiving and not the subject himself. But Emerson's eulogy seems particularly designed to present Thoreau's life as one of renunciation and withdrawal. Beginning with this allegation that Thoreau repudiated the pencil business and became absorbed in "endless walks," Emerson's account of Thoreau makes him a renouncer, an iconoclast, and, as Emerson forthrightly says, a "bachelor of thought and nature" and a "hermit and ascetic" ("Thoreau," 37, 39). Emerson no doubt felt the sting of Thoreau's disapproval of his own highly social and cultivated way of life, and managed to insinuate – while seeming to pay tribute to his iconoclasm – that Thoreau was perverse in his avoidance of society: "A fine house, dress, the manners and talk of highly cultivated people, were all thrown away on him" ("Thoreau," 37).

What Thoreau is *not* in Emerson's version is a writer. Remarkably, Emerson refers to Thoreau's writing only in passing, makes no mention of his career, and offers no description or evaluation of his books and principal essays. The only selections of Thoreau's prose that Emerson quotes are snippets from his then-unpublished Journal, a decision that reinforces the essay's subtext that Thoreau was chiefly a "character" who chose not to participate in the life of his times, someone who perversely produced his best writing for no audience but himself.

Having established Thoreau as a hermit and minimized his career as a writer, Emerson was able to reassert his fundamental criticism of Thoreau, one he had first written in briefer form in his journal in 1851:

Had his genius been only contemplative, he had been fitted to his life, but with his energy and practical ability he seemed born for great enterprise and for command: and I so much regret the loss of his rare powers of action, that I cannot help counting it a fault in him that he had no ambition. Wanting this, instead of engineering for all America, he was the captain of a huckleberry party. Pounding beans is good to the end of pounding empires one of these days, but if, at the end of years, it is still only beans!—("Thoreau," 53)

Although Emerson goes on to say that these "foibles" were "fast vanishing" in the growth of Thoreau's spirit, the residual force of his criticisms remains, and they have helped to perpetuate a myth that Thoreau wasted his talents and died without having accomplished what he might or ought to have done. More important, the lack of attention Emerson paid to Thoreau's writing career and the significance of his books no doubt retarded Thoreau's acceptance and kept him somewhat marginalized as a kind of counterculture figure for several generations of readers.

In the process of reading Thoreau's manuscript Journal in the months and years after his death, Emerson gradually came to recognize Thoreau's devotion to his craft, but he did not revise his memoir to reflect this recognition. Evidently, it could not overcome his belief that Thoreau had not followed the proper path. And since he was the survivor, it fell to him to write the history of his friend's life and accomplishments.

It is difficult to imagine how Thoreau could have gotten past the threshold of literary achievement without Emerson's generous support and assistance; at the same time it is difficult to imagine a eulogy by a close friend more damaging to a writer's reputation than Emerson's "Thoreau." But this sort of contradiction was typical of their relationship, and perhaps the tensions that were engendered between them were ultimately productive. The force, it may be, of their unspoken and unrealizable friendship, as well as the memory of its loss and each man's awareness of the other's disappointment in him, may have made each more determined than ever to play his part to the end.

NOTES

1   The most extensive treatment of the relationship is Joel Porte, *Emerson and Thoreau: Transcendentalists in Conflict* (Middletown, Conn.: Wesleyan University Press, 1966). Other notable studies include Paul Hourihan, "Crisis in the Emerson–Thoreau Friendship: The Symbolic Function of 'Civil Disobedience,'" in *Thoreau's Psychology: Eight Essays,* ed. Raymond D. Gozzi (Lanham, Md.: University Press of America, 1983), pp. 109–22; Richard Lebeaux, *Thoreau's*

Seasons (Amherst: University of Massachusetts Press, 1984); Mary Elkins Moller, *Thoreau in the Human Community* (Amherst: University of Massachusetts Press, 1980); William M. Moss, " 'So Many Promising Youths': Emerson's Disappointing Discoveries of New England Seer-Poets" (*New England Quarterly* 49 [1976]: 46–64); Leonard Neufeldt, "The Severity of the Ideal: Emerson's 'Thoreau' " (*ESQ* 58 [1970]: 77–84).

2   *The Journals and Miscellaneous Notebooks of Ralph Waldo Emerson*, ed. William H. Gilman, Ralph H. Orth, et al., 16 vols. (Cambridge: Harvard University Press, 1960–82), 5:453–4; hereafter cited parenthetically in the text as *JMN*.

3   *The Letters of Ralph Waldo Emerson*, ed. Ralph L. Rusk and Eleanor M. Tilton, 8 vols. to date (New York: Columbia University Press, 1939; 1990–), 2:182, 225; hereafter cited parenthetically in the text as *Letters*.

4   See Linck C. Johnson, *Thoreau's Complex Weave: The Writing of "A Week on the Concord and Merrimack Rivers"* (Charlottesville: University Press of Virginia, 1986), pp. 202–60; and Steven Fink, *Prophet in the Marketplace: Thoreau's Development as a Professional Writer* (Princeton: Princeton University Press, 1992), pp. 191–215, for detailed accounts of the writing of *A Week* and Thoreau's search for a publisher.

5   The discussion of the rift between Emerson and Thoreau that follows draws heavily on my " 'When He Became My Enemy': Emerson and Thoreau, 1848–49," *New England Quarterly* 62 (1989): 187–204.

6   "Experience," in *Essays: Second Series*, ed. Alfred R. Ferguson and Jean Ferguson Carr (Cambridge: Harvard University Press, 1983), pp. 30–1.

7   Joel Myerson, "Emerson's 'Thoreau': A New Edition from Manuscript," in *Studies in the American Renaissance 1979*, ed. Myerson (New York: G. K. Hall, 1979), pp. 17–55 (see especially pp. 28–30); subsequent references to "Thoreau" are to this edition and are cited parenthetically in the text.

8   *The Selected Letters of Louisa May Alcott*, ed. Joel Myerson and Daniel Shealy (Boston: Little, Brown, 1987), p. 74.

9   See Henry Petroski, *The Pencil: A History of Design and Circumstances* (New York: Knopf, 1989), pp. 104–25, for the best account of Thoreau's contributions to the pencil-making process.

10 That Emerson created the impression – while seeming to praise him – that Thoreau was willful and perverse, is corroborated by Julia Ward Howe's reaction to this passage in her *Reminiscences, 1819–1899:* "I remember hearing Mr. Emerson, in his discourse on Henry Thoreau, relate that the latter had once determined to manufacture the best lead pencil that could possibly be made. Having attained this end, parties interested at once besought him to make this excellent article attainable in trade. He said, 'Why should I do this? I have shown that I am able to produce the best pencil that can be made. This was all that I cared to do.' The selfishness and egotism of this point of view did not appear to have entered into Mr. Emerson's thoughts" (1899; rpt. New York: Negro Universities Press, 1969, pp. 290–1).

4

LINCK C. JOHNSON

A Week on the Concord and Merrimack Rivers

"There is nothing very good to tell you of the people here, no books, no poets, no artists; nothing but their incessant activity as pioneers & geographers," Emerson wrote an English friend in May 1849. Despite his usual complaint that the "material problem" of opening up new territories engrossed so much of the energy of Americans, Emerson expressed a hope that his country would nonetheless soon produce a major writer, adding: "I ought to say, however, that my friend Thoreau is shortly to print a book called 'A Week on the Concord & Merrimack Rivers,' which, I think, will win the best readers abroad & at home."[1] As that afterthought indicates, Emerson clearly did not believe that his young friend was the "great one" he prophesied. Even his tepid prediction that *A Week* would attract "the best readers" proved to be overly optimistic, for Thoreau's first book was read by very few people in either England or the United States. Now that Thoreau is widely viewed as one of the "classic" American authors, *A Week* has gained a larger audience. Yet it is probably his least familiar book, one that is almost completely overshadowed by *Walden*.

The relative neglect of *A Week* is not terribly surprising. For one thing, it is a very long book, nearly four hundred pages in the Princeton edition of *The Writings of Henry D. Thoreau*. What Dr. Samuel Johnson said of Milton's *Paradise Lost*, that "none ever wished it longer than it is," is perhaps equally true of *A Week*. Moreover, although it initially seems to be a fairly straightforward travel book, much of the text of *A Week* is devoted to a series of essays or "digressions" on subjects ranging from the Christian church and books ("Sunday"), through Hindu scripture ("Monday") and friendship ("Wednesday"), to writers like the Greek lyricist Anacreon ("Tuesday"), the Roman satirist Aulus Persius Flaccus ("Thursday"), and the British poets Ossian and Chaucer ("Friday"). "We come upon them like snags, jolting us headforemost out of our places as we are rowing placidly up stream or drifting down," James Russell Lowell complained in an otherwise laudatory review of *A Week*:

Mr. Thoreau becomes so absorbed in these discussions, that he seems, as it were, to *catch a crab*, and disappears uncomfortably from his seat at the bow-oar. We could forgive them all, especially that on Books, and that on Friendship, (which is worthy of one who has so long commerced with Nature and with Emerson,) we could welcome them all, were they put by themselves at the end of the book. But as it is, they are out of proportion and out of place, and mar our Merrimacking dreadfully. We were bid to a river-party, not to be preached at.[2]

Lowell's witty critique has been echoed by numerous critics, including some of Thoreau's most dedicated students and fervent admirers.[3] Such objections to the book's organization raise a fundamental question about *A Week*: what kind of book is it? The answer each reader offers to that question will profoundly influence his or her reading, since our response to any text is in large part shaped by our assumptions about the kind of book we are reading and, consequently, by the expectations different genres generate. (We do not, for example, read a lyric poem with the same expectations we bring to a novel.) If, as Lowell assumed, *A Week* is primarily a travel book, most of Thoreau's digressions are just that, turnings away from the main subject of the narrative. If, on the other hand, Thoreau's account of the voyage is either a part of or a metaphor for a larger quest, then the digressions are not turnings away but simply different approaches to the main subject of the book. The question about what kind of book Thoreau wrote may therefore be rephrased: does he bid us to "a river-party," as Lowell would have it, or does he invite us to join with him in an ambitious voyage of discovery, one that leads us far beyond the temporal and spatial boundaries seemingly established by the title *A Week on the Concord and Merrimack Rivers*?

Perhaps the clearest answer to that question is suggested by the history of the writing of the book, which occupied Thoreau on and off for nearly ten years.[4] The voyage described in *A Week* was part of a two-week boating and hiking trip he and his brother, John Thoreau, Jr., made to the White Mountains of New Hampshire in the late summer of 1839. In *A Week* Thoreau refers to writing "the journal of the voyage"; in fact, he jotted down only a few sketchy notes during the trip, which he evidently did not view as the subject even for an essay, and certainly did not view as one for a book. Although he had begun to keep a journal shortly after his graduation from Harvard College two years earlier, and had delivered two lectures at the Concord Lyceum, the only piece Thoreau had written for publication was a brief obituary printed in a local newspaper. Shortly after he and John returned from their vacation to the White Mountains in September 1839, Emerson and his fellow members of the "Hedge Club" – an informal group of Unitarian ministers and other intellectuals also known as the Transcendental Club – decided to establish a new journal, the *Dial*, where most of Thoreau's early writings would ultimately be published. In response to the establishment of the *Dial*, he began to plan essays on various subjects, including the excursion to the White Mountains. A list of essay topics he jotted down in 1840 included "Memoirs of a Tour – A Chit-chat with Nature," an awkward title Thoreau revised to "Merrimack & Musketaquid [the Indian name for Concord River]" when he drew up a new list of essay topics in 1841.

Together with some passages Thoreau drafted in the Journal, those titles offer some hints about his initial conception of the essay. "Memoirs" usually stands for a factual account written by a major participant in the actions, while the subtitle "A Chit-chat with Nature" suggests that Thoreau's account would focus on the casual "conversation" between the travelers and the natural world. The title reveals the influence of travel books, which he read avidly, and of Emerson, whose first book, *Nature*, was published in 1836.⁵ Thoreau's title does not, however, clearly indicate on which part of the brothers' "Tour" he planned to focus – their voyage on the Concord and Merrimack rivers or their week-long walking tour of the White Mountains. In a Journal entry dated June 11, 1840, he referred to the trip as their "White Mountain expedition," but the entry itself described their boat, their provisions, and the commencement of their voyage (*PJ* 1:124–6). The revised title he jotted down a year later, "Merrimack & Musketaquid," indicates that by 1841 he had clearly decided to focus on the river voyage rather than the tour of the White Mountains.

Characteristically, Thoreau was less interested in their destination than in the journey itself, which provided an occasion for the kind of inward exploration that most fully engaged him. "But we will not leap at once to our journey's end, though near, but imitate Homer, who conducts his reader over the plain, and along the resounding sea, though it be but to the tent of Achilles," he observed in "A Walk to Wachusett," an essay published in 1843. "In the spaces of thought are the reaches of land and water, where men go and come. The landscape lies far and fair within, and the deepest thinker is the farthest traveled."⁶ Thoreau thus established the intimate connection between literal and figurative travel, outward and inward exploration, the earthbound physical journey and the intellectual flights it inspired, sketching the contours of a literary form in which natural description and poetic meditation would be wedded, as they are in *A Week*. In his earliest "excursions," Thoreau also experimented with structural elements he would later incorporate into the design of *A Week*. "A Walk to Wachusett" is an account of his journey to and from a distant mountain,

Wachusett Mountain in western Massachusetts, which Thoreau and a friend ascended in the summer of 1842. "A Winter Walk," written the following year, describes a day-long ramble about his native town of Concord, Massachusetts. Thoreau would later exploit both patterns in *A Week,* in which each chapter describes the movement from morning to night, while the narrative as a whole charts the journey to and from Mt. Washington, the distant mountain the brothers ascend in "Thursday."

Although he began to plan a book about the trip as early as 1842, probably a few months after his brother's death in January, Thoreau did not actually begin to gather materials for *A Week* until 1844. By then, however, he had published numerous pieces that he later incorporated into the book. As his reference to Homer in "A Walk to Wachusett" indicates, and as any reader of *A Week* will immediately recognize, Thoreau was a very literary young man whose early writings were as deeply rooted in his voracious reading as in his close observation of nature. Many of the innumerable quotations in *A Week* were harvested from his "commonplace books," notebooks in which Thoreau jotted down choice passages from books he read. He was especially attracted to older writings, including ancient Hindu scriptures, the Greek and Roman classics, and English literature of the Middle Ages and Renaissance. The first issue of the *Dial,* for example, included his article "Aulus Persius Flaccus," a critique of the Roman satirist that Thoreau later inserted into "Thursday" (307–13). Several of his other contributions to the *Dial* also found their way into *A Week:* a number of his early poems, including "Sympathy" (260–1), "Stanzas" (285), "Friendship" (287–9), "The Inward Morning" (294–5), and "Sic Vita" (383–4); his translations of the minor Greek poet Anacreon (225–31); "Dark Ages," a brief essay on history he incorporated into "Monday" (154–8); and one of his longest essays in the *Dial,* "Homer. Ossian. Chaucer," which he divided between "Sunday" (91–5) and "Friday" (343–8, 366–77). In addition, *A Week* contains extracts from two early unpublished essays: an 1842 commentary on *The Laws of Menu,* one of the Hindu scriptures he praises in "Monday" (147–54); and an appreciative essay on the Renaissance writer and adventurer Sir Walter Raleigh. After delivering a lecture on Raleigh at the Concord Lyceum in 1843, Thoreau revised and expanded his manuscript for the *Dial.* But it ceased publication before the manuscript was printed, so the only portions of the essay on Raleigh published during Thoreau's life were those he later revised for the discussion of books in "Sunday" (90–109), the most extensive digression on literary matters in *A Week.*

Whereas the establishment of the *Dial* in 1840 prompted Thoreau to plan an essay on the voyage, the collapse of that journal in 1844 spurred him to begin his long-delayed book. He may also have been inspired to begin work on his first book by the completion of the first book by his friend and associate Margaret Fuller, whose travelogue, *Summer on the Lakes,* was published at the end of the summer of 1844. That fall, Thoreau began to gather material in what he called the Long Book, a large notebook in which he transcribed passages from his Journal of 1837–44. When he completed his transcriptions, Thoreau numbered each passage according to its projected place in the first draft of *A Week,* written after he moved to Walden Pond on July 4, 1845. As that painstaking process of composition suggests, *A Week* was less a product of direct observation during the voyage than of Thoreau's retrospective reconstruction of that journey, an effort in which he was aided by guide books such as the *New England Gazetteer.* Thoreau, however, did not set out to write simply a narrative of the brothers' voyage. Instead, he obviously intended to take full advantage of what had also attracted Fuller to the genre of travel writing: what Susan Belasco Smith has characterized as "the freedom of the form," the flexibility it offered "to explore summer wanderings both external and internal."[7] Even the first draft of *A Week,* which was much shorter than the published version, contained numerous poems and a series of extended digressions, including a descriptive catalog of the fish of Concord River in "Saturday," a meditation on freedom versus wildness in "Sunday," a discussion of Hindu scripture in "Monday," and, most significantly, a long essay on friendship in "Wednesday," where he celebrated the fraternal bond between the two brothers who had together voyaged on the Concord and Merrimack rivers.

In the first draft Thoreau lovingly evoked an idyllic past, but his account was ultimately shaped by the social and political conflicts of an increasingly troubled present. For several years before he moved to Walden Pond and began to write *A Week,* Thoreau had refused to pay his poll tax, an annual tax levied on all adult males in Massachusetts. His refusal was a protest against slavery, a divisive issue that was heightened by the annexation of Texas in 1845 and the subsequent outbreak of the Mexican War early in 1846. In July 1846, Thoreau was arrested and jailed for one night when he once again refused to pay his tax. Outraged by his imprisonment, he lashed out against what he called "dead institutions," the church and the state, in a Journal entry later revised for *A Week* (*PJ* 2:262–4; cf. *Week* 129–34). As he worked on the second draft during 1846–7, he also added a much longer and far more provocative critique of the Christian church to "Sunday." Consequently, although he reserved much of his social and political criticism for *Walden,* begun in late 1846, and for an 1848 lecture now widely known as "Civil Disobedience," Thoreau in *A Week* also vigorously challenged the values and institutions of antebellum America.

Even as he did so, Thoreau was becoming increasingly fascinated with American history, especially the history of Indian–white relations in New England. In the first draft of *A Week*, Thoreau paid scant attention to the rich history of the territories through which he and his brother had voyaged. In the second draft, however, he began to exploit the possibilities the account offered him to explore human as well as natural history. In fact, the voyage up the Merrimack came to symbolize a movement against the current of time and history, ever deeper into the American past. "It was . . . an old battle and hunting ground through which we had been floating," Thoreau observes shortly after the brothers enter the Merrimack, "the ancient dwelling-place of a race of hunters and warriors" (*Week* 82). As that remark suggests, he was fully aware that native Americans had a long history preceding what Thoreau in the first draft dismissed as accounts of "white men's exploits" – written histories of the settlement and conquest of New England by settlers from Europe. Nonetheless, his efforts to rewrite American history in *A Week* owed a great deal to such accounts, including histories written during the colonial period and the numerous local histories published during the nineteenth century, works like B. L. Mirick's *History of Haverhill, Massachusetts* (1832) and Charles J. Fox's *History of the Old Township of Dunstable* (1846). Fox's book provided Thoreau with more material than any other single source, while Mirick's inspired the most powerful historical narrative in *A Week*, his account in "Thursday" of Hannah Dustan's capture, captivity, and escape (*Week* 320–4), which he began to draft in the Journal in the spring of 1847 (*PJ* 2:377).

By then, Thoreau had also begun to incorporate into the second draft a good deal of material originally written without reference to *A Week*. Acting as Thoreau's agent, Emerson, in March 1847, wrote to a publisher that his friend had "just completed a book of extraordinary merit," then entitled "An Excursion on the Concord & Merrimack Rivers." Despite its title, Emerson emphasized that the "Excursion" was not a conventional travel book, since its narrative was "a very slender thread for such big beads & ingots as are strung on it." The book, he observed, would therefore not only be attractive "to *lovers of nature*," but also "to scholars for its excellent literature," because "It is really a book of the results of the studies of years."[8] As Emerson well knew, those "studies" had earlier produced the poems, translations, and articles Thoreau had published in the *Dial* and later incorporated into the manuscript of *A Week*. After failing to find a publisher in 1847, Thoreau continued to revise and expand the manuscript, and evidently added even more of his early writings. For example, in a letter written in March 1848 a friend praised "Aulus Persius Flaccus," Thoreau's first publication in the *Dial*, where it had appeared in July 1840. Thoreau replied that he had not read the article in years, so that he "had to look at that page again, to learn what was the tenor of my thoughts then" (*Corr* 214). Surprisingly, he, too, was apparently impressed by "Aulus Persius Flaccus," for a corrected version of the article appears in "Thursday." It joins a digression on another author, Goethe, whose *Italienische Reise (Italian Journey)* Thoreau had praised in an 1838 Journal entry he later developed for *A Week* (*PJ* 1:30; cf. *Week* 325–7).

Thoreau's own journeys during the 1840s also shaped *A Week*. On August 31, 1846 – on the same day he and his brother had embarked for the White Mountains seven years earlier – Thoreau set off on a trip to Maine, where he hoped to gain glimpses of native American culture and to immerse himself in the last surviving wilderness in New England. The centerpiece of his account of that trip, published as "Ktaadn, and the Maine Woods" in 1848, was the ascent of Mt. Katahdin, which he depicted as a vast, forbidding realm reminiscent of "the creations of the old epic and dramatic poets" (*MW* 64). Possibly as a result of that rugged experience, Thoreau omitted from *A Week* a guide-bookish description of the inns he and his brother had visited during their tour of the White Mountains, which were quickly becoming one of the major tourist attractions of New England. In the brief account of the White Mountains tour in "Thursday," where Thoreau describes the brothers' progress through "Unappropriated Land" to the fountain-head of the Merrimack, the New Hampshire mountains seem as remote, mysterious, and unexplored as Maine's Katahdin.

Within the larger journey depicted in *A Week,* Thoreau also offered brief accounts of trips to other mountains: his walk to Wachusett Mountain (*Week* 162–6); his ascent of Saddle-back Mountain (Mt. Greylock, in Massachusetts) which he climbed in 1844 (180–90); and an earlier episode during the latter trip, when he met Rice, the rude but hospitable man at whose farm in an isolated mountain valley Thoreau spent a night (202–9). At several places he refers to another trip he and a friend made to the valley of the Merrimack, in 1848, when he ascended Uncannunuc Mountain and climbed to the top of Hooksett Pinnacle (255, 302). The river voyage described in *A Week* is consequently punctuated by a series of ascents, preliminary pilgrimages to mountain tops that prepare for the ultimate climb to "the summit of AGIOCOCHOOK" – significantly, Thoreau adopted the Indian name for Mt. Washington – the highest peak in New England (314).

By the time he decided to publish *A Week* at his own risk in 1849, Thoreau had thus transformed what he had originally conceived as an essay mingling travel and natural history into a far more ambitious and complex work. One effect of the complementary excursions within the larger excursion depicted in *A Week* is to expand both its temporal and spatial boundaries. That effect is intensified by the numerous digressions, the meditations and essays in which Thoreau ranges from the ancient past to the troubled present, from India and Greece to New England – a heterogeneous array of materials that generates a sense of richness and profusion. Even for readers expecting something other than a straightforward travel narrative, however, such profusion may generate a good deal of confusion. Certainly the form of *A Week* – or, rather, its apparent lack of form – raises some crucial questions. What, for example, is the relation between the numerous digressions and Thoreau's account of the voyage? And what are the relations among those numerous digressions? In short, what, if anything, gives unity and coherence to a book that seems to defy all boundaries, either spatial or temporal, and that also seems to defy all generic conventions, mingling poetry and prose, narrative and meditation, natural history and local lore, a lofty essay on friendship, commentaries on writers and writing, and fierce polemics on the injustices of contemporary social institutions?

Some answers to those questions are suggested by the most traumatic event in Thoreau's early life, the death of John Thoreau, Jr., in January 1842. The loss of his brother not only prompted Thoreau to begin to plan a book about their 1839 voyage, it also profoundly influenced the form and contents of *A Week*.[9] Although Thoreau never explicitly refers to his brother's death, that event is obliquely evoked at various points, including his extended essay on friendship in "Wednesday." There, he celebrates friendship as the most ancient and natural of human relationships, an enduring bond that transcends death itself. "Even the death of Friends will inspire us as much as their lives" (*Week* 286), he declares near the end of the digression that, in fact, hints at one of the central concerns of *A Week*. Implicitly, John's death inspired him to write the book, which is perhaps best approached and most clearly understood as a prose version of the pastoral elegy, a poem expressing grief at the loss of a friend. Indeed, *A Week* bears some striking resemblances to Milton's "Lycidas," the most famous pastoral elegy in English. Just as Milton mourned his friend Edward King, a young man "dead ere his prime," Thoreau mourned the loss of his brother and closest friend, who died from lockjaw (a deadly form of tetanus) when he was only twenty-seven years old. Although Thoreau freely adapted the elegiac form, he incorporated some of the primary features of Milton's pastoral elegy, which includes an invocation of the Muse, a suggestion that the normal processes of nature have been impeded or reversed by the death of his friend, and flower symbolism. The pastoral elegy also featured digressions – in "Lycidas," the major digression is on the corruptions of the Church, subject of the extended digression in "Sunday" – as well as a consolation combined with an expression of belief in some form of immortality, which Thoreau affirms in various ways in his final chapters.

Thoreau echoes "Lycidas" at the very opening of *A Week*. In the final lines of his poem Milton envisages Edward King risen to heaven, "Where other groves, and other streams along, / With *Nectar* pure his oozy Locks he laves" (ll. 174–5). In some lines of verse jotted down on the first page of the Long Book and later used as the first of the epigraphs to *A Week*, Thoreau places his brother in a similarly transfigured landscape:

> Where'er thou sail'st who sailed with me,
> Though now thou climbest loftier mounts,
> And fairer rivers dost ascend,
> Be thou my Muse, my Brother – . (3)

Thoreau's invocation of John as his Muse, the poetic inspiration for the book that follows, illuminates the narrative strategies of *A Week*. In contrast to *Walden*, with its dominant and insistent "I," Thoreau limits the first person singular to digressions and to the introductory chapter, "Concord River." There, standing by the banks of his native stream at the beginning, he somberly meditates on time and the river, a symbol of the transience of all life. Describing the objects that float by, "fulfilling their fate," Thoreau in that chapter's final sentence observes, "at last I resolved to launch myself on its bosom, and float wither it would bear me" (*Week* 13). In the first sentence of "Saturday," he shifts from "I" to "we," the brothers who embark on the river journey: "At length, on Saturday, the last day of August, 1839, we two, brothers, and natives of Concord, weighed anchor in this river port" (15). As Jonathan Bishop has observed, "John disappears into the 'we' who together constitute the anonymous sensibility of the narrator."[10] Even when Thoreau describes their individual actions, he avoids using "I" and "he," making it impossible to distinguish which brother is doing what. For example, in his description of their swift passage through the Middlesex Canal, he observes that "while one ran along the tow-path drawing the boat by a cord, the other kept it off the shore with a pole" (62). Moreover, by referring to "our journals" and "our journal" of the voyage (332), Thoreau suggests that John, who had also shared his interest in books, nature, and native Americans, was the co-author of the account.

John thus remains a living presence, both during the voyage and during the writing of *A Week*. Nonetheless, his death is at least obliquely evoked in "Saturday." Although the voyage opens on a note of excitement and expectancy, on "a mild afternoon, as serene and fresh as if nature were maturing some greater scheme of her own" (15), Thoreau's descriptions of nature are poised between fruition and decay, permanence and transience, vitality and vulnerability. Near the end of a passage describing the rich array of flowers along the banks of Concord River, in which he observes that "nature seemed to have adorned herself for our departure," Thoreau sounded a more ominous note: "But we missed the white water-lily, which is the queen of river-flowers, its reign being over for this season. He makes his voyage too late, perhaps, by a true water clock who delays so long" (21). Shortly thereafter, he describes the brothers' pause at Ball's Hill, where they gather a few remaining berries, "hanging by very slender threads" (22).

Such indications of the apparent transience and fragility of life are underscored by Thoreau's initial digressions in *A Week*. In his descriptive catalog of Concord River fish in "Saturday," for example, he devotes particular attention to shad and other migratory fish, which "were formerly abundant here . . . until the dam, and afterward the canal at Billerica, and the factories at Lowell, put an end to their migrations hitherward" (33). In an intense apostrophe to the innocent shad, Thoreau dismisses "the superficial and selfish phil-*anthropy* of men" and asserts his solidarity with the fish (37). As he emphasizes in "Sunday," the so-called "development" of New England had an even more devastating impact on men, especially the Indians. In his brief history of Billerica, one of the oldest towns in Massachusetts, Thoreau depicts the European settlement of New England in terms of invasion, violation, and destruction, as the white man "rudely bridged the stream, and drove his team afield into the river meadows, cut the wild grass, and laid bare the homes of beaver, otter, muskrat, and with the whetting of his scythe scared off the deer and bear." Thoreau images the industrious white farmer as a figure of death, the grim reaper whose immediate victims are the indigenous inhabitants of the land. "The white man's mullein soon reigned in Indian corn-fields, and sweet scented English grasses clothed the new soil," he continues. "Where, then, could the Red Man set his foot?" (52–3).

A driving force in the early settlement of New England was religion, which, appropriately enough, is Thoreau's primary concern in "Sunday." Describing the ringing of the church bell in Billerica, he observes, "No wonder that such a sound startled the dreaming Indian, and frightened his game" (50). In effect, that bell had tolled the doom of native Americans and their culture, since the white settlers had dispossessed them of their religious traditions as well as of their land. Ironically, those "seeking 'freedom to worship God' in their way" (52) had consistently denied such freedom to others. Thoreau subsequently frames his extended critique of the Christian church in "Sunday" with incidents that illustrate his central point concerning the narrowness and bigotry of institutionalized Christianity. "As we passed under the last bridge over the [Middlesex] canal," he remarks, "the people coming out of church paused to look at us from above, and apparently, so strong is custom, indulged in some heathenish comparisons," since the brothers were breaking a religious law by traveling on the sabbath (63). The source of such an intolerant custom was the zealous Christianity of the Puritan founders of New England. The incident on the canal occasions Thoreau's critique of the church; he immediately follows it with an account of the conversion of Wannalancet, one of the chiefs of the Pawtucket tribe, near Wamesit, "where the Indians resorted in the fishing season," but which is "now Lowell, the city of spindles and Manchester of America" (83). As that pointed comment suggests, the religious conversion of Indians like Wannalancet went hand in hand with the "conversion," and consequent debasement, of their land, first into agricultural villages like Billerica and finally into cities like Lowell, both an illustration and the symbol of the industrialization Thoreau decried in both *A Week* and *Walden.*

As he recognized, however, converts like Wannalancet were the exception, for the Indians had not yielded their lands without a struggle. Beginning in "Monday" with an account of Lovewell's Fight, one of the most famous battles of the Indian wars, Thoreau deftly uses various incidents of local history to chart that struggle, offering a highly colored version of colonial history that culminates in his brilliant re-creation of the Hannah Dustan story in "Thursday" (320–4). As Harry Henderson has pointed out, the incidents depicted in *A Week* "are not merely local, but national in their communal resonance, and belong to the national legend of expansion into the wilderness as surely as do Filson's *Narrative* of Boone, the novels of Cooper, and the works of Parkman."[11] (Parkman's *The Oregon Trail* was published a few months before *A Week*.) Indeed, for Thoreau the destruction of the Indians was an integral part of one of the greatest catastrophes in history, a story with implications for all humanity. "This seems a long while ago, and yet it happened since Milton wrote his Paradise Lost," he observes in a meditation on history following the Hannah Dustan story (324). Implicitly, in the two centuries since Milton had written *Paradise Lost,* another paradise had been lost in America, where the hope for a new start for humanity had been blighted by the religious, cultural, and military conflict that had led to the destruction of the natives by the European settlers of New England.

Thoreau's excursions into colonial history are closely related to the central concern and the overarching drama of *A Week,* the concern with loss and the effort at recovery. Even as he mourns the passing of the Indians from the American scene – and his declaration of their extinction was more compelling than accurate – Thoreau displays his determination to vivify their spirit in his own life and writings. In a disquisition on freedom versus wildness in "Sunday," he insists that his own "genius dates from an older era than the agricultural," adding: "If we could listen but for an instant to the chaunt of the Indian muse, we should understand why he will not exchange his savageness for civilization" (54, 56). Significantly, however, Thoreau proclaims his allegiance to the Indians in a book, a means of expression that most clearly distinguished his own culture from that of the native inhabitants of New England. Despite his determination to attend to "the Indian muse," Thoreau's deepest inspiration came from books, so it is hardly surprising that he turns his attention to books at the end of "Sunday." In that extended digression, which may be understood as an effort to discover within his own culture and experience some correlative or equivalent to what he could only imagine to be the "spirit" that inspired the Indians, Thoreau includes an effusive paean to Homer. Just as he earlier remarks that the Indian "is admitted from time to time to a rare and peculiar society with nature" (55), so he insists that, in Homer, "It is as if nature spoke" (91–2). Similarly, just as he emphasizes the losses consequent upon the rise of civilization, in which "man degenerates at length" (56), so does he depict Homer as a primitive bard whose simplicity and naturalness expose the increasing artifice of the authors surveyed in later chapters of *A Week.*

Into his narrative of the 1839 journey, Thoreau thus wove two closely related historical narratives. In one, he offered what Robert Sayre has aptly described as "a condensed history, in an inferential, poetic form, of Indian–European relations in America, as represented in the little corner of northeastern Massachusetts and southern New Hampshire which is the book's microcosm."[12] In the other, Thoreau constructed an equally condensed and primitivistic history of Western literature, primarily by revising and arranging pieces he had earlier published in the *Dial.* Thoreau charts the decline from the epic poetry of the ancients through two traditions. In the classical tradition, he moves from Homer in "Sunday" through the minor Greek poet Anacreon in "Tuesday" to Aulus Persius Flaccus and Goethe in "Thursday." Emphasizing the "ethereal and evanescent beauty" of Anacreon's odes (226), Thoreau implies what his commentaries in "Thursday" explicitly indicate, the artistic costs of turning from nature to society. "Here is none of the interior dignity of Virgil, nor the elegance and vivacity of Horace, nor will any sybil be needed to remind you, that from those older Greek poets there is a sad descent to Persius," he observes of the Roman satirist. "You can scarcely distinguish one harmonious sound amid this unmusical bickering with the follies of men" (307–8). Even Goethe, a kind of culture hero among the Transcendentalists, is depicted as a victim of society, for his education "defrauded" him "of much which the savage boy enjoys" (327). In "Friday" Thoreau charts a similar declension in British poetry from the Celtic bard Ossian, who "reminds us of the most refined and rudest eras, of Homer, Pindar, Isaiah, and the American Indian" (344), to Chaucer and poets of more civilized periods, during which the poet had "come within doors, and exchanged the forest and crag for the fireside" (367).

Like his version of Indian–European relations, Thoreau's vision of literary history challenged the assumptions of most contemporary historians, who viewed the control of "primitive" forces as a necessary part of human progress and the triumph of civilization.[13] In *A Week* he carefully tallies the costs of that "triumph," opposing the idea of progress by emphasizing the decline in society, religion, and literature. Despite his emphasis on cultural decline, however, Thoreau suggests that such a debilitating process might be reversed. What connects his various digressions is his consistent effort to reclaim values that only seem to be lost. In contrast to the ruins of Egypt, "the death of that which never lived," he affirms that "the rays of Greek poetry struggle down to us, and mingle with the sunbeams of the recent day" (95). As his imagery suggests, Thoreau distinguished between cultural artifacts, which were subject to the ravages of time and history, and works like the *Iliad,* which were natural phenomena that shared the vitality and persistence of nature itself. (Not surprisingly, given his variant on the opposition between "culture" and "nature," Thoreau makes no reference to the scholars who edited and published classical texts, or to the controversy over the authenticity of the "Genuine Remains of Ossian," most of which was actually written by the eighteenth-century poet James Macpherson.) In passages that constitute a powerful counterweight to the theme of decline, Thoreau discovers numerous signs of enduring life and vitality, signs he reveals in various ways: in his descriptions of unspoiled nature, places where "the country appeared in its primitive state, and as if the Indian still inhabited it" (194); in his depictions of individuals who embody ancient virtues and values, men like Rice and the boatmen the brothers encounter on the voyage up the Merrimack; and in his hopeful commentaries on the kind of literature that might yet emerge in America, books that would revive the heroic spirit of ancient poetry, display the freedom and wildness he associated with native Americans, and celebrate the natural splendors of the New World.

Appropriately, in the major fruit of his literary apprenticeship, Thoreau in A Week defined his vocation as a writer. Books "must themselves be the unconstrained and natural harvest of their author's lives," he remarks in "Sunday" (98), anticipating there the autumnal imagery that dominates "Friday." Although he and his brother returned to Concord on September 13, eight days before the autumnal equinox, Thoreau devotes much of the final chapter of A Week to meditations on the autumnal scene. Those meditations serve two primary purposes. First, in contrast to his descriptions in "Saturday," where he emphasizes the frailty and transience of the summer flowers, Thoreau in "Friday" heralds the "floral solstice," a rich end-of-summer array that symbolizes the vitality and endurance of life itself (353–5). If A Week is read as an elegy, that passage may be interpreted as one of many indications of his movement from initial grief to final resolution, a resolution based on a recognition of nature's ongoing health and vitality. Second, by depicting autumn, not in terms of decay and death, but rather as a time of fruition and promise, Thoreau also finds in nature an inspiration for his own literary labors. "Thus thoughtfully we were rowing homeward to find some autumnal work to do, and help on the revolution of the seasons," he observes near the end of "Friday." "Perhaps Nature would condescend to make use of us even without our knowledge, as when we help to scatter her seeds in our walks, and carry burrs and cockles from field to field" (388–9). That work was the writing of A Week, the first substantial harvest of his own life, as well as a book he hoped would contain seeds that would germinate in the lives of his readers. Indeed, like Walden, A Week reveals Thoreau's profound faith in words, in the power of a text to transform the lives of readers and, consequently, to reform the institutions of society.

Thoreau's great hopes for his first book no doubt made its failure all the more painful to him. Certainly he had hoped A Week would fulfill the high expectations of his mentor, Emerson, who was obviously disappointed in the book and whose lukewarm response to its publication coincided with a breach between him and Thoreau that never completely healed. A Week generated even less enthusiasm outside Concord. Although it was designed as a memorial to his brother, the book was produced for the literary marketplace, in which Thoreau had struggled for nearly a decade to secure a foothold. He clearly hoped it would be his breakthrough, a work that would finally gain him a wide audience and establish him as a professional writer. Instead, the book was a complete flop. It received some respectful and respectable notices, but many reviewers were either dismissive or hostile, characterizing Thoreau as a mere imitator of Emerson or attacking his unorthodox religious views. Even the religious controversy *A Week* ignited among reviewers failed to attract readers: during the following four years the book sold only about two hundred of the thousand copies printed in 1849. Thoreau, who had expected to pay for the costs of publication out of his earnings from the book, was left with a debt of nearly $300, a significant amount of money at the time. The final indignity came in 1853, when his publisher returned the unsold copies to Thoreau. "They are something more substantial than fame, as my back knows, which has borne them up two flights of stairs to a place similar to that to which they trace their origin," he recorded in the Journal. "Is it not well that the author should behold the fruits of his labor? My works are piled up on one side of my chamber half as high as my head, my *opera omnia*. This is authorship; these are the work of my brain" (*J* 5:459).

Ironically, however, the book that gained Thoreau posthumous fame owed a great deal both to his work on and to the failure of *A Week*. Although even some recent critics have contrasted its apparent formlessness to the unified structure of *Walden*, others have argued that Thoreau's celebrated account of his life at Walden Pond was less a departure from than an outgrowth of the formal experiments he had undertaken in his first book. For example, calling attention to the various patterns in *A Week* – the movement away from and the return to Concord, the ascent and descent of mountains, and the cycles of the day, the week, and the seasons – Frederick Garber has affirmed that its design "is unsurpassed in Thoreau's work for the complex counterpoint of its components."[4] Moreover, had his first book initially received anything like the attention much later lavished on *Walden*, that acknowledged masterpiece would probably have been a radically different and far less compelling book. When he arranged to publish *A Week*, Thoreau originally planned to publish a much shorter version of *Walden*, which he apparently viewed as a kind of sequel, perhaps as an illustration of that "*natural* life" adumbrated in "Friday" (379–83). The failure of his first book delayed the publication of *Walden* until 1854, by which time Thoreau had transformed it into a richer, more resonant, and far more unified book, in part by more fully exploiting the kinds of structural patterns he had first developed in *A Week*. Yet even in its final form *Walden* is a less ambitious book than *A Week*, which, as Lawrence Buell has suggested, attempts "nothing less than to encompass the whole of Thoreau's intellectual and spiritual development, indeed to take in the whole cultural history of mankind." Buell is surely right to describe that as a "quixotic task"; I think he is also right to suggest that Thoreau's extraordinary ambitions in *A Week* place it "in the same category with those other American failures, from Melville to Dreiser to Williams, which together make up so much of what is interesting in our literary history."[5]

NOTES

1 *The Letters of Ralph Waldo Emerson*, ed. Ralph L. Rusk and Eleanor M. Tilton, 8 vols. to date (New York: Columbia University Press, 1939; 1990–), 4:145.

2 James Russell Lowell, review of *A Week on the Concord and Merrimack Rivers*, *Massachusetts Quarterly Review* 3 (December 1849): 40–51; rpt. *Thoreau Society Bulletin*, 35 (April 1951): 1–3. For a detailed discussion of the reception and later reputation of *A Week*, see Linck C. Johnson's "Historical Introduction" to the Princeton edition (*Week* 471ff.). All quotations from *A Week* are cited in the text.

3 See, for example, Harding's discussion of *A Week* in Walter Harding and Michael Meyer, *The New Thoreau Handbook* (New York: New York University Press, 1980), pp. 42–5.

4 The fullest account of his work on the book is Linck C. Johnson, *Thoreau's Complex Weave: The Writing of "A Week on the Concord and Merrimack Rivers," with the Text of the First Draft* (Charlottesville: University Press of Virginia, 1986).

5 For a discussion of Thoreau's life-long interest in travel literature, see John Aldrich Christie, *Thoreau as World Traveler* (New York: Columbia University Press, 1965).

6 Henry David Thoreau, *The Natural History Essays*, with an introductory essay and notes by Robert Sattelmeyer (Salt Lake City: Peregrine Smith Books, 1984), p. 33.

7 Susan Belasco Smith, "Introduction" to Margaret Fuller, *Summer on the Lakes, in 1843* (Urbana: University of Illinois Press, 1991), p. xii. Discussing its "miscellaneous character" and "digressive form," about which critics of *Summer on the Lakes* have frequently complained, Smith convincingly suggests that the structure of Fuller's book is better understood when it is read as part of "the tradition of portfolio and sketchbook writing that began at the turn of the nineteenth century" (pp. xii–xiv). Although he evidently sought and, I think, finally gained greater unity and coherence in *A Week*, Thoreau no doubt profited from the example of Fuller's work, which Smith describes as "a collection of autobiographical sketches, social criticism, inspirational passages, Transcendental meditations, and stories of her travels" on and around the Great Lakes (p. xiv).

8 Ralph Waldo Emerson, *Letters* 3:384. His description of *A Week* recalls a passage in *Summer on the Lakes*, where, observing that she would have liked to include additional extracts from some of the travel books she had studied in preparation for writing her own account, Fuller added: "I wish I had a thread long enough to string on it all these beads that take my fancy; but, as I have not, I can only refer the reader to the books themselves" (p. 148). Interestingly,

one of the books she especially commended was Alexander Henry's *Travels and Adventures in Canada and the Indian Territories* (1809), which Thoreau also highly praised in *A Week* (218–19, 274–5).

9 See Johnson, *Thoreau's Complex Weave*, pp. 41–84; and H. Daniel Peck, *Thoreau's Morning Work: Memory and Perception in "A Week on the Concord and Merrimack Rivers," the Journal, and "Walden"* (New Haven: Yale University Press, 1990), pp. 3–36.

10 Jonathan Bishop, "The Experience of the Sacred in Thoreau's *Week*," *ELH* 33 (1966): 89–90. For a more detailed discussion of the interplay between "I" and "we" in the book, see Steven Fink, "Variations on the Self: Thoreau's Personae in *A Week on the Concord and Merrimack Rivers*," *ESQ* 28 (1982): 24–35.

11 Harry B. Henderson, *Versions of the Past: The Historical Imagination in American Fiction* (New York: Oxford University Press, 1974), pp. 8–9.

12 Robert F. Sayre, *Thoreau and the American Indians* (Princeton: Princeton University Press, 1977), p. 28.

13 For a discussion of Thoreau's relation to the romantic historians of the period, see Joan Burbick, *Thoreau's Alternative History: Changing Perspectives on Nature, Culture, and Language* (Philadelphia: University of Pennsylvania Press, 1987), especially pp. 15–34.

14 Frederick Garber, *Thoreau's Redemptive Imagination* (New York: New York University Press, 1977), p. 193. One of the first critics to emphasize the artistry and unity of *A Week*, as well as its connections to *Walden*, was Sherman Paul, *The Shores of America: Thoreau's Inward Exploration* (Urbana: University of Illinois Press, 1958), pp. 191–233.

15 Lawrence Buell, *Literary Transcendentalism: Style and Vision in the American Renaissance* (Ithaca, N.Y.: Cornell University Press, 1973), p. 207.

5

ELIZABETH HALL WITHERELL

Thoreau as poet

In the Transcendentalist view, especially as articulated by Ralph Waldo Emerson in "The Poet" and in *Nature,* the poet's responsibility is essentially religious – by a finer organization, a greater sensitivity to truth and beauty, the poet perceives and interprets the eternal realm that stands behind the apparent reality of the material world. Thoreau aspired to this sacred and powerful vocation at least from the time he began keeping his Journal in October 1837. Emerson indicates that poetry is defined by the strength of its internal source rather than by the regularity of its external form,[1] but as a young man just beginning to explore the shape of his literary vocation, Thoreau, with Emerson's encouragement, was a dedicated writer of verse.

Thoreau's poetry is for the most part unremarkable in its subject and its form, and it suffers in comparison with even the quotidian prose of the Journal. In the poems, Thoreau often uses images provided by natural phenomena in and around Concord, and he applies the high standards of his idealism to aspects of the human condition – love, friendship, memory, the transitory nature of life. Nature is acknowledged as the source of inspiration, and provides analogies and tropes for Thoreau's perceptions and concepts. More than three quarters of the poems are written in the first person or foreground the speaker in some way. Despite this, in general they are quite bland. In many cases, the persona provokes only mild interest, and the situations lack drama.

In the structure of his poems, Thoreau displays a good deal of flexibility in constructing complex combinations of meter and rhyme within the simple standard forms, but only rarely does the content inevitably shape the form: instead, as he complains of "verse for the most part" in a Journal entry for April 2, 1842, "the music now runs before and then behind the sense, but is never coincident with it" (*PJ* 1:399). He wrote half his poems in stanzas, both symmetric and irregular, and half in verse paragraphs. In the stanzaic poems, he uses the quatrain most frequently, as Carl Bode notes;[2] the forms of the single verse paragraphs range from traditional stanza patterns to free verse, and most of them rhyme.

Some of Thoreau's poems are thought-provoking, and some are energetic and entertaining.[3] A number of the most interesting ones are obviously biographical.[4] Only a few, however, are remarkable as poetry.[5] It is in the context of Thoreau's literary ambitions that the poetry assumes special interest and importance: here and there in the early poems, one notes the beginning of the development of an original voice. The role poetry played in the creation of that voice is most clearly seen in what survives of the first twelve years of his Journal, in what was published in the Transcendentalist periodical the *Dial,* and in his setting of poetry into a prose context, as is most obvious in *A Week on the Concord and Merrimack Rivers.*

These three documentary sources – the Journal, the *Dial,* and *A Week* – reveal, by what they exclude as well as what they include, the progress of Thoreau's career as a writer of verses. The period of his most sustained interest in writing poetry began in 1837 and was over by the end of 1844 (of this period, Bode justly says "when he wrote the most poetry, he was writing the best poetry" [*CP* viii]). His initial intention seems to have been to produce poems that would stand alone, and even to present himself to the public primarily as a poet, which he did in the *Dial* – although to the small and select public of Transcendentalist subscribers. During this time, he may have been keeping his poems in a separate notebook or portfolio. Sometime after an unusually intense period of poetic composition in the late summer and fall of 1841, however, he shifted his concentration away from poetry. Although he continued to compose poems in 1842 and 1843, and in the fall of 1842 sent three that had been published in the *Dial* to Rufus Griswold for *The Poets and Poetry of America* (*Corr* 54; Griswold did not publish them), there is no evidence that he sought to publish poems alone after the *Dial* came to an end in 1844. Instead, he found another use for his poems: they went into his first book, *A Week on the Concord and Merrimack Rivers,* to intensify and dramatize the exposition and give it depth as his quotation of the poetry of other authors does. In *A Week,* he quotes in entirety or quotes partially from over sixty of his poems, by far the largest number to appear anywhere in his lifetime. Most of these survive in manuscript versions that Thoreau composed before 1845. He recycled twelve from the *Dial.* Finally, after a brief flurry of poetry-writing in the late summer of 1850 (*PJ* 3:103–14), he essentially gave up the form: neither later published writings nor the Journal from 1850 to 1861 contains more than a handful of poems.

Thoreau's surviving manuscript Journal provides the evidence that he began writing poetry seriously enough to keep the results in 1838, when he was twenty-one years old, and continued serious versifying until 1850, when he was thirty-four. However, conclusions about numbers and dates of poems in the Journal cannot be definitive: Thoreau culled and copied the contents of the Journal from October 1837 to the beginning of February 1841 from two earlier, original Journal notebooks; his Journal from April 1842 until summer 1845, and also from late 1846 until late 1850, survives only in fragments, in manuscript volumes out of which many leaves have been cut, and in manuscript volumes with mostly undated entries.[6] There were probably many more poems than can be read in the Journal in its present form; nevertheless, enough have survived to demonstrate the importance of the Journal in Thoreau's poetic development.

He did not draft poetry in his Journal; very early rough drafts by Thoreau are not commonly found there for any of his writings, and his Journal is itself the polished result of deliberate artistic effort. F. B. Sanborn describes Thoreau composing verse by copying stanzas written separately into the Journal and later collecting and "arrang[ing] them in the form of a single piece."[7] Comparing several versions of the same poem often reveals examples of this accretive method at work. One of the few extant, very early drafts, on a leaf in the Huntington Library (in HM 13201), shows one process by which he constructed the smaller units. There Thoreau has blocked out stanzas by positioning the rhyming words at the ends of each of eight lines; these words appear at the ends of lines 3, 6, 15, 16, 19, 20, 21, and 22 in "To the Mountains" (CP 200).

In his Journal, Thoreau usually entered poems as finished products, standing alone and set off from the surrounding prose. In the Journal volumes dating from 1838 through 1840, poems are often titled, and many of them start at the top of a new page. This privileging of poetry may reflect the arrangement of the poems in the two original Journals from which he copied them – a few leaves, probably from the first of those original Journals, contain only poems (PJ 1:617–8). Or it may indicate that poetry was especially significant to him.

Those leaves of poetry from the first of the original Journals may have survived because they belonged to a collection of poems that Thoreau kept apart from his Journal during these years. They may have been in a portfolio or in a separate notebook that he later destroyed. The existence of such a collection is suggested by the fact that, of almost one hundred poems in the Journal from 1838 through 1844, Thoreau mentions only four in the indexes that he made, and none is identified as a poem – the indexes give only the subjects. He was working hard at his poetry during this time; beginning in late 1839 he was preparing poems for submission to the *Dial*, which published its first issue in July 1840. How did he locate the texts he had written, scattered as they were through several hundred pages, without index entries? A separate collection of poetry, separately indexed, would have given him easy access to his poems.

If Thoreau kept such a collection, it may have contained many more poems than the Journal did. Emerson's comment in a journal entry from the fall of 1842 about the quantity of Thoreau's verses suggests large numbers. After indicating that Thoreau's poetry is not in the highest class, he notes, "But it is a great pleasure, to have poetry of the second degree also, & mass here as in other instances is some compensation for superior quality for I find myself stimulated & rejoiced like one who should see a cargo of sea-shells discharged on the wharf[,] whole boxes & crates of conchs, cypraeas, cones, nerites, cardiums, murexes, though there should be no ⟨single⟩ pearl oyster nor one shell of great rarity & value among them."[8]

The existence of such a collection would help to explain an account Sanborn gives of Thoreau's having done away with much of his poetry: "He told me in his last illness that he had destroyed many of his early verses because Emerson criticised them." Sanborn is a notoriously unreliable editor, and Thoreau scholars who have accepted his account have nevertheless wished for some corroboration. He goes on to say that other versions of the poems Thoreau destroyed "seem to have been preserved by friends to whom he had given them in their early forms; and in different connections from those in which he afterwards preserved stanzas that he thought good enough to print."[9] Perhaps, then, what Thoreau destroyed was the collection of his poetry that he had gathered separately, and what survives in the Journal and other manuscripts and in publications are only versions of those poems preserved by having been copied out before the destruction.[10]

After Emerson's early encouragement of Thoreau as a poet, his negative judgment might well have stung enough to provoke Thoreau to destroy copies of his early poems. In legend, poetry plays an early role in the relationship between Emerson and Thoreau: Thoreau is said to have delivered a copy of his poem, "Sic Vita" ("I am a parcel of vain strivings tied," *CP* 81–2), wrapped around a bunch of violets, to Emerson's sister-in-law, Lucy Jackson Brown, in May 1837. Brown supposedly showed the poem to Emerson.[11] That story may be apocryphal, but Emerson's initial delight in Thoreau's poetry is documented in his journal and in letters. In early February 1839, he wrote to Margaret Fuller, who was to become the editor of the *Dial*, that Thoreau had "broke out into good poetry & better prose."[12] Emerson's first recorded response to a poem by Thoreau was to "Sympathy" (*CP* 64–6), and it was studded with superlatives: "a beautiful poem," "the purest strain & the loftiest, I think, that has yet pealed from this unpoetic American forest," "I hear his verses with . . . triumph" (*JMN* 7:230–1). Emerson liked the poem so well that he sent a copy to his friend Samuel Gray Ward, and, in November, simply announced to Fuller that the poem would be in the first number of the *Dial* (*Letters* 7:360, 2:234).

Emerson praised Thoreau's poetry to other correspondents as well. In September 1839, he confided to his brother William his high hopes for Thoreau's success in the *Dial*: "My Henry Thoreau will be a great poet for such a company, & one of these days for all companies" (*Letters* 2:225); he wrote to Christopher Cranch in March 1840, inviting him to visit and see "Walden Pond, and our Concord Poet too, Henry Thoreau" (*Letters* 7:374). During the first two years of the *Dial*, Emerson kept Fuller supplied with Thoreau's poems, enclosing or referring in letters to "When winter fringes every bough" (*CP* 14; *Letters* 2:320), "The Mountains in the Horizon" ("With frontier strength ye stand your ground," *CP* 47–50; *Letters* 2:435), "The Fisher's Son" (*CP* 121–3; *Letters* 2:442), "Sic Vita" (*Letters* 2:395), "Nature doth have her dawn each day" (*CP* 70; *Letters* 2:315), and "Friendship" ("Let such pure hate still underprop," *CP* 71–3; *Letters* 2:442). Emerson undoubtedly conveyed others to her as well, and Thoreau sent some to her directly.

Fuller published only four of Thoreau's poems standing alone – the last three listed above, and "Sympathy." Judging from her response to "The Mountains in the Horizon" (*Corr* 56–7), her criticism of both the poem and the poet, though not unsympathetic, was rigorous and objective. The tone of her letter contrasts markedly with the warmth of Emerson's praise. In the first number of the *Dial* for which he acted as editor, published in October 1842, Emerson seemed to be making up to Thoreau all at once for Fuller's rationing. That issue contains eight of Thoreau's better poems,[13] and two of his best, "Smoke" ("Light-winged Smoke, Icarian bird," *CP* 27) and "Haze" ("Woof of the sun, ethereal gauze," *CP* 59), appeared in the April 1843 issue.

But even as he was providing Thoreau with a forum for his poetry, Emerson's enthusiasm was fading. He may have been influenced by Fuller's opinions; as time passed, he may have decided that Thoreau was not going to fulfill the potential Emerson had found in the first few poems he read. The burgeoning "scholar & . . . poet" whom Emerson described to his brother William in June 1841 as being "as full of buds of promise as a young apple tree" (*Letters* 2:402) had become by the fall of 1842 the poet of high quantity and only medium quality. Emerson indexed the journal entry quoted a few paragraphs above as, "H.D.T.s poetry; . . . mass a compensation for quality" (*JMN* 8:257, n19). In that same journal entry he expresses his realization that, after five years of writing verse, Thoreau's "gold does not yet flow pure, but is only drossy & crude. The thyme & marjoram are not yet made into honey" (*JMN* 8:257). Though he professed in his journal to be pleased "by the honest truth, and by the length of flight & strength of wing" of Thoreau's poetry, respecting it for its "rude strength" and depth of thought, his reservations are obvious (*JMN* 8:257). Emerson's summary of Thoreau's poetic gift was a response to an oral presentation by Thoreau ("Last night H. T. read me verses" [*JMN* 8:257]). Emerson may have expressed his analysis directly to Thoreau at the time, or Thoreau may have read it later – it was not uncommon for those in the Transcendentalist group to exchange journals. The change in Emerson's attitude was probably expressed in many ways; one expression of it may have been that no more of Thoreau's poems appeared standing alone in the remaining four numbers of the *Dial*.

In the poems that Thoreau is known to have submitted to the *Dial* and in those that appeared in it during the four years of its publication, Thoreau introduces himself to a circle of readers whose opinions he valued and whose assumptions he shared. These poems take on an added dimension of meaning when read as the results of his own judgment about his best work. But it is also significant that, in the cases in which dated manuscript versions survive, the poems submitted were not composed for the *Dial*, but had been written months and sometimes years before their publication. As Thoreau continued to review and rework his poetry for publication, he was also developing a more complex and even ambivalent attitude toward verse.

The Journal from February 1841 onward contains evidence that Thoreau was beginning to see his poems in another way. They are less often titled, and the pattern of interaction between prose and poetry that will prevail in *A Week* appears occasionally. The entry for April 4, 1841, is the first example of it:

The rattling of the tea-kettle below stairs reminds me of the cow bells I used to hear when berrying in the Great Fields many years ago – sounding distant and deep amid the birches. That cheap piece of brass which the farmer hangs about his cow's neck – has been more to me than the tons of metal which are swung in the belfry.

> They who prepare my evening meal below
> Carelessly hit the kettle as they go
> With tongs or shovel,
> And ringing round and round,
> Out of this hovel
> It makes an eastern temple by the sound.

> At first I thought a cow bell right at hand
> Mid birches sounded o'er the open land,

Where I plucked flowers
Many years ago,
Spending midsummer hours
With such secure delight they hardly seemed to flow. (*PJ* 1:296)

The poetry rings several changes on the prose account, and also makes explicit the reason for the impact of these commonplace sounds: the intensity of the speaker's delight produced a mystical experience in which he seemed to be outside of time. Each description emphasizes different features of the experience, and each glosses the other.

Ironically, Thoreau's first strong expressions of doubt about the possibilities of poetry are found in Journal entries that appear in the late summer and fall of 1841, just before and then just after the most intense period of poetic composition he ever experienced. On August 18, 1841, he wrote, "The best poets, after all, exhibit only a tame and civil side of nature – They have not seen the west side of any mountain. Day and night – mountain and wood are visible from the wilderness as well as the village – They have their primeval aspects – sterner savager – than any poet has sung. It is only the white man's poetry – we want the Indian's report. Wordsworth is too tame for the Chippeway" (*PJ* 1:321). Thoreau continued to idealize the poetry of bards such as Homer – the beauty and force of the ancient epics were enhanced for Thoreau by their proximity to the era when language was created, when "the poets made all the words" (*Essays* 13). However, he is beginning, in the Journal discussion of wildness and tameness, to elaborate the standard of nature as a measure for poetry that is more fully articulated in "Walking."[14]

A comment in his Journal in late November, while he was in Cambridge copying from the works of the English poets in the Harvard College Library for an anthology he was planning,[15] indicates Thoreau's surprise at finding that so little of the poetry he had judged to be great was actually inspiring to him: "When looking over the dry and dusty volumes of the English poets, I cannot believe that those fresh and fair creations I had imagined are contained in them. English poetry from Gower down collected into one alcove – and so from the library window compared with the commonest nature seems very mean" (*PJ* 1:337–8).

In the three and a half months between writing these passages, Thoreau composed a group of interrelated poems that make up his least known but most significant poetic work. This group explores one of the primary themes in much of his later writing – the relationship between nature and the conditions of the writer's creative life – using images that will recur in both his literary and scientific work.[16] In Thoreau's development as a writer, this group of poems functions as a kind of fulcrum: his early desire to become a poet culminated in his work on them, and yet, of the hundreds of lines involved, he published in full only one version of one poem in the group ("Independence"). The group is also significant for giving the fullest picture available of Thoreau at work on his poems.

The group consists of five titled poems (each exists in several versions, and for each there is at least one fair-copy version in ink that provides the title): "Independence," "Cock-crowing," "Inspiration," "The Soul's Season," and "The Fall of the Leaf." Also there is a draft version of a sixth that combines stanzas from the other five. The sixth poem, untitled, provides the textual evidence for Thoreau's plan to revise and combine the titled five into one: it is made up of leaves that contain pencilled drafts of stanzas from the other five and that Thoreau arranged by numbering the leaves in ink.

Each of the first five poems deals with an aspect of the experience of the true poet. The theme of "Independence" (*CP* 132) is the poet's fundamental freedom in the face of worldly temptations such as material goods, political power, and public recognition, a freedom which has its source in divine approval of his work. Inspiration is the subject of both "Cock-crowing" and "Inspiration." "Cock-crowing" (Witherell, 70–3) describes the music of nature that prepares the way for inspiration, the actual experience of which, described in "Inspiration" (Witherell, 73–80), is sudden and overwhelming, extending the limits of the poet's physical senses and calling his soul out of temporality by "a clear and ancient harmony." It is a rebirth, an awakening in which the poet knows himself to be alive for the first time: "Then chiefly is my natal hour, / And only then my prime of life." The effect on his modes of perception is profound, as described in a quatrain that appears in all of the versions of the poem and that summarizes the transcendental experience in general:

> I hearing get, who had but ears,
> And sight, who had but eyes before,
> I moments live, who lived but years,
> And truth discern, who knew but learning's lore.

In "The Soul's Season" (Witherell, 80–2) the poet's preparation for the experience of inspiration is explicitly connected with autumn, suggesting an association between artistic and seasonal maturity; "The Fall of the Leaf" (Witherell, 82–91) is a catalogue of autumn events.

The sixth poem, which Thoreau apparently did not complete, begins with the drafts of stanzas from "The Soul's Season" and "The Fall of the Leaf" to set the scene in autumn, and then incorporates the description of the morning sounds of Concord from the draft of "Cock-crowing" (because of the context, they are now identified as fall sounds). This detailed description of particular sounds that are sources of inspiration leads to a warning (from the draft of "Inspiration") that too strong an attachment to "the general show of things" can temporarily interfere with inspiration. Yet the poet's "true love and wonder" in response to the phenomena of nature do not prevent inspiration altogether, for

> . . . soon there comes unsought unseen
> Some clear divine electuary
> And I who had but sensual been
> Do sensuous grow and as God is am wary

An account of the experience of inspiration follows. The poem closes with an assertion of the artist's autonomy, taken from the draft of "Independence." Following the exalted tone of the poet's description of his response to inspiration, this statement rings with triumph and even defiance:

> Ye princes keep your realms
> And circumscribed power
> Not wide as are my dreams
> Nor rich as is the muses dower

"Independence" is the only poem in the group that was published in full (several stanzas of "Inspiration" appear in *A Week*). Emerson included it in the October 1842 issue of the *Dial* as "The Black Knight" (lines 16–29 of "Independence," CP 132). Nothing survives to indicate whether or not Thoreau tried to publish the other poems in the group, although Emerson clearly knew about them and probably discussed them with Fuller (Witherell, 58–9). Perhaps Thoreau offered them to Fuller and she rejected them; perhaps the tragic deaths of Emerson's son Waldo and Thoreau's brother John in early 1842 so occupied Emerson and Thoreau that poetry was temporarily forgotten. Perhaps when Thoreau measured them against the standard he articulated in his Journal in November, he realized that he could not achieve that standard in his own poetry.

With the April 1844 number, the *Dial* ceased publication, and Thoreau lost the only reliable outlet he had for his writing. The alternative was to create his own forum, and in the fall he began work on his first book, *A Week on the Concord and Merrimack Rivers.*[17] *A Week* is an extended elegy for his brother John, with whom he had taken the voyage that provides the narrative structure. That poetry remained important to him is indicated by his inclusion of poetic epigraphs, beginning with an invocation of John as his muse (*Week* 3), and of a number of his own poems from the material he collected for the book from his earlier Journal (*PJ* 2:3–120). More of them appeared in the first draft, completed sometime in 1845 (Johnson, 223–4 and 289–393). As the book grew, the ratio of his poetry to the prose remained steady.

The poems in *A Week* are, for the most part, firmly embedded in the prose. Even those that stood alone in the *Dial* have been incorporated into the prose context, serving to resonate with and enhance it, while the prose extends and explicates the poetry. As he matured as a writer, and refocused his artistic energies on prose, Thoreau learned that his poems would not stand alone, but that they had their uses: "These humbler, at least, if not those higher uses" (*Week* 287). Indeed, Thoreau includes in *A Week* a concealed farewell to his youthful ambition: a passage that includes a poem in its Journal incarnation (*PJ* 2:32–3) and in the first draft (Johnson, 387) appears as follows in the final, nostalgic chapter of the published work:

> To an unskilful rhymer the Muse thus spoke in prose:
> The moon no longer reflects the day, but rises to her absolute rule, and the husbandman and hunter acknowledge her for their mistress. Asters and golden-rods reign along the way, and the life-ever-lasting withers not. The fields are reaped and shorn of their pride, but an inward verdure still crowns them. The thistle scatters its down on the pool, and yellow leaves clothe the vine, and naught disturbs the serious life of men. But behind the sheaves, and under the sod, there lurks a ripe fruit, which the reapers have not gathered, the true harvest of the year, which it bears for ever, annually watering and maturing it, and man never severs the stalk which bears this palatable fruit.
>
> (*Week* 378)

Thoreau's progress away from writing verse was gradual but inexorable. While he did not analyze his motives for the change, a few comments in the Journal and in letters serve to chart its course. In February 1843 he wrote to Emerson, "As for poetry, I have not remembered to write any for some time," though he went on to characterize this lapse as only a temporary "drought" (*Corr* 88). In 1847, responding to a request from the secretary of his Harvard class, which was planning a ten-year reunion, he listed a number of his paying jobs: "a Schoolmaster – a private Tutor, a Surveyor . . . a Painter, I mean a House Painter . . . a Day-Laborer, a Pencil-Maker, a Glass-paper Maker" – and he concluded with "a Writer" and the disparaging "sometimes a Poetaster" (*Corr* 185–86). By 1852, Thoreau was describing a permanent state of affairs in his Journal: "The strains from my muse are as rare now a days – or of late years – as the notes of birds in the winter" (*PJ* 4:357). During the twelve years between 1850 and his death in 1862, he wrote only twenty poems in his Journal; several of these are epigrams in couplet form ("When the toads begin to ring, / Then thinner clothing bring / or Off your greatcoat fling" [*J* 6:222] and "Any fool can make a rule / And every fool will mind it" [*J* 13:125] are examples; for more, see CP 187). *Walden* contains only four of his own poems, all fully integrated into the prose;[18] "Wild Apples" contains a poem that seems to have been written for the essay, "In two years' time 't had thus" (*NH* 191; *CP* 20), whose subject is unintelligible without the surrounding prose.

In *A Week*, elaborating a couplet that first appeared in an August 1842 Journal passage, Thoreau announced his philosophy of artistic creation:

> The true poem is not that which the public read. There is always a poem not printed on paper, coincident with the production of this, stereotyped in the poet's life. It is *what he has become through his work*. Not how is the idea expressed in stone, or on canvass or paper, is the question, but how far it has obtained form and expression in the life of the artist. His true work will not stand in any prince's gallery.

> My life has been the poem I would have writ,
> But I could not both live and utter it. (*Week* 343)

The effort to "both live and utter it" occupied Thoreau throughout his life: the success he achieved came to him in the writing of prose, but when he began his career as a writer, his commitment to writing verse was deep. In the light of his completed career, poetry was less important as a product than as a discipline that prepared Thoreau to fulfill in the medium of prose the role that Emerson (*Essays* 21) had described for the poet: "He . . . shall draw us with love and terror, [he] sees, through the flowing vest, the firm nature, and can declare it."[19]

NOTES

1 In "The Poet," Emerson writes, "For it is not metres, but a metre-making argument, that makes a poem, – a thought so passionate and alive, that, like the spirit of a plant or an animal, it has an architecture of its own, and adorns nature with a new thing" (*Essays: Second Series*, ed. Alfred R. Ferguson and Jean Ferguson Carr [Cambridge: Harvard University Press, 1983], p. 6; hereafter cited as *Essays*).

2 Carl Bode, "Henry Thoreau as a Poet, with a Critical Edition of the Poems" (Ph.D. diss., Northwestern University, 1941), p. lxxxv. Bode's dissertation was published as *Collected Poems of Henry Thoreau* (Chicago: Packard, 1943; enl.

ed., Baltimore: Johns Hopkins Press, 1964). Some new poems, as well as newly edited versions of those in *Collected Poems,* will be presented in the volume forthcoming in *The Writings of Henry D. Thoreau,* but for now, *Collected Poems* is the only collection that approaches completeness. It contains almost two hundred verse texts printed in full, with a complete textual apparatus that gives variants as well as dates and sources, and an introduction that summarizes the history of Thoreau's reputation as a poet and discusses his poetic theory. *CP* in the text and notes refers to the enlarged 1964 edition of *Collected Poems;* I have included Bode's title for a poem when it differs from that of the version under discussion.

3   "Conscience is instinct bred in the house" (*CP* 42–3), "Though all the fates should prove unkind" (*CP* 46), "Rumors from an AEolian Harp" (*CP* 53), and "Wait not till slaves pronounce the word" (*CP* 198–9) all deal poetically with intriguing ideas. "The respectable folks" (*CP* 32), "The Peal of the Bells" (*CP* 111), "The Assabet" (*CP* 113–5), and "The Breeze's Invitation" (*CP* 116) are good examples of this liveliness.

4   "Low in the eastern sky" (*CP* 38–9), "Lately, alas, I knew a gentle boy" (*CP* 64–6), "The Poet's Delay" (*CP* 78), "I am a parcel of vain strivings tied" (*CP* 81–2), "The Cliffs & Springs" (*CP* 92), "The Bluebirds" (*CP* 93–6), and "I'm guided in the darkest night" (*CP* 124) all center on significant experiences or relationships. Two of these are particularly poignant, "Brother, where dost thou dwell" (*CP* 151–2), written after the death of his brother John in 1842, and "Farewell" (*CP* 215), for his sister Helen, who died in 1849. See Walter Harding, *The Days of Henry Thoreau* (New York: Knopf, 1965; enl. and corr. ed., Princeton: Princeton University Press, 1982) for discussions of some of these poems and the events that prompted them.

5   The best of these are "Light-winged Smoke, Icarian bird" (*CP* 27), "Woof of the sun, ethereal gauze" (*CP* 59), "Low-anchored cloud" (*CP* 56), and "On fields oer which the reaper's hand has pass[e]d" (*CP* 142).

6   For more detailed descriptions of the manuscript volumes that make up the Journal through 1850, and for information about Thoreau's use of those volumes, see the historical and textual introductions to *PJ* 1 (pp. 592–643), 2 (pp. 445–83), and 3 (pp. 478–508).

7   F. B. Sanborn, *Henry David Thoreau* (Boston: Houghton, Mifflin, 1882), p. 286.

8   *The Journals and Miscellaneous Notebooks of Ralph Waldo Emerson,* ed. William H. Gilman, Ralph H. Orth, et al., 16 vols. (Cambridge: Harvard University Press, 1960–82), 8:257; hereafter cited as *JMN.*

9   F. B. Sanborn, *The Life of Henry David Thoreau* (Boston: Houghton, Mifflin, 1917), p. 129.

10   If Thoreau did indeed destroy a collection of his poems, when is a problematical question. It seems unlikely that he would have done so while the *Dial* was still being published; it had provided a forum and might again. Perhaps his hopes were finally dashed only when he read Emerson's statement in "The Poet" (in *Essays: Second Series,* of which Emerson gave Thoreau a copy on October 15, 1844, just after it was published): "I look in vain for the poet whom I describe" (pp. xxxii, 21). It may be significant that Thoreau's index for one of the Journal volumes he filled at Walden from the summer of 1845

through February 1846 (*PJ* 2:197–229), one in which there are only three poems, does include two of these identified as poems ("The Recluse poem ... poem on travelling" [*PJ* 2:387]).

11 Henry Seidel Canby, *Thoreau* (Boston: Houghton Mifflin, 1939), pp. 71–3.

12 *The Letters of Ralph Waldo Emerson*, ed. Ralph L. Rusk and Eleanor M. Tilton, 8 vols. to date (New York: Columbia University Press, 1939; 1990–), 2:182.

13 "The Black Knight" ("Independence," *CP* 132–3); "The Inward Morning" (*CP* 74–5); "Free Love" ("My love must be as free," *CP* 68); "The Poet's Delay" (*CP* 78); "Rumors from an AEolian Harp" (*CP* 53); "The Moon" (*CP* 11); "To the Maiden in the East" ("Low in the eastern sky," *CP* 38–9); and "The Summer Rain" ("My books I'd fain cast off, I cannot read," *CP* 76–7).

14 See Henry David Thoreau, *The Natural History Essays* (Salt Lake City: Peregrine Smith, 1980), pp. 119–22; hereafter cited as *NH*.

15 See Robert Sattelmeyer, "Thoreau's Projected Work on the English Poets," in *Studies in the American Renaissance 1980*, ed. Joel Myerson (Boston: Twayne, 1980), pp. 239–57.

16 The connections among the poems in this group have only recently been described in print: see Elizabeth Hall Witherell, "Thoreau's Watershed Season as a Poet: The Hidden Fruits of the Summer and Fall of 1841," in *Studies in the American Renaissance 1990*, ed. Joel Myerson (Charlottesville: University Press of Virginia, 1990), pp. 49–105; hereafter cited as Witherell.

17 Linck C. Johnson, *Thoreau's Complex Weave: The Writing of "A Week on the Concord and Merrimack Rivers"* (Charlottesville: University Press of Virginia, 1986), pp. 220–1; hereafter cited as Johnson.

18 These are "Men say they know many things" (*W* 42; *CP* 24), "What's the railroad to me?" (*W* 122; *CP* 25), "It is no dream of mine" (*W* 193; *CP* 26), and "Light-winged Smoke, Icarian bird" (*W* 252–3; *CP* 27).

19 In addition to sources referred to in the endnotes, the following contain useful discussions of Thoreau as a poet and the Transcendentalist interpretation of the poet's vocation.

Lawrence Buell, *New England Literary Culture from Revolution Through Renaissance* (Cambridge: Cambridge University Press, 1986), especially pp. 105–36.

Richard Lebeaux, *Young Man Thoreau* (Amherst: University of Massachusetts Press, 1977).

Joel Myerson, *The New England Transcendentalists and "The Dial"* (Rutherford, N.J.: Fairleigh Dickinson University Press, 1980).

Robert D. Richardson, Jr., *Henry Thoreau: A Life of the Mind* (Berkeley: University of California Press, 1986).

Elizabeth Hall Witherell, "The Poetry of Henry David Thoreau: A Selected Critical Edition" (Ph.D. diss., University of Wisconsin, 1979).

Helen Hennessy, "The *Dial*: Its Poetry and Poetic Criticism," *New England Quarterly* 31 (March 1958): 66–87.

Fred W. Lorch, "Thoreau and the Organic Principle of Poetry," *PMLA* 53 (March 1938): 286–302.

Richard J. Schneider, "Henry David Thoreau," in *Critical Survey of Poetry*, ed. Frank N. Magill, 8 vols. (Pasadena, Cal., and Englewood Cliffs, N.J.: Salem Press), 7:3364–73.

Henry W. Wells, "An Evaluation of Thoreau's Poetry," *American Literature* 16 (May 1944): 99–109.

Paul O. Williams, "The Concept of Inspiration in Thoreau's Poetry," *PMLA* 79 (1964): 466–72.

Paul O. Williams, "Thoreau's Growth as a Transcendental Poet," *ESQ: A Journal of the American Renaissance* 19 (1973): 189–98.

6

STEVEN FINK

Thoreau and his audience

The question of who constitutes a writer's audience is most usefully and fully understood if we begin with the premise that an audience is determined by the intersection of the literary marketplace with the writer's own ambitions and self-definition as a writer. On the one hand, we want to consider the relationship from the author's point of view: What kind of influence did Thoreau hope to have on his readers? Who did he hope or think would read his works or hear his lectures? How did he hope to attract and engage an audience, or, conversely, what expectations or demands did he make of his audience? On the other hand, we also want to consider the relationship from the point of view of the audience, or potential audience, for his works: What was the status of writers in American society of the time? What expectations and demands did the reading public make of authors writing in the particular genres Thoreau worked in, or through the particular media he employed (such as the monthly magazines, or the lyceum lecture system)? Moreover, we need to ask who *could* have constituted Thoreau's audience? Who was literate? Who could afford to buy books and magazines? What constraints on the geographical distribution of print material defined Thoreau's potential audience? Who had access to the lyceums?

Thoreau's career as a writer coincided with a period of remarkable growth and change in the production, distribution, and consumption of literature in the United States; and while Thoreau generally affected indifference or hostility to the literary marketplace he could not remain untouched by it or by the changes it was undergoing. The first condition enabling the rapid expansion of the literary marketplace was, of course, the existence of a reading public. By the time of Thoreau's graduation from Harvard in 1837, basic literacy rates in the United States were the highest in the world. By 1850, basic literacy in the U.S. was at 90 percent for white adults (compared to about 60 percent in Britain), though it was by no means uniform: literacy rates were significantly higher for men than women, and also significantly higher in the northeastern states than in the south or west.¹ Equally important were the advances made at the time in the production and distribution of printed matter: The development of stereotyping (1811) and then electrotyping (1841) meant that the slow and expensive process of setting type by hand needed only be done for a first edition. Printing and marketing multiple editions became, over a more extended period of time, feasible and economically attractive to publishers. The development of the flatbed steam press by Isaac Adams (1830–6) and then the cylinder press by Robert Hoe (1847) meant that printed matter could be produced in large quantities, at high speed, and at low costs not to be compared with earlier methods.² The third important factor was the development of new and more efficient means of geographic distribution of literature, which transformed the literary marketplace from a local to a national one. The Erie Canal (1825) was of major importance, but even more significant was the development and expansion of the railroads, beginning in the 1830s, but especially in the 1840s and 1850s.³

This process of rapid commodification and commercialization of literature, and the concomitant professionalization of authorship, created both opportunities and obstacles for writers, neither of which were lost on Thoreau as he viewed the literary landscape from his vantage point as a Harvard student in the 1830s. In a college essay written in April 1836, Thoreau railed against this commercialization of literature: "Utility is the rallying word with us; we are a nation of speculators, stock-holders, and money-changers; we do every thing by steam, because it is most expeditious, and cheapest in the long run ... The question with us is whether a book will take – will sell well, not whether it is worth taking, or worth selling; the purchaser asks the price, looks at the binding, the paper, or the plates, without learning the contents. The press is daily sending forth its thousands and tens of thousands, for the publisher says 'tis profitable. To judge from appearances rather than facts, to mistake the profitable for the useful, are errors incident to youth; but we are fast hardening into the bone of manhood" (*EEM* 39). Thoreau's response strikes a chord he would repeat throughout his career, challenging the value of merely material progress. To some extent, Thoreau's high-minded idealism here reflects the influence of Emerson and the Transcendentalists, whom Thoreau was just now discovering. But it also reflects, to some extent, a more conservative reaction, shared by the college-educated Brahmin class generally,⁴ to the shifting locus of cultural power engendered by the emerging market economy, and, more specifically, it reflects the anxiety shared by this class in the face of the rapidly changing role of the author in society from that of gentleman amateur to professional writer for the marketplace.

Yet Thoreau also recognized new opportunities made available by these changes. In another college essay assignment, on "Methods of gaining or exercising public influence," Thoreau responded by claiming that the preacher's influence was both "narrow and circumscribed," and also tainted by "inveterate custom" which makes for uncritical auditors: "He, on the other hand, who addresses his fellow men through the medium of the press, is so far a stranger to the mass of his readers, as not to be exposed to the effects of those prejudices which a personal acquaintance would be inevitably attended by. His field of labor is the universe," and "The thousands of newspapers that circulate throughout the United States develope different sorts of editors" (*EEM* 86–7). Thus, in spite of Thoreau's more familiar and more persistent hostility toward the press and toward the commercial spirit of the age generally, his acknowledgment here of potential advantages of the popular press should also be kept in mind as we examine his subsequent relationship with the literary marketplace of the day.

Thoreau's literary apprenticeship, however, was served as Emerson's protégé, with the Transcendentalists' journal the *Dial* as their forum, and this profoundly shaped Thoreau's sense of himself as a writer and of his proper audience. Emerson's view of the *Dial's* intended audience implies both its ambitions and its limitations: "With the old drowsy Public which the magazines address, I think we have nothing to do; – as little with the journals & critics of the day. . . . This Journal has a public of its own; its own Thou as well as I; a new-born class long already standing waiting for this voice & wondering at its delay."[5] Indeed, the *Dial* was distinct from both the established and scholarly quarterly journals and from the more recently established high-circulation popular monthly magazines, but the "new-born class" waiting for a Transcendentalist journal was in fact very small. A month before the first number appeared, Margaret Fuller informed Emerson that the *Dial* had only thirty Boston subscribers, and in its four years of existence its subscription list never seems to have exceeded three hundred[6] (though it did achieve a greater notoriety than these numbers might suggest).

It was not simply that the "new views" had inherently limited appeal. Part of the problem was that, because of their emphasis on the spontaneous and intuitive nature of the highest artistic expression, the Transcendentalists tended to regard any active consideration of audience as adulterating or debasing the work, even as they hoped it would exercise broad public influence. Thoreau fully shared these views, and we find his Journal from this period peppered with such comments as, "The flowing drapery of genius is too often tucked up and starched lest it offend against the fashions of the time"; or "Those authors are successful who do not write down to others, but make their own taste and judgment their audience. . . . It is enough if I please myself with my writing – I am then sure of an audience." Yet Thoreau also shared the ambition for public influence, and so we find in his Journal from the same period his confession, "I would fain communicate the wealth of my life to men – would really give them what is most precious in my gift. . . . I have no private good – unless it be my peculiar ability to serve the public" (*PJ* 1:185, 388, 393). The tension between these impulses generates the complex, demanding, and often antagonistic rhetorical stance toward his audience that characterizes much of Thoreau's work throughout his career.[7]

Both the Transcendentalist philosophy and the literary style affected by the *Dial*'s contributors elicited a considerable amount of scorn from the popular press. In general, Thoreau's contributions to the *Dial* were not exempt from this criticism, but his nature and travel sketches were an important exception. Thoreau's first piece of nature writing, "Natural History of Massachusetts," won the admiration of readers not accustomed to praising the *Dial*. Like all of Thoreau's nature and travel writings, "Natural History" was a celebration of the American landscape, and so contributed to the self-conscious literary nationalism of the day. Moreover, readers found the precision and concreteness of Thoreau's observations a welcome relief from the mystical and obscure oracles they had come to associate with the *Dial,* and several reviews of this issue of the *Dial* singled out Thoreau's essay for special praise. Thoreau's even more genial and engaging nature essay "A Winter Walk," printed in the *Dial* for October 1843, won similar approval in the popular press, the reviewer for the *Knickerbocker Magazine* noting significantly, "There is much less of the new style of verbal affectation in the present than in preceding numbers of 'the Dial,' and it is just in this proportion the more readable and attractive."[8]

Such concessions, however, were not enough to win for the *Dial* a sufficient audience, and the magazine folded in mid-1844. It was too radical and outré for most of the intellectual establishment and yet too scholarly and esoteric for the masses. The *Dial* aroused the curiosity of various outsiders, but finally it spoke primarily to its own coterie. Thoreau remained an active and loyal contributor to the *Dial* until its end, especially after 1842, when Emerson took over as editor. Yet it was at just this time that Thoreau also initiated a series of efforts to break into the popular periodical press. Thoreau's first piece published outside the *Dial,* "A Walk to Wachusett," appeared in the January 1843 issue of the *Boston Miscellany of Literature and Fashion.* Established in 1842, the *Boston Miscellany* maintained a high standard of literary quality for the monthly magazines, but like the other monthlies it aimed at a fairly broad, popular audience, and each number included two pages of colored plates of the latest fashions and a page of sheet music. Recognizing that "there was no class of readers who could sustain creditably a purely literary magazine," the publishers sought to attract the "great many factory girls in the country for whom there was no journal of fashion," and "there was great glee in the counting-room when it was announced that a thousand copies of the magazine had been sold in Lowell."⁹ That is, the magazine was designed for the entertainment of both New England gentility and those who admired or aspired to that class, with a deliberate emphasis on female readers. Nevertheless, and in spite of the fact that the *Boston Miscellany* was very highly regarded by reviewers, the magazine folded just one issue after Thoreau's essay appeared. Like most of the monthly magazines of the day, the *Boston Miscellany's* subscription rate was three dollars per year, and we need to recognize that this was still a substantial sum. Skilled male day-laborers typically earned not more than $1.25 per day at this time, and female laborers earned substantially less. The *Boston Miscellany* undoubtedly appealed to the Lowell factory girls, but a subscription might cost them a week's wages.

A stylish magazine of genteel literature and fashion may not seem a likely vehicle for Thoreau's writing, but in fact "A Walk to Wachusett" was not at all out of place there. Thoreau's account conformed to the current vogue for picturesque travel narratives and for works contributing to the spirit of literary nationalism. In his ascent of the mountaintop and his call for a westering America at once more spiritualized and naturalized, Thoreau assumes the mantle of the prophet so attractive to the Transcendentalists, but for the most part, "A Walk to Wachusett" remained within the conventions of the romantic excursion quite familiar in the magazine literature of the day: a fairly detailed account of the sights and scenes of the tour, peppered with the thoughtful observations and reflections of the sensitive and literate traveler.

Thoreau made a more determined assault on the literary marketplace when he spent the period from May to December of 1843 in New York, even though he managed to sell only two pieces to the magazines there. By the time of Thoreau's move, New York had clearly become America's pre-eminent literary marketplace, far surpassing both Philadelphia and Boston – its nearest rivals – in both magazine circulation and book publishing.¹⁰ Yet all the literary activity masked the fact that it was still a very precarious and unstable market. It was run on little capital; magazines had yet to use advertising effectively and so were cripplingly dependent upon subscription sales; and book publishing was fiercely competitive, with American authors severely handicapped by the absence of international copyright laws. The result was that while a great deal was printed, magazines rose and fell rapidly, both book and magazine publishers depended heavily on pirated reprints of foreign works for which they paid nothing, and American writers often went begging, being poorly paid or unpaid when they found their way into print at all. Thoreau discovered this firsthand and reported his frustration to Emerson: "Literature comes to a poor market here, and even the little that I write is more than will sell. I have tried the Democratic Review, the New Mirror, and Brother Jonathan. The last two, as well as the New World, are overwhelmed with contributions which cost nothing, and are worth no more. The Knickerbocker is too poor, and only the Ladies' Companion pays" (*Corr* 139). As he explained it, somewhat more colorfully, to his mother, "My bait will not tempt the rats; they are too well fed" (*Corr* 141). Indeed, the reading public had an abundance of popular and relatively inexpensive literature to choose from, and Thoreau's letters make it clear that he actively sought an outlet in both the popular weekly and monthly magazines aimed at a broad, general audience. But the marketplace proved inhospitable, not just to Thoreau but to the American writer generally, and in the end Thoreau's only success was with John L. O'Sullivan's *Democratic Review*, which eventually published Thoreau's review essay "Paradise (to be) Regained" and his sketch "The Landlord."

The United States Magazine, and Democratic Review, as its full title indicates, was something of a hybrid periodical, combining the characteristics of the monthly magazine and the quarterly review. The "review" side of the *Democratic Review* was the self-proclaimed organ of the liberal component of the Democratic party, and its target audience was potential sympathizers to its political causes. The "magazine," or more purely literary side of the journal was nonpartisan, and O'Sullivan was able to make it one of the highest quality literary magazines of the day. In 1843, the *Democratic Review* had a circulation of about 3,500; this was a respectable figure, putting it in the same class as the *Knickerbocker Magazine*, for example, though this was only about one-tenth of the circulation of the most popular magazines of the day, *Graham's* and *Godey's*.¹¹

Of the two pieces Thoreau published in the *Democratic Review*, "Paradise (to be) Regained" belonged to the "review" category, and "The Landlord" to the "magazine" category. The first was a review of a utopian tract based on the communitarian principles of Charles Fourier. There was clearly an audience interested in debating the merits of the various communitarian projects being initiated or advocated at the time, but O'Sullivan was at first reluctant to print Thoreau's essay because it was at odds with O'Sullivan's sympathetic view of communitarian experiments. Thoreau's second piece, a purely literary sketch, encountered no such opposition. "The Landlord" is a light sketch in which Thoreau facetiously celebrates the Tavern and its Landlord as epitomizing the true spirit of hospitality. There is an underlying seriousness in Thoreau's sketch, advocating a version of the spiritualized and highly moral democratic sensibility that emerges as the prophetic vision in so much of Thoreau's writing. But Thoreau's sketch, with its wit and light humor, was clearly an attempt to accommodate the tastes of magazine audiences – it was, as he noted, "a short piece which I wrote to sell" (*Corr* 142).

Unable to support himself in New York by his pen, Thoreau returned to Concord. He helped Emerson with the last issues of the *Dial* and, by the end of 1844, began making plans to take up residence on a piece of property Emerson had bought on the shores of Walden Pond. Thoreau's major writing project at the pond was a book-length account of a river journey he had taken with his brother John in 1839. This was an ambitious and, in many ways, highly personal project, one he would not complete until 1847 and would not publish until 1849, as *A Week on the Concord and Merrimack Rivers*. But Thoreau also worked on several other literary projects. He not only began shaping the record of his life at the pond into lecture material that would eventually become the basis for *Walden,* but he also wrote lectures on Thomas Carlyle, on his excursion to Mt. Katahdin and the Maine woods, and on his night in Concord jail for refusing to pay his poll tax. Each of these was, in turn, revised for publication in periodicals. During this period, then, Thoreau was shaping his work for three related but distinct modes of publication – the lecture, the periodical, and the book – and so also for three related but distinct audiences.

Thoreau had long been an active member and supporter of the Concord Lyceum, one of the oldest and most successful of the many loosely connected lecture societies that proliferated especially throughout New England, beginning in the late 1820s.[12] He delivered his first lecture there, "Society," in 1838, and he was an occasional performer there and at some of the neighboring lyceums during the following years. Prior to the 1848–9 lecture season, however, when he read exclusively from his Walden material, Thoreau was not particularly aggressive in seeking out lecture opportunities through the lyceum system. Thoreau read his Carlyle and his Ktaadn lectures only once each, for example, before attempting to sell them to magazines.

Rather than attempting to sell his wares directly, however, as he had in New York, he now sought the assistance of someone who had greater knowledge of and access to the marketplace: in the summer of 1846, Thoreau sent his Carlyle essay to Horace Greeley (whom he had met in New

York), asking for his help in selling it. Greeley agreed, and so began his long-standing role as Thoreau's unofficial literary agent. Greeley saw that the Carlyle essay was too long for the paying monthlies (and he never tired of asking for shorter, more easily digestible pieces from Thoreau, as better suited to the tastes of the magazine audiences), but he rather surprisingly managed to sell Thoreau's essay to *Graham's Magazine* for the substantial sum of seventy-five dollars. It appeared in two parts, as *Graham's* lead article, in March and April of 1847.

G. R. Graham had earned a reputation for paying contributors well, and so was able to enlist the most popular and prominent writers of the day; but as Greeley told Thoreau, his essay's "appearance there is worth far more to you than money" (*Corr* 173–4). *Graham's* circulation at the time was fifty thousand or more, and it addressed a popular audience of both sexes. Whereas it published some of the very best writers of the day, *Graham's* relied heavily on high-quality, original illustrations as well as lighter literary fare as the basis of its broad appeal. As Emerson noted in his journal several years earlier, "Cheap lit. makes new markets. We have thought only of a box audience or at most of box & pit; but now it appears there is also slip audience, & galleries one, two, three; & backstairs, & street listeners, besides. Greeley tells me that Graham's Magazine has 70,000 subscribers. And I may write a lecture, if I will to 70,000 readers."[13] *Graham's* was not in fact an example of the very cheapest literature available; as a three-dollar-a-year monthly, *Graham's* was still out of reach for many of the lower class. But its attractive representation of middle-brow gentility was an affordable luxury for the literate and advancing middle class. Thoreau's essay on Carlyle was not typical *Graham's* fare, but Greeley had managed to sell it by arguing, "I know it is unlike the general staple of your Magazine, but I think it will on that account be relished and give zest to the work. . . . I am confident that it would attract many new readers to the Magazine." Greeley closed by suggesting that if Graham did not want it he would sell the piece to their chief competitor, *Godey's*.[14] Thoreau's essay almost certainly failed to have the effect Greeley promised, but its publication at least gave Thoreau prominent exposure to the largest audience yet available to him.

In the spring of 1848, Thoreau again enlisted Greeley's help in placing his long account of his excursion to the Maine woods, and Greeley succeeded in selling it (also for seventy-five dollars) to the *Union Magazine of Literature and Art*, a New York publication newly established on the model of *Graham's*: though never rivaling *Graham's* in circulation, it too was a fifty-page, three-dollar-a-year monthly, featuring prominent literary contributors and high-quality illustrations. "Ktaadn, and the Maine Woods," printed serially from July through November 1848, was – except for its length – an ideal offering for the monthly magazines. A serious and provocative essay on man's relation to nature, it nevertheless always remains within the bounds of the adventure narrative and travel guide, and it was clearly popular. Greeley was extravagant in his praise for it in his *Tribune* reviews; Emerson admired it, yet extracts were also reprinted in the juvenile magazine *The Student;* and over the next several years various writers began alluding to Thoreau's essay in their own accounts of the Maine woods.[15]

Thoreau always found audiences most receptive to his travel and nature writings, and later in his career he would continue to find outlets for these works in the very best of the literary monthly magazines. But Thoreau's ambition was never to become merely a popular writer; he also demanded that he be taken seriously as a social critic and moral reformer, and the lecture platform proved to be a more direct and more readily available outlet for controversial views that magazine editors were reluctant to print. With his lectures on "Resistance to Civil Government" and then on his life at the pond, Thoreau began to acquire a reputation as a radical social critic and as a genuine eccentric.

Thoreau lectured exclusively on his Walden experiment during the 1848–9 lecture season. He spoke at lyceums throughout Massachusetts – in Concord, Lincoln, Gloucester, Salem, Worcester – and in Portland, Maine, as well. As Carl Bode has pointed out, New England towns were the heart of the lyceum movement, drawing their clientele from among skilled laborers and the merchant class – tradespeople, clerks, managers, merchants – as well as from among middle- and upper-class professionals, such as lawyers and ministers.[16] Ronald Zboray describes the typical lyceum audience as "mostly native-born, lower-middle-class, and in their twenties or thirties."[17] These descriptions of the typical audience suggest that, for all the novelty of his experiment, Thoreau often found himself speaking to people not much different from himself. Lyceum lecturers themselves were usually ministers, professors, politicians, writers, travelers, or reformers, and lectures were typically published after they had been tested and refined in the lecture halls or whenever the lecturer had developed a sufficient stock of new material. Here, too, Thoreau falls within the general model, though he did not always take full advantage of the system.

Lyceum audiences demanded that lectures be original and either instructive or amusing. When Thoreau's lectures were successful, they were praised in just these terms. A reporter for the *Salem Observer,* for example, described Thoreau's lecture on the "economy" of his life at the pond as "sufficiently queer to keep the audience in almost constant mirth, and sufficiently wise and new to afford many good practical hints and precepts,"[18] and his lectures received similar responses elsewhere. At times, however, he was regarded either as too imitative of Emerson to be considered original or, conversely, as exceeding the bounds of desirable originality with his eccentricity. At times, too, his humor eluded his audiences, and his Transcendentalism was dismissed as impractical moonshine. A Worcester, Massachusetts, reviewer dismissed Thoreau by saying, "Such philosophers illustrate the absurdities the human mind is capable of. What would a forest of them be good for?"[19] Several reviewers acknowledged the mixed responses of Thoreau's audiences, as did a Salem reviewer who observed, "The diversity of opinion is quite amusing. Some persons are unwilling to speak of his lecture as any better than 'Tom-foolery and nonsense,' while others think they perceived, beneath the outward sense of his remarks, something wise and valuable."[20]

Thoreau's accounts of his Walden experiment aroused curiosity and sparked controversy; aided by the numerous reviews in local papers, he acquired the image of the eccentric hermit of Walden Pond. Thoreau affected indifference to the reviews, claiming "whatever they say of me is not to the purpose only as it serves as an advertisement of me. There are very few whose opinion I value" (*Corr* 234). But Thoreau was not entirely indifferent to his audiences' reactions, and he came increasingly to distinguish between those who only saw "Tom-foolery" and those who recognized the wisdom of his words.

While Thoreau was lecturing on his Walden experiment, he also agreed to Elizabeth Peabody's request to include his 1847 lecture on "Resistance to Civil Government" in her new journal, to be called *Aesthetic Papers*. Peabody had been closely associated with the *Dial*, and *Aesthetic Papers* was to be a similarly idealistic forum for a wide range of views. It also had similar problems attracting an audience. The first issue found only fifty subscribers, and so no subsequent issues were ever printed. A few politely appreciative reviews appeared, but more often critics dismissed the entire project, and Thoreau's contribution was either ignored completely or roundly condemned as (to use one critic's word) "crazy."[21] Thoreau's essay, calling for committed resistance to laws that violated one's conscience and moral convictions, was addressed to those New Englanders already opposed to the Mexican War and to slavery but who Thoreau felt had not sufficiently acted upon their principles. As such, his essay anticipated his subsequent uncompromising antislavery lectures, "Slavery in Massachusetts" and "A Plea for Captain John Brown," which won Thoreau an audience in abolitionist circles. Eventually, of course, "Resistance to Civil Government" became Thoreau's best-known and most influential work, next to *Walden,* but, published in *Aesthetic Papers* in 1849, Thoreau's essay was unknown beyond a very small circle of friends and sympathizers, and only after his death did the essay become widely known.

Thoreau was also preparing his first book for publication at this time. After two years of unsuccessful attempts to find a publisher, *A Week on the Concord and Merrimack Rivers* was finally published by James Munroe & Co., of Boston, in May of 1849. Nominally a travel book, filled with carefully rendered descriptions of the landscape and of local historical associations, *A Week* was also so laden with extended digressions and meditations on such diverse subjects as Christianity, poetry, and friendship that it strained the conventions of the genre to the breaking point. It is almost as if Thoreau employed the travel narrative merely to entice a popular audience to his book, only to insist that his readers then respond to the more rigorous demands of a higher and more original kind of literature. With some readers, this strategy seems to have worked: the review in *Godey's* described *A Week* as "just the book to read in the idleness of summer, when wishing to enjoy the pleasures of journeying."[22] Others felt misled: James Russell Lowell complained in his review of *A Week* that Thoreau's meditations and digressions "are out of proportion and out of place, and mar our Merrimacking dreadfully. We were bid to a river-party, not to be preached at."[23] Still others tolerated and even enjoyed the digressions, but condemned Thoreau's pantheism and his attack on Christianity.[24] Yet within the pages of *A Week* Thoreau also gives notice of the kind of book he has written and of his expectations of his audience: "Certainly," he warns his readers, "we do not need to be soothed and entertained always like children. He who resorts to the easy novel, because he is languid, does no better than if he took a nap. . . . Books . . . such as an idle man cannot read, and a timid one would not be entertained by, which even make us dangerous to existing institutions – such call I good books" (*Week* 96). Thoreau would offer a similar critique of popular literature and make similar demands on his audience in the "Reading" chapter of *Walden.* Yet he clearly wanted to attract a popular audience; when Thoreau first tried interesting a publisher in his book, Emerson noted that he was "mainly bent on having it printed in a cheap form for a large circulation."[25]

Thoreau's desire proved painfully ironic, for though it won some critical admiration, *A Week* was an unequivocal failure commercially. Four and a half years after its publication, only slightly over two hundred copies had been sold out of an edition of one thousand (*J* 5:459). The eccentricities of *A Week* might well lead one to expect that it would attract only a limited audience; but to understand the reasons for such an absolute commercial failure we must also recognize the crucial role played by the publisher in mediating (or failing to mediate) between a book and its potential audience. Thoreau had been unable to find any publisher willing to print *A Week* at its own risk; Munroe & Co. finally agreed, however, to deduct the printing costs from initial sales rather than requiring him to pay in advance. Thoreau accepted their terms. An edition of one thousand copies was printed, though to save on initial costs only half were bound at first. At $1.25 a copy, *A Week* was actually priced at the higher end of the normal range for a decently bound hardcover work of belles lettres. When we recognize that a schoolteacher might make only $500 a year, a custom house surveyor about $1,200 a year, and a Harvard professor about $1,500 a year, it is clear that such books were simply unaffordable for many and still something of a luxury even for middle-class readers, especially when entire pirated novels were available in the weekly story papers or in cheap paperbound "supplements" for a tenth of the price. But the price was not the main obstacle. Printing a book at the author's rather than the publisher's expense meant that the publisher had no vested interest in advertising, promoting, or distributing the book, and this was especially true for a provincial and conservative publisher like Munroe & Co. As a result, *A Week* was simply not easily available even to the limited potential audience whom reviews suggest it might have attracted.

Thoreau soon realized how badly he had been served by his publisher, but the low point came in 1853, when Munroe asked Thoreau to take the 706 remaining unsold copies off his hands, leaving the author, as he wryly noted, with "a library of nearly nine hundred volumes, over seven hundred of which I wrote myself" – and with a debt to Munroe for $290 (*J* 5: 459, 521). *A Week* remained out of print until the end of Thoreau's life, but after the modest success of *Walden* in 1854, Thoreau found himself selling individual copies of *A Week* to admirers unable to find copies of his first book anywhere else.[26]

Munroe had originally agreed to publish Thoreau's *Walden* after *A Week* but, with the failure of the first book, backed out of their agreement for the second. By the time *Walden* was published, five years later, by the Boston firm of Ticknor & Fields, it was a much revised and expanded version. Thoreau did not, in fact, publish anything at all for three years after the publication of *A Week,* but that did not really signal a renunciation of his ambitions as a public writer. In the autumn of 1849, and again in the summer of 1850, Thoreau traveled to Cape Cod, and he quickly transformed his notes into lectures which he read to appreciative audiences at lyceums in Massachusetts and Maine. He also made an excursion to Montreal and Quebec City, in the autumn of 1850, and this too he worked up into a lecture for the following season. In the spring of 1851, Thoreau also read the first version of a new lecture on "The Wild." By the 1851–2 lecture season, Thoreau was also lecturing from new *Walden* material. Increasingly, however, Thoreau came to distinguish between his travel material, which could satisfy the tastes of popular audiences, and his more extravagantly transcendental meditations, which appealed to a more select few. He read from *Walden* and "The Wild" most willingly in places like Concord, or in Worcester, where his admirer Harrison Blake had gathered a loyal audience for Thoreau, or in Plymouth, where another friend, Marston Watson, had organized a lecture series for an audience responsive to unconventional and progressive material. Thus, Thoreau responded to Thomas Wentworth Higginson's invitation to lecture in Boston in 1852 by explaining, "what makes me hesitate is the fear that I have not another [lecture] available which will *entertain* a large audience, though I have thoughts to offer which I think will be as worthy of their attention" (*Corr* 278–9). Yet, later that year, when Watson invited him to return to Plymouth (having lectured there the year before on both Walden and "The Wild"), Thoreau declined, explaining that "at present I have nothing to read which is not severely heathenish, or at least secular. . . . When I have something of the right kind, depend upon it I will let you know" (*Corr* 290–1).

When Thoreau turned again to the monthly magazines as an outlet, therefore, it was with his new travel pieces. Greeley had trouble selling Thoreau's "Excursion to Canada" because of its length, but it was finally sold to the new *Putnam's Monthly Magazine,* edited by Thoreau's friend George William Curtis, and Thoreau quickly sent him the first half of his Cape Cod material as well. The first of five proposed installments of his "Excursion to Canada" appeared in the very first issue of *Putnam's* in January 1853. *Putnam's* was an instantly popular monthly of the very highest literary quality, notable on several counts. As an adjunct to Putnam's book publishing firm, the magazine was following the lead of Harper Brothers, which had established *Harper's Monthly Magazine* three years earlier. Whereas *Harper's* had built its business largely on cheap reprints of British fiction, *Putnam's* explicitly announced itself as a forum for American writers. It was a godsend for Melville's waning career, and its early issues also included works by Henry Wadsworth Longfellow, James Fenimore Cooper, William Cullen Bryant, James Russell Lowell, and many other popular but less well-remembered writers. *Putnam's* circulation never exceeded 20,000, and so never really rivaled the even more successful *Harper's,* but it was a nearly ideal forum for Thoreau's work.[27]

Or so it would have seemed. Unfortunately, Curtis chose to delete some lines about the Catholic Church which he thought too inflammatory, and, unable to resolve the ensuing dispute, Thoreau had Putnam return his Canada manuscript after only three of five installments were printed, along with his unpublished Cape Cod manuscript. Thoreau's Canadian journey was a fairly straightforward account of a commercial tourist excursion, fleshed out with material from the extensive reading Thoreau did upon his return, and pretty clearly intended for a popular audience. Already inclined to accuse himself of compromising his principles and his higher ambitions when he wrote to entertain, Thoreau was perhaps particularly sensitive when an editor insisted on further accommodations. As a result, Thoreau's Canadian journey was not published in its entirety until after his death.[28]

Early in 1854, Thoreau took his new version of *Walden* to the Boston publishing firm of Ticknor & Fields. Thoreau had declined their offer to publish it in 1849, preferring to publish *A Week* first, but now he readily accepted their generous terms. Printed at the publisher's risk, *Walden* was printed in an edition of 2,000 handsomely bound copies, and Thoreau would receive a fifteen-percent royalty on the retail cost of one dollar per copy.[29] More important, Ticknor & Fields had become the most successful and prestigious publisher in New England, the publisher of John Greenleaf Whittier, Oliver Wendell Holmes, Longfellow, Nathaniel Hawthorne, and, later, Emerson. Thoreau's association with this firm, and with these authors, now began playing a crucial role in both finding and defining Thoreau's audience.

Because Ticknor & Fields was aggressive in promoting its books through review copies, advertisements, and wide distribution, *Walden* was reviewed far more widely and prominently than *A Week* had been, and it was also more readily available to readers once they were made aware of it. Reviews appeared in a wide array of magazines and newspapers, in the South and West as well as in the North.[30] As the reviewer for *Graham's* noted, "Whatever may be thought or said of this curious volume, nobody can deny its claim to individuality of opinion, sentiment, and expression. Sometimes strikingly original, sometimes merely eccentric and odd, it is always racy and stimulating."[31] And indeed, *Walden* was sometimes dismissed as mere foolishness, though more often the reviews were positive, and occasionally extravagantly so. Among the most enthusiastic reviewers were Lydia Maria Child, in the *National Anti-Slavery Standard*, and Thomas Starr King, in the *Christian Register* – both notable authors in their own right.

Sales of *Walden* were fairly brisk in the first six months after publication, and at the end of a year only 256 copies remained unsold, though the book was not entirely out of print until 1859.[32] Who read *Walden*? In the book itself Thoreau identifies several potential audiences. He says (as he did in his early lecture versions) that he is speaking to his neighbors, responding to their curiosity about his experiment, on the one hand, and telling them what he knows about their own lives, on the other. He assumes their impoverishment, telling them "I have no doubt that some of you who read this book are unable to pay for all the dinners which you have actually eaten, or for the coats and shoes which are fast wearing or are already worn out"; but we learn quickly that for Thoreau poverty is really a spiritual condition, and his "economy" a spiritual economy, so he redefines his audience as "the mass of men who are discontented." Having first suggested that "Perhaps these pages are more particularly addressed to poor students," he therefore subsequently adds, "I also have in mind that seemingly wealthy, but most terribly impoverished class of all, who have accumulated dross, but know not how to use it, or get rid of it, and thus have forged their own golden or silver fetters" (W 3, 6, 16). Thoreau projects into his narrative an implied audience that is essentially benighted, trapped by their own materialism and expediency; but in so doing he implicitly invites his actual readers to identify with the alternative values represented by his own search for spiritual enrichment.[33]

Some readers, then, may have been attracted to *Walden* as a mere curiosity, the account of the hermit of Walden Pond; others merely on the recommendation of its Ticknor & Fields imprint; but it is not surprising to find that many of *Walden*'s actual audience seem to have had more in common with the author, for all his eccentricities, than with the impoverished students or obtuse farmers he projects rhetorically into his narrative: they were necessarily highly literate, if not literary or scholarly themselves; sufficiently free from genuine poverty to afford the book and the leisure to read it; already prone to be nature lovers or questers after spiritual fulfillment; believers in the virtue of self-culture, and dissatisfied with the merely conventional.

The book naturally won the approval of fellow Transcendentalists and personal friends like Bronson Alcott, William Ellery Channing, and H. G. O. Blake. Those of his friends and acquaintances with considerable influence in the literary world, including Greeley, Higginson, Curtis, Hawthorne, and Emerson, all admired his book and also introduced it to new readers, through reviews, private correspondence, or by word of mouth.

Thoreau's correspondence gives us some further insight into *Walden*'s readership, although those who were sufficiently affected by the book to write to Thoreau are not necessarily typical. Daniel Ricketson was a New Bedford Quaker, trained as a lawyer but living off a private income; a nature lover and an abolitionist, he too had built himself a rustic cabin, though he also had a wife and children. He learned of Thoreau's book from Greeley's *Tribune* and wrote to Thoreau as soon as he had finished it, initiating a lifelong correspondence and becoming one of Thoreau's most devoted admirers. B. B. Wiley and D. W. Vaughn were both Providence, Rhode Island, bankers who wrote to Thoreau for copies of *A Week* after having read *Walden;* Wiley kept up a correspondence with Thoreau, revealing himself as an earnest seeker after spiritual nourishment not provided by his career. Thoreau established a similar correspondence with Calvin Greene, of Michigan, who also wrote for a copy of *A Week,* and he received an admiring letter from Abbe Adrien Roquette, of New Orleans, "an authority on monastic solitude, a friend of the Choctaw Indians, and a writer on nature."[34]

There were, of course, more casual readers, and not all readers bought Thoreau's book. Ronald Zboray's research into the library records of the New York Society Library, for example, discovers a twenty-one-year-old Leonard Wyeth checking out *Walden* at the end of 1854 along with such eclectic titles as to defy characterizing his tastes – immediately after *Walden* he checked out a book titled *Modern Flirtations.* Whether this young reader had heard of the hermit of Walden Pond, or merely took it as a wilderness adventure, we cannot know. These records do tell us that *Walden* was purchased by libraries early on, but we should also note that, as Zboray points out, memberships in subscription libraries like the New York Society library were sufficiently expensive as to limit their clientele to the merchant and professional classes.[35]

Walden is sometimes characterized as appealing principally to a male audience, especially as it is seen as a retreat from the female domestic sphere into the masculine wilderness; but Thoreau's critique of the commercial spirit and valorization of individual moral reform actually had much in common with the reform ethos of many women of his day, so it is not entirely surprising to note that several of *Walden*'s favorable reviews were written by women (Lydia Child, Elizabeth Barstow Stoddard, George Eliot), or that Higginson reported to Thoreau that he had just bought a copy for Harriet Prescott, "to whom your first book has been among the scriptures, ever since I gave her that" (*Corr* 336).

Higginson's principal reason for writing in this case was actually to thank Thoreau for his powerful abolitionist lecture, "Slavery in Massachusetts," attacking the Fugitive Slave Law in the wake of the Anthony Burns affair. Higginson had led a failed attempt to rescue Burns, and Thoreau had read the speech at an abolitionist meeting in Framingham, Massachusetts, on July 4, 1854. This lecture, printed in the *National Anti-Slavery Standard,* the *Liberator,* and the *New York Tribune,* just a month before *Walden* was published, established another important audience for Thoreau among the abolitionists. Thoreau's family had long been active in the antislavery movement; Thoreau had defended abolitionist speakers at the Concord Lyceum; he had assisted runaway slaves on their way to Canada; and he had explained his principles of noncompliance in "Resistance to Civil Government"; but "Slavery in Massachusetts" was a more direct and powerful attack and was actually more widely heard and read at the time than "Resistance." It clearly put Thoreau in the camp of the active abolitionists, anticipating his even more radical speeches in defense of Captain John Brown in 1859, and winning for Thoreau an audience at least partly distinct from the audience for his less controversial nature and travel writings (though Higginson, both an abolitionist and nature writer, represents the frequent overlap of the two).

After 1854, then, Thoreau had a modest but established reputation on the margin of the New England literary establishment. He was now part of the constellation of Ticknor & Fields writers. An entry on Thoreau was included in Scribner's 1855 *Cyclopaedia of American Literature,* designed to provide "notices of the Lives and Writings of all American authors of importance."[36] Thoreau tried to arrange a lecture tour to the West to build on his successes, but this fell through. He continued to lecture actively in New England, but his modest successes in fact underscored his ambivalence about success. In the winter of 1854, after reading one of the earliest versions of a lecture eventually published as "Life Without Principle," Thoreau recorded in his Journal, "After lecturing twice this winter I feel that I am in danger of cheapening myself if by trying to become a successful lecturer, i.e., to interest my audiences. I am disappointed to find that most that I am and value myself for is lost, or worse than lost, on my audience. I fail to get even the attention of the mass" (*J* 7:79). Eventually these sentiments found their way into the lecture itself: "If you would get money as a writer or a lecturer," he says, "you must be popular, which is to go down perpendicularly. Those services which the community will most readily pay for it is most disagreeable to render" (*RP* 158).

This unease about his relation to his audience was present from the beginning of his career, but it seems particularly characteristic of the post-*Walden* period, when he actually achieved a modicum of success. In the summer of 1855, George William Curtis began printing Thoreau's long-deferred essay on Cape Cod in *Putnam's* – perhaps to capitalize on the momentum of *Walden*'s recent publication. Yet, as with the "Excursion to Canada," the last installments were never printed in the magazine, and this excursion too remained unpublished in its entirety until the posthumous book version of 1864. In this case, it is not quite clear why the printing was aborted, but the pattern was repeated yet again in 1858, when James Russell Lowell, then editor of the *Atlantic Monthly,* asked Thoreau for an account of his most recent excursion to the Maine woods.

The *Atlantic Monthly* was established in 1857 in association with the Boston publishing firm of Phillips, Sampson & Co., and it was conceived as a forum for New England's brightest literary lights and for the articulation of their strong abolitionist views.[37] Longfellow, Holmes, Lowell, Emerson, Higginson, James Elliot Cabot, and Edward Everett Hale were all consulted in organizing the magazine, and writers including Thoreau, Whittier, and Harriet Beecher Stowe were targeted from the outset as important potential contributors. With its philosophical and critical essays, in addition to the literary pieces, and its lack of illustrations, the *Atlantic* appealed to a more select audience than did popular monthlies like *Graham's, Godey's,* or *Harper's,* but it still began with sales of 20,000 and rose steadily from there.

Thoreau responded to Lowell's request by sending him "Chesuncook," an account of his 1853 excursion to Maine, which was printed in installments from June through August 1858. After the second installment, however, Thoreau saw that Lowell had omitted a line about the immortality of a pine tree, and he immediately shot off an angry letter to Lowell: "I do not ask anybody to adopt my opinions, but I do expect that when they ask for them to print, they will print them, or obtain my consent to their alteration or omission. . . . I am not willing to be associated in any way, unnecessarily, with parties who will confess themselves so bigoted & timid as this implies" (*Corr* 515–6). The last installment of "Chesuncook" did appear in the August issue, but Thoreau would have nothing more to do with the *Atlantic Monthly* while Lowell remained its editor.

For the next two years, Thoreau found his audience from the lecture platform. In 1859 Thoreau's fiery lectures on John Brown attracted considerable attention, but he also repeated his lectures on "Walking" and "Life Without Principle," and he began reading new lectures based on his careful observation of natural phenomena – he first read "Autumnal Tints" in 1859, and "Wild Apples" and "The Succession of Forest Trees" in 1860. Nevertheless, it was the *Atlantic Monthly* that gave Thoreau his audience at the end of his life.

The magazine was purchased by Ticknor & Fields in 1859, and James T. Fields became editor in 1861. By this time Thoreau was already quite ill with the tuberculosis that would shortly take his life, but when Fields wrote to him asking if he could print some of Thoreau's recent lectures, Thoreau readily agreed, providing his health held out – adding only, "Of course, I should expect that no sentiment or sentence be altered or omitted without my consent" (*Corr* 635–6). In his final year, then, Thoreau found himself in the enviable position of being asked to contribute to a distinguished magazine owned by his successful publisher. Ticknor & Fields and the *Atlantic Monthly* were in fact just the right vehicles for Thoreau to reach his most appreciative audience. As he revised his lectures on "Walking," "Life Without Principle," "Autumnal Tints," and "Wild Apples," he was also negotiating for the reprinting of both *A Week* and *Walden*. Fields agreed, and he carefully began orchestrating the apotheosis of Henry Thoreau. Even before Thoreau died, in May of 1862, Fields solicited a tribute to Thoreau from Bronson Alcott, which appeared in the *Atlantic* in April under the title "The Forester."[38] Both of Thoreau's books were back in print within a month of his death – albeit in limited numbers. "Walking" was printed in the *Atlantic* for June, "Autumnal Tints" and "Wild Apples" appeared in the fall, and "Life Without Principle" a year later. Fields followed this with additional Thoreau material: "Night and Moonlight" in November of 1863, and the following year the two unpublished segments of his Cape Cod account, "The Wellfleet Oysterman" and "The Highland Light." In the meantime, Ticknor & Fields published a collection of his essays under the title *Excursions in Field and Forest* in 1863, and they published *The Maine Woods* in 1864, *Cape Cod* and *Letters to Various Persons* in 1865, and *A Yankee in Canada and Reform Papers* in 1866.

To a considerable extent Thoreau needed to define himself in opposition to his audience – whether it was his actual audience or his rhetorically constructed audience. Yet his ambitions – as a reformer, as a prophet of Transcendentalism, or as a professional writer – demanded that he never simply dismiss or ignore his audience. He never tired of complaining that his audiences appreciated only the least valuable part of what he had to offer, yet at the end of his life Thoreau had succeeded in entrusting his writings to those who would see that they found their proper audience.[39]

NOTES

1 These data are summarized and astutely contextualized in Ronald Zboray, *A Fictive People: Antebellum Economic Development and the American Reading Public* (New York: Oxford University Press, 1993); see pp. 36, 83–5, and 196–201.

2 See Zboray, *A Fictive People*, pp. 9, 31.

3 Zboray, *A Fictive People*, pp. 12–14; William Charvat, *Literary Publishing in America, 1790–1850* (Philadelphia: University of Pennsylvania Press, 1959), pp. 17–30.

4 As Robert D. Richardson, Jr., points out in his *Henry Thoreau: A Life of the Mind* (Berkeley: University of California Press, 1986), Harvard was a small, provincial college in Thoreau's day, but a college education still defined a very

small class of Americans: "In the 1840s there was, in New England, one college student for every 1,294 people in the general population" (p. 10). Thus, even though Thoreau was the son of a pencil-maker who could afford to attend Harvard only with the aid of a scholarship, he became a member of the cultural elite. Even though he often bristled at Harvard and its values, Thoreau's attitude toward literature shared the antimarket bias of the Brahmin class.

5 *The Letters of Ralph Waldo Emerson,* ed. Ralph L. Rusk and Eleanor M. Tilton, 8 vols. to date (New York: Columbia University Press, 1939; 1990–), 2:285–6.

6 See Joel Myerson, "A Union List of the *Dial* (1840–1844) and Some Information About Its Sales," *Papers of the Bibliographical Society of America* 67 (3rd Quarter 1973): 322–8; and Myerson, *The New England Transcendentalists and "The Dial"* (Rutherford, N.J.: Fairleigh Dickinson University Press, 1980), pp. 48, 74, 88, 90.

7 Thoreau's apprenticeship with the *Dial* and his subsequent relationship with the marketplace are the subject of my *Prophet in the Marketplace: Thoreau's Development as a Professional Writer* (Princeton: Princeton University Press, 1992).

8 "Editor's Table, 'The Dial,'" *Knickerbocker Magazine* 23 (November 1843): 486–7.

9 Edward Everett Hale, *James Russell Lowell and His Friends* (Boston: Houghton, Mifflin, 1899), p. 83. On the *Boston Miscellany,* see Frank Luther Mott, *A History of American Magazines, 1741–1850* (Cambridge: Harvard University Press, 1959 [1930]), pp. 718–720; and *American Literary Magazines: The Eighteenth and Nineteenth Centuries,* ed. Edward E. Chielens (Westport, Conn.: Greenwood Press, 1986), pp. 70–3.

10 Mott, *American Magazines,* p. 375; see also Charvat, *Literary Publishing,* pp. 17–37; and John Tebbel, *A History of Book Publishing in the United States,* vol. 1 (New York: R. R. Bowker, 1972), pp. 203, 206; and Fink, *Prophet in the Marketplace,* pp. 86–121.

11 *American Literary Magazines,* ed. Chielens, p. 427.

12 On the lyceum system, see Carl Bode, *The American Lyceum* (New York: Oxford University Press, 1956).

13 *The Journals and Miscellaneous Notebooks of Ralph Waldo Emerson,* ed. William H. Gilman, Ralph H. Orth, et al., 16 vols. (Cambridge: Harvard University Press, 1960–82), 8:343.

14 *Passages from the Correspondence and Other Papers of Rufus W. Griswold,* ed. W.M. Griswold (Cambridge: W.M. Griswold, 1898), p. 207.

15 On the publication, reception, and influence of "Ktaadn," see Fink, *Prophet in the Marketplace,* pp. 150–187.

16 Bode, *The American Lyceum,* pp. 132–3.

17 Zboray, *A Fictive People,* p. 107.

18 "Salem Lyceum," *Salem Observer,* November 25, 1848.

19 Quoted in Hubert Hoeltje, "Thoreau as a Lecturer," *New England Quarterly* 19 (December 1946): 489–90.

20 *Salem Observer,* March 3, 1849.

21 On subscription numbers, see George Willis Cooke, *An Historical and Biographical Introduction to Accompany "The Dial,"* 2 vols. (Cleveland: Rowfant

Club, 1902), 1: 193; on reviews of *Aesthetic Papers,* see Fink, *Prophet in the Marketplace,* pp. 206–10.

22 [Sarah Josepha Hale], Review of *A Week on the Concord and Merrimack Rivers, Godey's Lady's Book* 39 (September 1849):223.

23 [James Russell Lowell], "*A Week on the Concord and Merrimack Rivers,*" *Massachusetts Quarterly Review,* 3 (December 1849):40–51.

24 For other reviews of *A Week,* see Linck C. Johnson's "Historical Introduction" to *A Week;* and *Emerson and Thoreau: The Contemporary Reviews,* ed. Joel Myerson (New York: Cambridge University Press, 1992), pp. 341–70.

25 Emerson, *Letters,* 8: 122.

26 See *Corr* 377, 349, 406, 425, 431, 453, 577, 583, 611, 634.

27 On *Putnam's,* see Frank Luther Mott, *A History of American Magazines, 1850–1865* (Cambridge: Harvard University Press, 1957 [1938]) pp. 419–31; and *American Literary Magazines,* ed. Chielens, pp. 328–33.

28 On the publication of "Excursion to Canada," see Walter Harding, *The Days of Henry Thoreau* (New York: Dover, 1982), pp. 282–3; and Stephen Adams and Donald Ross, Jr., *Revising Mythologies: The Composition of Thoreau's Major Works* (Charlottesville: University Press of Virginia, 1988), pp. 104–26.

29 See Ellen Ballou, *The Building of the House: Houghton Mifflin's Formative Years* (Boston: Houghton Mifflin, 1970), pp. 150–1; *The Costbooks of Ticknor and Fields and Their Predecessors, 1832–1858,* ed. Warren S. Tryon and William Charvat (New York: Bibliographical Society of America, 1949), pp. 289–90; and on Ticknor & Fields, see Tebbel, *A History of Book Publishing,* pp. 394–401.

30 On reviews of *Walden,* see *Critical Essays on Henry David Thoreau's "Walden,"* ed. Joel Myerson (Boston: G. K. Hall, 1988); and Bradley P. Dean and Gary Scharnhorst, "The Contemporary Reception of *Walden,*" *Studies in the American Renaissance 1990,* ed. Joel Myerson (Charlottesville: University Press of Virginia, 1990), pp. 293–328.

31 Review of *Walden, Graham's* 45 (September 1854): 298–300.

32 Harding, *The Days of Henry Thoreau,* p. 340.

33 On Thoreau's rhetorical relationship with his audience, see especially Stephen Raillton's chapter on *Walden* in *Authorship and Audience: Literary Performance in the American Renaissance* (Princeton: Princeton University Press, 1991), pp. 50–73.

34 Harding, *The Days of Henry Thoreau,* pp. 340, 343–5; *Corr* passim.

35 Zboray, *A Fictive People,* pp. 171–2.

36 *Corr* 326; *Cyclopaedia of American Literature,* ed. Evert A. and George L. Duyckinck, 2 vols. (New York: Scribner's, 1855), 2:653–66.

37 On the *Atlantic Monthly,* see Mott, *A History of American Magazines 1850–1865,* pp. 493–515; and *American Literary Magazines,* ed. Chielens, pp. 50–7.

38 Harding, *The Days of Henry Thoreau,* pp. 458–9.

39 On the subsequent role of Thoreau's publishers in bringing him into the canon of classic American authors, see Lawrence Buell's "Henry Thoreau Enters the American Canon," *New Essays on "Walden,"* ed. Robert F. Sayre (New York: Cambridge University Press, 1992), pp. 23–52; on Thoreau's reputation more generally, see Walter Harding's essay in this collection.

7

RICHARD J. SCHNEIDER

Walden

In *Walden* Thoreau writes of the traveler approaching a swamp who asked a boy if the swamp was passable, if it "had a hard bottom." The boy, Thoreau says, "replied that it had. But presently the traveller's horse sank in up to the girths, and he observed to the boy, 'I thought you said that this bog had a hard bottom.' 'So it has,' answered the latter, 'but you have not got half way to it yet' " (*W* 330).

So it is with *Walden* itself. Most readers approach *Walden* assuming that they will find the "hard bottom" of its truth in the popular cultural myth of Thoreau as the hermit sitting meditatively by Walden Pond. It is a myth of retreat, a myth of a return to Eden, a myth of stasis, and it is a very appealing myth to a postindustrial society faced with overwhelming change. That myth is in *Walden,* to be sure, but the alert reader will find that it does not take him or her any more than halfway to the full significance of the book. A closer reading of *Walden* reveals a Thoreau who is often less interested in stasis than in change, less interested in meditation than in a journey of exploration.

Thoreau's own journey in *Walden* took him physically no farther than Walden Pond, a mile and a half outside Concord. The plan to live alone by a pond had been on his mind for years. In 1837 during the summer after his senior year at Harvard, he lived in a bachelor cabin with his friend Charles Stearns Wheeler (Harding 49). As early as 1841 he wrote in his Journal of building his own cabin by a pond (Sandy Pond, at first): "I want to go soon and live away by the pond. . . . But my friends ask what I will do when I get there? Will it not be employment enough to watch the progress of the seasons?" (*PJ* 1:347). His first published essay, "Natural History of Massachusetts" (1842), had indicated his interest in studying and writing about nature. Living by a pond would be convenient for the nature study, which might lead to other publishable essays.

Foremost in his mind by 1845, however, was a plan for another writing project, a book about the boating trip that he and his brother John had taken up the Concord and Merrimack Rivers in 1839. This book would be a labor of love in memory of his brother, who had died in 1842 of lockjaw. Privacy for writing was scarce in the Thoreau household, because Thoreau's mother took in boarders and behind the house his father ran a pencil factory in which Henry was frequently required to work. A separate cabin by the pond offered the peace and quiet he needed to write.

Thoreau's third purpose was to conduct an experiment in economic independence. Seeing the "quiet desperation" involved in his father's running of the pencil factory, he must have sensed that there should be a saner, less stressful alternative to the capitalistic emphasis on constantly increasing production. The trick, he decided, would be not to work six days and rest one day, but to reduce one's needs enough and work efficiently enough so that one day's work would be sufficient to allow six days of leisure for more important pursuits.

Such plans led his neighbors to conclude – logically enough by their standards – that he wanted to loaf. Their subtle accusations as well as their open curiosity about his life at the pond led him to write the series of lyceum lectures that was to become *Walden* to try to dispel such misconceptions. He hoped to demonstrate that none of his purposes for going to the pond allowed for loafing. There were all of the Concord woods to study, a book to write, and in the summer a bean-field to be hoed. Thoreau's own famous statement of purpose in *Walden* is remarkable for the vigor of its verbs: he intends, he says, "to live deliberately, to front only the essential facts of life." He does not "wish to practice resignation"; rather he wants "to live deep and suck out all the marrow of life," "to live . . . sturdily," "to put to rout all that was not life, to cut a broad swath and shave close, to drive life into a corner" (W 90–1). This is not the language of a lazy man. For Thoreau, intellectual and spiritual labor were every bit as strenuous as physical labor. They were essential to a journey of what Sherman Paul has called "inward exploration."

Thoreau himself presents *Walden* as, among other things, a travel book, which was a popular genre of his day, and himself as the tour guide. But it is not to be an account of mere tourism; it is to record the quest of a student, a seeker after truth. It is to be "a simple and sincere account of his own life . . . some such account as he would send to his kindred from a distant land" (W 3). Thoreau claims to have traveled a good deal . . . in Concord, and he writes "not so much concerning the Chinese and Sandwich Islanders" as about "you who read these pages, who are said to live in New England" (W 4), for whom he advises their own inward journey.

These words alert the reader to two elements of the journey that will affect crucially what we see: the persona of our guide and the way he uses language to guide us through the book.

The passage reveals a complex narrator. Most obviously he is a lecturer and tour guide announcing his topic, but almost immediately after beginning the tour he turns the tables on his audience. Although he will describe "where he lived and what he lived for," he is just as interested in describing and critiquing how his audience lives. The reader finds himself or herself in the situation of a tourist signing on to tour a strange land, only to find the tour guide heading toward the tourist's own home. He is a guide who can be sternly didactic and judgmental, preaching that "The mass of men lead lives of quiet desperation" (W 8). But he can also be hilariously ironic, as when he describes the farmer who insists that Thoreau cannot live on a vegetable diet because it provides "nothing to make bones with" while at the same time he walks behind two oxen who "with vegetable-made bones" jerk him powerfully across his field (W 9).

He can be exasperatingly contradictory. He rejects all advice from his elders (W 9) but offers himself with his book as an elder mentor to "poor students" (W 4). He seems supremely confident in his own wisdom, but occasionally he reveals his insecurity, as in "The Bean-Field" where he admits that some of the seeds of virtue that he planted in himself "did not come up" (W 164). Thus, our guide, who seems most of the time to know so clearly where he is going, sometimes becomes one of us and shares our uncertainty. His search becomes ours as well.

Thoreau's humor expresses this same combination of confidence and insecurity. In the title-page epigraph that begins *Walden* he establishes the image of himself as the comically brash "chanticleer . . . standing on his roost, if only to wake his neighbors up." Although he seems confidently prepared to risk alienation by arousing his readers rudely from their moral slumber, at the same time his humor allows him to present himself playfully as one of them, someone who knows them well enough to poke fun at them. As Stanley Cavell suggests, Thoreau's problem concerning his readers "is not to learn what to say to them; that could not be clearer. The problem is to establish his right to declare it" (Cavell 11). His humor is the main tool through which he establishes this right. As he admits elsewhere, "the transcendental philosophy needs the leaven of humor to render it light and digestible" (*EEM* 235), a lesson that had been driven home to him by his failure to attract readers with *A Week on the Concord and Merrimack Rivers*.

While through his humor he subtly solicits the approval of his neighbors, Thoreau also requires of his readers that they prove worthy of the guidance he offers. Reading, he insists, "requires a training such as the athletes underwent, the steady intention almost of the whole life to this object. Books must be read as deliberately and reservedly as they were written" (W 100–1). The main test of a reader's worthiness is the ability to understand fully Thoreau's use of language. When, for instance, he describes his audience as those "who are said to live in New England," he is saying several things at once, depending on where one chooses to put the emphasis. To emphasize "said" suggests that it may be only a rumor that there is life in New England; to emphasize "live" suggests that what is called life in New England may not be genuine living; and to emphasize "New" raises the question of whether life in New England really is any different from life in "old" England. That Thoreau intended such playful use of emphases is made clear by the early pages of the first version of the *Walden* manuscript (see W 354, "Notes on Illustrations").

Throughout *Walden* Thoreau uses other kinds of language that compound his meaning. The book is filled with puns, so many (and many of them very bad) that even the most alert reader is likely to miss a few. When he writes of a fisherman who, after fishing a long while, has concluded that "he belonged to the ancient sect of Coenobites" (W 173), how many readers will read "see no bites" in the name? Thoreau also frequently uses his own twists on clichés and aphorisms: "As if you could kill time without injuring eternity" (W 8), or (referring to a postfuneral auction) "When a man dies he kicks the dust" (W 68). At times these resuscitated bits of language serve as parodies of the American dependence on oversimplified moral maxims in the tradition of Ben Franklin's Poor Richard. They are also much more than that, however; they are a crucial part of Thoreau's search for the hard bottom of truth that he believed could be found in language.

Recently critics (see West, Gura, Dillman, and Dettmer) have demonstrated Thoreau's conviction, based on his reading of Charles Kraitsir and other linguists and rhetoricians of his time, that all language has a common origin in the past and in nature. To find original truths one must dig through the corruptions of meaning that have encrusted themselves on words through the centuries. Etymology thus becomes a philosophical and spiritual search for truth. The most famous example of this theory is in the passage on the thawing sand bank in "Spring," in which Thoreau explores the etymology of the word "lobe" and its relation to the word "leaf" as part of his demonstration that "this one hillside illustrated the principle of all the operations of Nature" (W 304–9). This belief in the essential core of truth in language as reflecting a similar core of truth in nature is in one sense affirmed by his discovery of apparently fresh meanings through puns and revived clichés, because the "new" meanings might, in fact, be a re-discovery of the old, the original meanings. The job of the writer is to rediscover and revive the original truths of language.

On the other hand, the fact that words can have multiple meanings in a pun or take on additional meanings when Thoreau shifts emphases or places a cliché in a new context completely undercuts his attempts to find certainty in language. If words can have more than one meaning at the same time, how can they also have only one original meaning? For Thoreau, then, language is both a hard bottom and a slippery surface. The more our guide tries to lead us to hard bottom of truth with language, the more mysterious and distant that truth sometimes becomes.

The verbal terrain through which Thoreau guides us shares this ambiguity structurally also. One "map" of the structure of *Walden* reveals an apparent clarity and symmetry in the book's organization. From this viewpoint the chapter on "Economy" provides a prologue to the book proper, and the "Conclusion" provides the epilogue. To shift metaphors briefly, in "Economy" Thoreau provides the diagnosis of the spiritual and economic disease besetting his neighbors, and in "Conclusion" he describes the prognosis. The main body of the book prescribes the cure, which involves both an inward and an outward pilgrimage. "Where I Lived, and What I Lived For" begins the pilgrimage by establishing Thoreau's "point d'appui" (*W* 98), his home base at the cabin by the pond, and "Spring" presents the revelatory arrival at his spiritual destination.

Between these first and last chapters, *Walden* progresses in dialogic pairs of chapters on contrasting topics: quiet vs. sounds ("Reading" and "Sounds"), solitude vs. society ("Solitude" and "Visitors"), country vs. town ("The Bean-Field" and "The Village"), purity vs. degeneration ("The Ponds" and "Baker Farm"), spiritual vs. animal impulses ("Higher Laws" and "Brute Neighbors"), present vs. past ("House-Warming" and "Former Inhabitants; and Winter Visitors"), animal life in nature vs. human exploitation of nature ("Winter Animals" and "The Pond in Winter").

Yet to point out these pairings is to oversimplify Thoreau's scheme, for within chapters still other contrasts occur. This insistence on contrasting views is an essential part of Thoreau's purpose. As he says in "Economy," "The life which men praise and regard as successful is but one kind. Why should we exaggerate any one kind at the expense of the others?" (*W* 19). The purpose of the pilgrimage is to expose us not just to new scenic views but also to new ways of life, often ways directly opposed to the status quo.

He makes this strategy of absolute opposition clear from the outset: "The greater part of what my neighbors call good I believe in my soul to be bad, and if I repent of any thing, it is very likely to be my good behavior" (*W*

10). We are so stuck in our ways, he warns us, that we do not even know there is any other way: "it appears as if men had deliberately chosen the common mode of living because they preferred it to any other. Yet they honestly think there is no choice left" (*W* 8). Rather than one way of living, or even two, there are, he says, "as many ways as there can be drawn radii from one centre" (*W* 11). This strategy of first subverting the status quo with its opposite and then opening up infinite possibilities from that opposition point of view is crucial to *Walden,* as we shall see more clearly as we journey further into the book.

Thoreau's circular metaphor contrasts with a linear concept of travel to create another structural tension in *Walden.* On the one hand, the goal of Thoreau's pilgrimage – and presumably the reader's – is spiritual progress, to explore beyond the restricted boundaries of our materialistic lives to find new truths and thus to become a new person. To walk in the woods is to "saunter," to go "a la Sainte Terre, to the Holy Land" ("Walking" 205). At other times Thoreau defines this linear journey as vertical rather than horizontal. The truth is to be sought by diving to the bottom of the pond like a loon or delving to hard bottom in the earth (see Boone). Yet, though the reader is a pilgrim who is to progress to a new destination, Thoreau reminds us that finally "Our voyaging is only great-circle sailing" (*W* 320) and that the reader's task is to " 'Direct your eye sight inward,' " and " 'be expert in home-cosmography' " (*W* 320).

This circle of inward spiritual and psychological exploration in *Walden* is reflected in its chronological structure, the cycle of the seasons. Thoreau condenses his two years at the pond into one to emphasize the process of death and rebirth that the reader's journey involves. In "Where I Lived," he builds his cabin in the summer as the base for his exploration of nature and of self, and he moves in on Independence Day. The next ten chapters record his explorations (natural and spiritual) of Walden Pond and of the plants, animals, and people in its environs through summer and early fall. In "House-Warming," he makes an October retreat inward to the womb/tomb of the cabin and its fireplace. This retreat gives him time to reflect on the past ("Former Inhabitants; and Winter Visitors"). The pond's complementary retreat in being sealed over with ice affords Thoreau (in "Winter Animals" and "The Pond in Winter") "new views . . . of the familiar landscape" by allowing him to walk over its surface, measure it with surveying tools, and observe the new uses to which men and animals put it. Thoreau then comes full circle with his vision of nature resurrected in "Spring": "Walden was dead and is alive again" (*W* 311).

Thoreau superimposes on these linear and circular travel structures a complex mixture of other "maps" based on allusions to other genres of writing, including heroic epics, pastoral poetry, treatises on domestic economy, natural history, fiction (the *bildungsroman*), autobiography, history (for a discussion of these, see Johnson), and young men's guides (see Neufeldt). With these multiple structures he suggests what his own travels by the pond have taught him, that there is more than one way to get where we are going and that we must be prepared to consider multiple viewpoints on any issue.

Equipped with some combination of these "maps" of *Walden,* each reader is ready to consider the topic of economy, the methods and materials for traveling through life that are most likely to get us to the destination we set for ourselves. Thoreau sums up his idea of economy in his advice to "Simplify, simplify" (W 91). Like world travelers today, it is wisest for us to ask not "How much should we take?" but "How little can we take?" to get through life successfully. "Shall we always study to obtain more of these things," he asks, "and not sometimes less?" (W 36). This advice strikes to the heart of capitalist economics by asserting that less is more and that it is not material objects but spiritual development that we should seek. One travels through life best by simplifying bodily needs to leave more time and energy for pursuing transcendental reality. Through his experiment at Walden Pond, Thoreau attempts "to live a primitive and frontier life, though in the midst of an outward civilization, if only to learn what are the gross necessaries of life and what methods have been taken to attain them" (W 11).

Thoreau's short list of "necessaries" conspicuously omits the essential element of capitalism: money. "Money," he asserts, "is not required to buy one necessary of the soul" (W 329). If money is unessential, then so is work, which Thoreau defines as any activity done solely to obtain money. By this definition, "As for work, we haven't any of any consequence" (W 93). Any activity done out of true necessity or love then becomes "not a hardship but a pastime, if we will live simply and wisely" (W 70).

Thoreau defines a necessity as anything "so important to human life that few, if any, whether from savageness, or poverty, or philosophy, ever attempt to do without it" (W 12). These he reduces at first to four: clothing, shelter, food, and fuel. Clothing, he complains, has become more fashion than necessity. People are more concerned, he finds, "to have fashionable, or at least clean and unpatched clothes, than to have a sound conscience" (W 22). We do not need new clothes for our journey, because "a man who has at length found something to do will not need to get a new suit to do it in" for "if there is not a new man, how can the new clothes be made to fit?" (W 23).

New England tastes in housing also run to the merely fashionable and luxurious, he complains, while not more than half the families actually own their own houses. Whereas some build palaces without having the noble character to deserve them, others live in unheated shanties that, Thoreau points out (W 34–35), line the railroad tracks throughout New England. Thoreau's one-room cabin with its six modest pieces of furniture thus becomes the antithesis of the fancy homes described in house pattern books by such architects as Andrew Jackson Downing (see Masteller).

Regarding food Thoreau was not a complete vegetarian – he records experimenting with woodchuck meat – but he describes his diet at Walden as consisting mostly of such simple staples as "rye and Indian meal without yeast, potatoes, rice, a very little salt pork, molasses, and salt, and my drink water" (W 61). Even when he dined with his family in town, his mother served excellent bread, vegetables, fruit, and occasionally pies or puddings, but not meat (Harding 86).

Clothing, shelter, and food all finally serve the one purpose of fuel, however, "to keep the vital heat in us" (W 13). The key to living therefore becomes to maintain our physical vital heat by the most economical (that is, the simplest) method, thereby producing the maximum amount of the only capital that is ultimately real: time. "The cost of a thing," he reminds us, "is the amount of what I will call life which is required to be exchanged for it, immediately or in the long run" (W 31). As an example of the superiority of valuing time rather than money, he uses the example of traveling thirty miles, a typical day's travel in his day. He argues that by walking the thirty miles, which he can do in one day, he will cover that distance more quickly than the traveler who travels by railroad but must first spend a day earning the ninety cents for a ticket. As he walks he can enjoy the landscape and people along the way as well (W 53). The true value of time, however, is not in producing material goods or services such as railroad travel but in producing spiritual and psychological capital in the form of self-culture. Thoreau holds up several examples of neighbors – the young men who have inherited farms (W 5) and John Field, the Irish laborer (W 204–209), for instance – who are so caught up in the economy of production that they have no time for self-culture and can see no way out of the endless round of working, eating, and sleeping with no purpose other than physical survival or monetary profit.

Thoreau thus undermines the materialistic ideas of two of the classical economists whom he specifically mentions, Jean-Baptiste Say and Adam Smith, but he does so by diverting their own theories from materialistic to spiritual ends. If Say advised that saving money was a form of production in that it made possible new monetary investment, Thoreau advises us to save our time instead to make possible more investment in spiritual self-culture. If Smith argued that economic growth depends upon freedom for individuals to exercise enlightened self-interest, Thoreau shows his fellow travelers through life that they have choices (freedom) about how to use their time of which they are unaware. This freedom, if used wisely, can allow them to seek their full spiritual rather than monetary potential (see Birch and Metting 590–9).

For Thoreau the purpose of life's journey is to explore this potential, and nature provides the world, the moral landscape, in which to explore it. True, a Transcendental idealist should not need nature, what Emerson identified as "Not Me," for, as Thoreau asserts in "Higher Laws": "man flows at once to God when the channel of purity is open" (W 220). Most readers find "Higher Laws," the most obviously Transcendentalist chapter in the book, to be exasperating in its puritanic insistence on the virtues of a vegetarian diet and sexual chastity and in its apparent denial of the value of Nature. We are shocked to read Thoreau saying that "Nature is hard to overcome, but she must be overcome" (W 221). But "Higher Laws" represents only one side of the issue for Thoreau. We must take seriously his embrace of nature's duality at the beginning of the chapter: "I found in myself, and still find, an instinct toward a higher, or, as it is named, spiritual life, as do most men, and another toward a primitive rank and savage one, and I reverence them both. I love the wild not less than the good" (W 210). "Higher Laws" is one chapter in praise of the good in a book full of praise of the wild.

Most of the time Thoreau does not see nature as Emerson seems to, as only a physical means to a spiritual end. For Thoreau spirit is found *in* nature, not *through* it – a crucial distinction. His most obvious counterpoint to the Transcendentalism of "Higher Laws" occurs when he parodies idealism in his comic dialogue between the Hermit (Thoreau) and the Poet (his friend Ellery Channing) at the beginning of "Brute Neighbors." The Hermit abandons his meditation to go fishing, thereby affirming that spirit is to be found by experiencing nature, not by retreating into the mind. Once one recognizes this dualistic debate between the Transcendentalist and the naturalist in Thoreau's attitude, every natural object that he describes takes on a double meaning, one physical and one symbolic.

Thoreau's descriptions of animals illustrate this sense of nature's double meaning. In "Winter Animals," he presents his animals realistically, without any obvious symbolic meaning. His description of a fox hunt is a lively narrative but with no hint of symbolism. Descriptions of owls, jays, and rabbits in this chapter also remain at the level of naturalistic observation, as if the starkness of winter stripped his observations down to clear, simple fact. The title of the "Brute Neighbors" chapter, on the other hand, is ironic, because the animals described cease to be merely brutes as they symbolically take on spiritual meaning. They become "all beasts of burden, in a sense, made to carry some portion of our thoughts" (*W* 225). While the famous ant war passage is a masterpiece simply on the level of narrative and of factual observation, Thoreau moves smoothly to the symbolic level using mock epic conventions. The ants take on human characteristics as Greek "Myrmidons" (Greek for "ants"), and the fierce encounter between two small red ants and their much larger black ant adversary (*W* 229–30) reveals both humanity's courage and its tragic pride. Such animals as the ants and the "winged cat" in the same chapter suggest Thoreau's belief that seeking out natural facts and observing them carefully could yield important symbolic insights.

The loon which dominates the last pages of the chapter is a more ambiguous and troubling symbol, however. Thoreau plays "checkers" with the loon, trying to guess where it will resurface after it dives, but he always loses. The loon is depicted as a teasing but friendly adversary, but Thoreau also describes its typical sound as "demoniac laughter" (*W* 236), thereby suggesting a darker side to the animal's significance. Because the loon is able to dive to the deepest part of the pond, where humans cannot venture, it represents nature's dark, unknowable secrets, which may or may not be benign.

Walden Pond, Thoreau's central symbol, shares this dual significance, representing nature as both knowable and unknowable. Its symbolic meaning is in some ways very clear, especially when he describes it through the metaphors of the pond as mirror and the pond as "earth's eye" (*W* 186). As a mirror, the pond symbolically mediates between the material and spiritual worlds represented by the earth and the sky. In "Where I Lived" he speaks of the pond's "smooth reflecting surface" and emphasizes its ability to reflect the sky, thus becoming a "lower heaven" (*W* 86). It demonstrates that heaven is not distant in time or place but immediately under our feet here and now.

In reflecting the shoreline also, the pond reveals new views to the alert observer and provides an art gallery of nature's masterpieces: "Each morning the manager of this gallery substituted some new picture, distinguished by more brilliant or harmonious coloring, for the old" (*W* 240). The reflections, Thoreau finds, are never mere duplicates of the scene reflected, however. The air and the water always add something new. Thus the pond represents as well the eye of the artist/writer, whose task is to connect the material and the spiritual and thereby reveal new and beautiful truths to others. As a metaphor for the writer's own artistic eye, the pond's "crystalline purity," emphasized in "The Ponds," also suggests a moral purity against which the writer or the reader can "measure the depth of his own nature" (W 186). The pond as metaphor for humanity's moral nature is developed in "The Ponds in Winter," where the map of the pond's depths becomes a symbol of "the height or depth of [a person's] character" (W 291), a comparison more clever than clear, but one that emphasizes the importance to Thoreau of finding moral implications in nature.

To a traveler, being able to measure depths, distances, and objects is important as a way of asserting mastery over what has been seen. At the same time, however, Thoreau realizes that measuring the allegedly bottom-less depths of the pond physically is not the same as mastering its full symbolic meaning. Symbolically, the pond remains bottomless, because people want to believe in the infinite: "While men believe in the infinite some ponds will be thought to be bottomless" (W 287). The imagined depth of the pond is as close as Thoreau gets to taking us into the wilder-ness, a kind of landscape that had already disappeared around Concord and that he would explore in *The Maine Woods* and in "Walking." Both the wilderness and the pond's "bottomlessness" are symbols of human po-tential, reminders of truths yet to be discovered. The crux of *Walden* is perhaps to be found in Thoreau's recognition of this dual goal of humanity: "At the same time that we are earnest to explore and learn all things, we require that all things be mysterious and unexplorable, that land and sea be infinitely wild, unsurveyed and unfathomable by us because unfathom-able" (W 317–8).

Thus Walden Pond is both a port of departure and a port of call for our travels, both the place from which we begin to "travel farther than all travellers" (W 322), by following the ancient advice to "Explore thyself" (W 322), and the destination where we discover that "There is a solid bottom every where" (W 330), even if it is inaccessible to us in this life. The location of the pond proves ideal for exploring multiple perspectives. It is far enough away from town to provide solitude for inward exploration, yet close enough for periodic excursions into town for contact with people whose customs, viewed objectively from outside, seem stranger than those of the Chinese and Sandwich Islanders. It also allows Thoreau to adopt a subversive "carnival" attitude (see Schueller). He lives on the borders of the town, so he is not always expected to follow its rules – his neighbors consider him a bit odd. But he is still close enough to them physically and enough part of them culturally for him to hope that his irony and humor will strike home and undermine their most deeply held assumptions. Im-plied, of course, is that each reader should seek his or her own equivalent of such a stance.

Thoreau occasionally seems hopeful that his neighbors might join him on his exploration, as when he proposes that villages like Concord become true universities by hiring "all the wise men in the world to come and teach her" (*W* 110). Nonetheless, throughout his life he preferred to explore the woods alone, and throughout *Walden* he indicts his neighbors for their misplaced priorities and inability even to consider new ways. The overwhelming evidence in *Walden* is that his neighbors are not properly prepared for true exploration, because they do not yet know how to see truly. (Presumably he hopes his readers, his fellow travelers, will be the exception.) Living becomes a matter of self-culture, because – as he discovered during his night in jail (which occurred while he was living at the pond) – one's neighbors can seldom be coaxed into exploring new views. Life with principle can be a lonely journey.

The capacity for vision becomes the key to a successful and necessarily solitary journey of inward exploration. The crucial choice he puts to us is "Will you be a reader, a student merely, or a seer?" (*W* 11). Being a seer means, of course, not only to see physical reality accurately, which he certainly wants us to do, but to see in the mystical sense, to perceive the spiritual truths in and beyond nature. Most of us, he chides, are not even awake on our journey: "I have never yet met a man who was quite awake. How could I have looked him in the face?" (*W* 90).

Our first goal, he reminds us in "Where I Lived," must be to wake up to our potential and to maintain the morning mood of expectation. Even if they are awake enough for physical effort, most people see only surfaces: "our vision does not penetrate the surface of things. We think that *is* which *appears* to be" (*W* 96). Throughout the book, morning and the light it brings become dominant symbols of rebirth, even in the Christian sense, and of our potential for effective living. Of the light that announces the arrival of spring (the "morning" of the year) he exclaims, "All things must live in such a light. O Death, where is they sting? O Grave, where was thy victory, then?" (*W* 317).

Through this imagery of light we come as close to our destination, the hard bottom of truth, as Thoreau seems able to take us. The light reflected from the pond's pure surface and the light that floods through the window in spring remind us symbolically of a transcendent source from which they emanate. Thoreau seems confident that such a source exists, as the tone of the book's conclusion suggests. Yet he also reminds us in his conclusion that "The light which puts out our eyes is darkness to us" (*W* 333), that we cannot look directly into the truth of the sun, just as we can measure the depth of the pond physically but cannot dive, like the loon, directly to its bottom. Thoreau can show us the pond as a point of departure for a journey to the truth, he can advise us to open our eyes truly to what we can see outwardly and inwardly on the way, but he cannot tell us what we will see when we arrive, for he himself has not arrived. "Not one of my readers," he reminds us, "has yet lived a whole human life" (W 331); but neither had he when he wrote those words. Only death can provide a destination, and there might even be further journeying beyond that. There is in that sense always "more day to dawn" (W 333).

From one point of view, *Walden* is, as Michael Gilmore suggests, "a book at odds with its own beliefs" (Gilmore 36): a book that attacks capitalism, by an author who presumably hopes to make at least a modest profit from his book; a book about the truths to be found in nature that nonetheless cautions us to overcome nature; a book that seems confident that transcendent truth exists, while acknowledging repeatedly that everyone must find his or her own truth. Such contradictions reveal Thoreau's struggle to move beyond dualities to a full appreciation of life's variety.

An influential theory of cognitive development developed by William G. Perry suggests that children begin by believing that the one view they have been taught on any topic is necessarily the only truth. Later students go through most of high school and college as dualistic thinkers needing to see actions and ideas as either good or bad and unable to admit the possibility of uncertainty about which to prefer (Rodgers, "Teaching"). By the time they are graduated from college, only a few, perhaps 15 percent at most, move beyond dualism to consider the possibility that multiple views of actions and ideas might be equally valid or that there might be no absolute truth (Rodgers, Workshop).

The contradictions of *Walden* reveal that Thoreau is not always in that 15 percent either, that he sometimes adopts the dual vision of the reformer. The dualistic Thoreau insists that his neighbors' standards are bad and that his own are good, that the physical world is an illusion and that the spirit is the only ultimate reality. This Thoreau, of course, attracts the most readers to *Walden,* because we readers are mostly dualists too, longing for certainties in an impossibly complex world, even if those certainties are only the opposite of those that dominate our culture. We like the idea of tossing aside all of our old assumptions and trading them in for new ones, leaving the hubbub of the city to find the tranquility of nature beside a pond, to return to Eden.

But as Robert Sattelmeyer found in his study of the genesis of *Walden,* as Thoreau wrote the book his own thinking evolved so that he came "to regard his experience at Walden less as an example to misguided reformers and more as a personal quest involving doubt and uncertainty as well as discovery" (Sattelmeyer 62). Even Thoreau did not stay at Walden Pond; two years there were enough for him, because he found that he had worn a path from the hut to the pond, a sign that he could fall into a rut in the woods as well as in Concord. Although his life by the pond gave him "a success unexpected in common hours" (W 323), it was nonetheless only a preparation for further voyaging. Our journey into *Walden* should not end at Walden Pond either. *Walden* is, as Martin Bickman suggests, essentially "a book concerned with transitions, with passage" (Bickman 57).

In the part of this passage that is *Walden,* Thoreau as seer constantly deconstructs his own certainty, questions the meanings of the world around him, and reminds himself and us that there might be as many truths as there are points of view. He begins the lifelong passage to multiplistic thinking by emphasizing the variety of views that nature offers to the observer who is awake. Like the rest of us, Thoreau never completed the passage; on some topics, such as economics and slavery, he became even more dogmatic as the years went on. But his Journal after the Walden years records most often the explorations of a man fascinated, and perhaps at times overwhelmed, by the multitude of views that life has to offer. *Walden* proves finally to be about the potential passage – both Thoreau's and ours – from one kind of vision, and thus one kind of life, to another. As a challenge to move beyond dual certainties to an exploration of multiple possibilities, *Walden* is as fine a companion for a lifelong journey as one is likely to find. It reminds us that we too have "several more lives to live" (W 323).

WORKS CITED

Bickman, Martin. *Walden: Volatile Truths.* New York: Twayne, 1992.

Birch, Thomas D., and Fred Metting. "The Economic Design of *Walden," New England Quarterly* 65 (1992): 587–602.

Cavell, Stanley. *The Senses of "Walden."* New York: Viking, 1972.

Dettmer, Kevin J. H. "Ransacking the Root Cellar: The Appeal to/of Etymology in *Walden," Strategies: A Journal of Theory, Culture, and Politics* 1 (1988): 182–201.

Dillman, Richard. "The Psychological Rhetoric of *Walden," ESQ* 25 (1979): 79–91.

Gilmore, Michael T. *American Romanticism and the Marketplace.* Chicago: University of Chicago Press, 1985.

Gura, Philip F. "Henry Thoreau and the Wisdom of Words," in *Critical Essays on Thoreau's "Walden",* ed. Joel Myerson, pp. 203–14. Boston: G. K. Hall, 1988.

Harding, Walter. *The Days of Henry Thoreau.* New York: Knopf, 1965.

Johnson, Linck C. "Revolution and Renewal: The Genres of *Walden,"* in *Critical Essays on Thoreau's "Walden,"* ed. Joel Myerson, pp. 215–34. Boston: G. K. Hall, 1988.

Masteller, Richard N., and Jean Carwile. "Rural Architecture in Andrew Jackson

Downing and Henry David Thoreau: Pattern Book Parody in *Walden*," *New England Quarterly* 57 (1984): 483–510.

Neufeldt, Leonard N. *The Economist: Henry Thoreau and Enterprise.* New York: Oxford University Press, 1989.

Paul, Sherman. *The Shores of America: Thoreau's Inward Exploration.* Urbana: University of Illinois Press, 1958.

Perry, William G. *Forms of Intellectual and Ethical Development in the College Years.* New York: Holt, Rinehart and Winston, 1970.

Rodgers, Robert F. "Teaching to Facilitate Critical Thinking: A Cognitive-Developmental Perspective," in *Critical Thinking, Interactive Learning, and Technology,* ed. Thomas J. Freca. Chicago: Arthur Anderson and Company, 1992.

Rodgers, Robert F. Workshop presentation at Wartburg College, 4 January 1993.

Sattelmeyer, Robert. "The Remaking of *Walden*," in *Writing the American Classics,* ed. James Barbour and Tom Quirk, pp. 53–78. Chapel Hill: University of North Carolina Press, 1990.

Schueller, Malini. "Carnival Rhetoric and Extra-vagance in Thoreau's *Walden*," *American Literature* 58 (1986): 33–45.

Thoreau, Henry D. "Walking," in *The Writings of Henry David Thoreau,* 20 vols., 5:205–48. Boston: Houghton, Mifflin, 1906.

West, Michael. "Scatology and Eschatology: The Heroic Dimensions of Thoreau's Wordplay," *PMLA* 89 (1974): 1043–64.

8

LEONARD N. NEUFELDT

Thoreau in his Journal

When an anonymous interlocutor asked Thoreau, "Do you keep a journal?" one of Thoreau's responses was to begin one. This Journal turned out to be his largest work by far and, in his estimation, possibly his most important project as a writer. According to Thoreau, the inquiry about keeping a journal was preceded by another question: "What are you doing now?" (PJ 1:5). There was something familiar and quite unfamiliar in starting a journal. Journal as private genre, as popular, published genre, as a miscellany in which various versions of this popular form appeared in the company of many other kinds of writings, and as a feature of daily and weekly newspapers with their miscellaneous and detailed reports were all familiar to him. Yet how should he initially proceed after taking note of the question of whether he kept a journal? What was he instating with his first entry?

The twin questions are also Thoreau's questions, and they are ours as well: why should he as an aspiring writer keep a journal, what are the doings that warrant reporting, what is his relation to them, and what is he doing in reporting them? Others, the questioner implies, are keeping journals. Many others, we might add. Lawrence Buell reminds us that when Harvard professor of rhetoric Edward Tyrell Channing assigned an essay on "The Advantages of Keeping a Journal" Thoreau "dutifully ... noted three."[1] Despite Thoreau's familiarity with the term "journal," he wondered what he was doing in commencing his project. As he filled early notebooks and then cannibalized and transcribed them, drafted major essays in later volumes, borrowed phrases, sentences, and pages from these volumes for his other writings, and came to understand his journal notebooks as increments in an independent, self-justifying work, his reflections on his journalizing produced incommensurable and imprecise observations. Yet he returned to these volumes as he did to his essay drafts, to revise them with the eyes of an editor mindful of readers. The question that opens the Journal invites us to revisit the term "journal," to engage the authorial voice, to track and, if possible, to locate "Thoreau" in his Journal, to address the issues of textuality in this infinitely complex document, and, in these undertakings, to track scholars who have been tracking the Thoreau of the Journal.[2]

Thoreau's "failure" to be definitive on the purpose of his journalizing is part of a pattern noticeable throughout his Journal and in keeping with an entry he made early on. "Of all strange and unaccountable – things," he admitted, "this journalizing is the strangest, it will allow nothing to be predicted of it." This statement is framed by two paragraphs on friendship that with their two metaphors make a twice-told message into two different messages on unpredictability. The first of these two paragraphs begins: "Friends will have to be introduced each time they meet. They will be eternally strange to one another, and when they have mutually appropriated their value for the last hour, they will go and gather a new measure of strangeness for the next." In the second of these paragraphs Thoreau declares, "Men lie behind the barrier of a relation as effectually concealed as the landscape by a mist; and when at length some unforeseen accident throws me into a new attitude to them, I am astounded, as if for the first time I saw the sun on the hill-side" (*PJ* 1:236–7). Strange and unaccountable, indeed, is this journalizing – as unaccountable as strangeness between friends and relations who must always reach beyond barriers and find themselves anew. The question that opens the Journal, "What are you doing now?" is a remarkably compact preface, and more than a preface, to Thoreau's project. It establishes a kind of provenance for what will follow – years of journalizing and occasional reflections on his project.

Nonetheless, the story of Thoreau's journalizing has its familiar aspects. Scholarship inclined to see the works of nineteenth-century American Transcendentalists as exceptional, if not unique, has inclined to the view that "literary" journal-keeping like Thoreau's is a characteristic and perhaps peculiar New England Transcendentalist or Emersonian performance. Yet the habit of journal-keeping was prevalent outside of nineteenth-century Concord and New England in both America and Europe. Published journals and surviving manuscripts and records indicate that journal-keeping was done in seventeenth-century continental Europe, England, and colonial America – it was widely practiced by English and colonial Puritans – and that the practice spread over the next two centuries. In the Old World as much as in the New, formats, contents, and purposes varied from journal to journal. Eighteenth- and nineteenth-century types include general logbooks of events, simple recitations of activities (for example, domestic operations and details), reading records, travel narratives, accounts of or reflections on one's personal economy, memorandum books on one's business, astronomical records, notes on changes of seasons or weather, medical observations of patients and treatments, observations of flora and fauna, testimonies of particular providences, introspective registers of one's spiritual state or one's moral or intellectual improvement, notes on political or other social and institutional goings-on, private histories of one's ideas and reconsiderations of those ideas, and, of course, combinations of several, perhaps many, of these. Many such journals or portions of them have survived in manuscript form; others, especially those considered to have special edifying value, were published and widely read.

In 1803, in his new *Literary Magazine and American Register,* Charles Brockden Brown took special note of a journalizing which only the French could have invented, "to present the public with their character, and this fashion seems to have passed over to our country. . . . Every writer then considered his character as necessary to his preface. I confess myself much delighted with these self-descriptions."[3] The first volume of *Literary Magazine* includes memoirs and a travel journal, the second a diary. Private literary journals of various kinds were common features in many of the American cultural and literary journals established in the first half of the nineteenth century. More common were devotional and edificatory journals, particularly of the kind Margaret Fuller was given by her hosts during her vacation in Bristol in 1839, to read in her free time. She put it aside after a few pages, presumably to work on her own journal.[4] It was not the material she pushed aside at Bristol but the kind of journal that she, Thoreau, and other Transcendentalists kept that Brockden Brown had had in mind.

It was to be expected that members of leading families and the educated middle class in colonial and early national America kept journals. The journal of his great-grandfather that Emerson consulted has apparently been lost, but some of the journals kept by his grandfather and father have survived. Moreover, his aunt Mary Moody Emerson and some of his brothers kept journals (the first and thirteenth issues of *Dial* featured posthumous extracts from Charles Emerson's journal). Most of the members of the Transcendental club who attended its meetings in its first year (1836) are known to have kept journals. Nearly all members of the Alcott family (including Alcott's mother and at least one cousin) kept a journal, as did Nathaniel Hawthorne, Fuller, Ellery Channing, and many other temporary or resident Concordians. Indeed, in Concord, clergy, teachers, naturalists, businessmen, lawyers, housewives, unmarried women, students, and farmers left journals behind ranging from a few page fragments to Bronson Alcott's fifty neatly bound volumes of approximately five million words. In subject matter, these journals present a similarly wide range of diversity.

As for the journals of Transcendentalists, at the most general level one can agree with Lawrence Rosenwald's characterization of them as "stubborn individualists." "Fuller's," he goes on to say, "is the diametric opposite of Thoreau's, a brilliant account of social interactions; Hawthorne's is an exercise book in scene painting; Alcott's is in diligence if not in gusto almost Pepysian, faithfully recording the events of the day, reflections upon them, and so to bed." Unlike any of these, Emerson's refused to adhere to what Rosenwald calls "the rhythm of the calendar," was inclined to use the second and third person, and so forth.[5] Much as Alcott desired, in his words, to "forget chronologies and annals, and dwell on the spiritual pedigrees of things,"[6] he couldn't escape the historical sequence of days and weeks. Thoreau, on the other hand, felt comfortable with days and weeks, and with seasonal calendars, and used them to his advantage. Many other differences might be noted among these journalists, including the degree and kind of note-taking for use in journal entries, the relative amount of spontaneous or unpremeditated journalizing, favorite sources for one's journal, typical length of entries, patterns of intermittent or continuous journalizing, the continuity or discontinuity of materials from entry to entry, the presence or absence of cross-referencing and other internal linkages, the extent of current and subsequent authorial revision, the relation of notebooks to each other, and the relation of one's journal to one's published work.

Differences also characterize any journal practice of long duration. For example, in the early 1850s Thoreau acknowledged that his Journal had changed in style, contents, and purpose.[7] The reader recognizes in the Journal of this period several other modifications – a greater number of entries, longer entries, and a decreasing number of days not accorded an entry. Alcott not only became increasingly encyclopedic, but also changed his format in 1837 from daily to weekly units. For some time thereafter he seems to have kept a number of preliminary "day notes" and on the weekend composed a weekly unit from them. As for Emerson, the purpose to which he dedicated his series of "Wide World" notebooks changes somewhat with each volume. One is not surprised, therefore, by his habit of simultaneously keeping several kinds of journals, some of which also exhibit significant changes over the years.

Whereas the practices of individual journal writers may have changed and may have differed from writer to writer, there is evidence that several Transcendentalists, including Thoreau, "were surely considering the prospect of posthumous independent publication and, thus, inevitably thinking of their diaries *as books*."[8] Although in 1843 Thoreau refused a request of the editor of the *Democratic Review* to send him journal extracts for publication, a few years later he was referring to his Journal in the same terms he used for his published work and even imagined it published unabridged. In this vision he had company. Like Benjamin Franklin, Alcott wrote of his massive journal that it "gathers up the fragments, and preserves in transcript, whatever there may be, for future value & use, so that nothing of life shall be wantonly contemned or irretrievably lost. . . . The history of one human mind . . . would be a treasure of inconceivably more value to the world than all the systems which philosophers have built concerning the mind up to this day."[9] Neither self-address nor an exchanging of journal notebooks or portions thereof, a favorite method of literary sharing among Transcendentalists – whose circle of exchange also included Fuller, Elizabeth Peabody, Mary Moody Emerson, and Elizabeth Hoar – could finally satisfy Thoreau. Nor did it satisfy Alcott, whose journal at times became a local lending library, and who complained that "As yet my principles and purposes, have not found admission into the public Journals."[10]

Ellery Channing, who hoped to see his own journal notes published, went so far as to persuade Emerson and Thoreau to allow him to combine extracts of journals of all three of them in book form – he had also considered including Alcott's journal, but Emerson vetoed that part of the plan.[11] Channing eventually used many of his gleanings from Thoreau's Journal in his *Thoreau: The Poet–Naturalist* (1873). Fuller's journal, too, was eminently publishable in the view of Emerson, William Henry Channing, and James Freeman Clarke, who drew heavily on it for their *Memoirs of Margaret Fuller Ossoli* (1852). Cabot did the same with Emerson's journals when he wrote *A Memoir of Ralph Waldo Emerson* (1887).

Not only did Concord's Transcendentalists imagine that a readership would some day engage their journals as dutifully as Transcendentalist writers read each other's journals; they also often imagined general and particular readers as they wrote. Thus the reader of Thoreau's Journal can easily make too much of his possibly descriptive, possibly prescriptive, notations, "Say's I to my-self should be the motto of my Journal" and "Speak though your thought presupposes the non existence of your hearers" (*PJ* 4:177, 224). These comments, made a little more than a month apart, were followed shortly by the less cryptic observation, "I do not know but thoughts written down thus in a journal might be printed in the same form with greater advantage – than if the related ones were brought together into separate essays. They are now allied to life – & are seen by the reader not to be far fetched" (*PJ* 4:296).

These writers' view of their journals as important literary projects, Buell has noted, helps to account for why the journals of several of the Transcendentalists, Thoreau's included, "are less intimate than those of their forebears."[12] That generalization is particularly persuasive if one restricts the focus to, say, those Transcendentalist journal-keepers whose Puritan ancestors kept religious diaries. On the other hand, Charles Brockden Brown seemed to have more literary journals in mind when he observed that there "once prevailed the custom of a man's journalizing his own life. Many of these journals yet remain in their MS. state. . . . The pleasures of memory are delicious; its objects must, however, be proportionate to the powers of vision." If blessed by such powers, "diaries form that other self, which Shaftesbury has described every thinking being to possess; and which, to converse with, he justly accounts the highest wisdom."[13]

In a sense, then, Thoreau stands in a long tradition of forming that "other self," in his case a rich combination of selves and voices, in his Journal. Such a project must be undertaken in a deliberate and disciplined way. "No day will have been wholly misspent, if one sincere thoughtful page has been written," Thoreau early on confided to his Journal (PJ 1: 151). "How many communications may we not lose through inattention?" asks the guarded journalist in another entry. "I would fain keep a journal which should contain those thoughts & impressions which I am most liable to forget that I have had" (PJ 3:178). What one finds, or seeks out, "it is important in a few words to describe" (J 7:171), thus safeguarding potentially important communications. Such accounting "is a record of experiences and growth, not a preserve of things well done or said. . . . The charm of the journal must consist in a certain greenness, though freshness, and not in maturity" (J 8:134). To preserve greenness and enhance the sense of immediacy – "as though a green bough were laid across the page" (Week 104) – Thoreau usually wrote his reports in the present tense, although he often drafted them several days after the fact. Occasionally he lapsed into the past tense only to alter it to the present. At times one present tense competes with another, as when he describes a walk along a brook and also comments on "the sound of the piano below as I write this" (PJ 4: 433–4).

But it is in Thoreau's multiple understanding of the "field" of his Journal rather than in his regimen of journal-writing that we discern qualities distinguishing his Journal from others'. "Field" also serves to distinguish the earlier from the later Journal. "Might not my Journal be called 'Field Notes?' " he asks rhetorically in an entry in 1853 (J 5:32). A year earlier he had recorded, "I commit my thoughts to a diary even on my walks" (PJ 4:426). Brief notations made while surveying, sauntering, hiking, botanizing, and so forth, frequently provided the origins of journal entries. Yet the entries commonly include reflections, ruminations, conclusions, reconsiderations, and other forms of expansion and conceptualizing. Apparently referring to the expansion of individual entries as well as to the addition of new entries, he declares, "Each thought that is welcomed and recorded is a nest egg – by the side of which more will be laid. Thoughts accidentally thrown together become a frame – in which more may be developed – & exhibited. Perhaps this is the value of writing – of keeping a journal. . . . Having by chance recorded a few disconnected thoughts and then brought them into juxtaposition – they suggest a whole new field in which it was possible to labor & to think. Thought begat thought" (*PJ* 4:277–8). A related meaning of "field" is the setting or the special condition generating an entry – a moment of fascination, attention, mystery, and inspiration he refers to as "the cavern" (*PJ* 4:296–7). Yet, to the extent that experiences are taken out of that field and placed in another one, they take on a second life, which assumes its own time and place that may strongly recall the original time and place or largely erase it. According to Thoreau, some records of important events in his life "are not dated" (*J* 8:64). Generally speaking, this mode of composition is more familiar to the creative writer, the personal essayist, and the impressionistic and inventive journalist than to the professionally trained research scholar.

All these meanings of "field" are involved in the following passage: "I would fain make two reports in my Journal, first the incidents and observations of to-day; and by to-morrow I review the same and record what was omitted before, which will often be the most significant and poetic part. I do not know at first what it is that charms me. The men and things of to-day are wont to be fairer and truer in to-morrow's memory" (*J* 9: 306). In the more affected and self-conscious early Journal he declares that although his journalizing represents "gleanings from the field," he must live not for that field but for the gods. "I am clerk in their counting room, and at evening transfer the account from day-book to ledger. It is as a leaf which hangs over my head in the path – I bend the twig and write my prayers on it" (*PJ* 1:259). Whereas these passages emphasize an active seeking, finding, textualizing, and retextualizing, they also denote a recipient who admits that which finds him and admits to being charmed by it. No diagrams or maps can fix these transactions. "From all points of the compass from the earth beneath and the heavens above have come these inspirations and been entered duly in such order as they came in the Journal" (*PJ* 2:205). Addressing both himself and his generation of writers, he encourages a discipline practiced "as if thy time was short. . . . Use & commit to life what you cannot commit to memory." Having kept a Journal for almost a decade and a half, he adds, "I feel as if I then [in the early years] received the gifts of the gods with too much indifference – Why did I not cultivate those fields they introduced me to?" Intimations of mortality, we might say – the transitoriness of writer and writing ability. Such complaints usually are found near admissions of writing difficulties in the present, admissions often countered in the same notebook by reports of success and gratitude. Nonetheless, the typical condition against which he registers regret for lost opportunities is the transience of what he calls the "rhythmical mood." "I cannot draw from it – & return to it in my thought as to a well – all the evening or the morning – I cannot dip my pen in it" (*PJ* 4:281–2).

"Field" as multiple world, as unpredictable inspiration, as only partially taught textualizations gathered and revisited on changing terms, and as unpredictable, relatively atomistic, heterogeneous, often inconsistent anthologizing – this plurality distinguishes both Thoreau's Journal and Thoreau in his Journal. "Where also will you ever find the true cement for your thoughts?" he asks himself as journalist (*PJ* 4:297). The answer lies not in journal-keeping, and perhaps not even in Thoreau's other kinds of writing, whether or not these grew out of the Journal. As a young writer, however, he assumed that his other writings would eventually "stand, like the cubes of Pythagoras, firmly on either basis; like statues on their pedestals," like separately framed, individual works such as paintings in an artist's exhibit (*PJ* 2:205-6). The conundrum generated by these partially contradictory metaphors has to do with relationship. One cannot expect to find "the true cement" or a definitive framing principle or a generic law of the Journal. Yet this very impossibility implies a greater degree of mutuality among parts than that between individual literary exhibits such as nature essays, *A Week,* and *Walden.*

Thus "field" might be said to comprise disciplined seeking, spontaneity, vagrance, and surprise in a dialectic of everydayness; but "field" must also be understood as the conjoining of this dialectic with traditional myths, values, and practices that repeatedly produce tensions and contradictions between a journalizing heavily marked by cultural inscription and reports of immediate evidence. What we might refer to as the ideological in the Journal includes both, of course. Therefore, the ideological cannot be reduced simply to a cultural text or to presumed sparks of a unique unconsciousness, apperception, and imaginative energy free of culture, community, or any other kinship, influence, or mediation. Nor should we expect cultural inscriptions simply to reproduce themselves in familiar forms. But in recognizing that the field of the Journal assumes the form of a distinguishable, multivoiced persona, and that the text of this persona solicits several kinds of reading in order to compass the field, the reader has discerned Thoreau's version of Shaftesbury's "other self."

At this point it has become necessary to address more directly the implications of multiple mappings for the multifield of the Journal, implications that reach toward questions of the homogeneity–heterogeneity and unity–fragmentation of the Journal. Because these issues have the potential to swallow the essay, let me suggest somewhat reductively four mappings that, despite potential overlap in their conclusions, yield different results: (1) the microlinguistic, (2) the intratextual, (3) the multitextual, and (4) the intertextual. Of course, answers to the question of what the Journal looks like as a whole, given its many parts, depend on one's charting.

(1) "Say's I to my-self should be the motto of my Journal," Thoreau informs himself, potential readers, or both (*PJ* 4:177). This declaration might seem unproblematic – identifying the Journal as autobiography, indeed an autography constructing a self for purely private purposes. As such it would be a record of an identifiably stable "I." This "I" is also a characteristic kind of mediator between self as subject and object (no matter where we happen to open the Journal), and the originating power as well as the center of the Journal. But this motto can also be considered as a rule of performance, an act of speaking which attempts to construct both a self and a regulation of self. To consider self-construction as both subject and object of journalizing complicates Thoreau's statement considerably, as does the suggestion of separation between "I" and "my-self," a separation possibly confirmed and doubled by the hyphen as divider. Yet the hyphen also raises the possibility of alliance. How unitary and stable is such a "self," and, for that matter, the "I" as negotiator and mediator of a potentially fragmented and multiple self? What are the means and possibilities of relation, not to mention integrity? The "should" that follows "my-self" seems to register a similar separation in that it reports desire yet stops short of achievement. Likewise the double meaning of "motto" can refer to text or pre-text. In the latter case it stops short of and therefore distinguishes itself from text, unless pre-text, also understood as pretext, is the text of the Journal. And the relation of the final "my" to the earlier "my" and "self" is subject to, and subject of, all these deconstructions.

(2) Microlinguistic examination of the Journal, especially of the kind claiming our deconstructive attention by focusing on what Frederick Garber calls "slippage" within words and between proximate words,[14] continues to be a marginal practice in the scholarship. Much more common is what I refer to as intratextual analysis, by which I mean the scholarship that for years has established relatedness between various Journal entries by identifying certain recurrent structural properties, themes, and motifs. These make it possible to speak of the Journal both as parts and whole. Scholarly favorites in the list of unifying structural properties have included a characteristic spatiality (for example, "I"-centeredness, the horizon as

angle of vision or circle; linear or concentric exploration; nearness or remoteness), characteristic temporality (for example, diurnal, seasonal, annual, or calendar – of a life, vocation, or intellectual history); the Journal as a writer's storehouse; the negotiations between facts and transformation or transcendence of facts; and an essential kind of nature writing. Themes offered as integrating principles have included the pure subjectivity of the "I" persona, the objective subjectivity of tracing oneself in one's world, sensuousness, nature, organicism, increasing empiricism, time, and various avatars of truth. Commonly noted motifs include the seasons, the wild, the simple, the immediate, and forms of quest or mythic movement. Although these continue to be important in current scholarship, several scholars have teased out what they perceive as competing impulses and claims in Thoreau's alliances and, discernibly, in the Journal's structures or in Thoreau's treatment of themes and use of motifs – most notably Daniel Peck in a dialectical analysis and Sharon Cameron in a more radically deconstructive way. With some justification scholarly reaction to radically deconstructive approaches has ranged from respect for close reading, lucid exposition, and illuminating diagrams to exasperation over a reading equivalent of climbing a greased pole.

To date most scholarship on the Journal has searched out unifying principles. In a statement such as the following, Thoreau seems to anticipate this approach: "Every man thus *tracks himself* through life, in all his hearing and reading and observation and travelling. His observations make a chain. The phenomenon or fact that cannot in any wise be linked with the rest which he has observed, he does not observe." But this passage comments on the act of perceiving and recording. And Thoreau adds, "By and by we may be ready to receive what we cannot receive now" (*J* 13:77). That concluding observation undoubtedly contains several signals, one of which is that in various ways the Journal is not consistent but may feature genealogies of change, competing claims, and unpredictable claims within, between, and among entries as a variable observer sounds his multiform world.

A few examples will illustrate the point just made. As reader of America's past, Thoreau can be found in the thralls of a triumphal revolutionary republican historiography, that popular progressivist Whig view of the colonial and early national experience that served both as paradigm for the notable histories of his day and as the core of civil religion in his New England. At other times his relation to this interpretation of past and present is ironic, even contemptuous. One also recognizes impulses to construct what Joan Burbick has called an "alternative history." Occasionally he dismisses history altogether in favor of myths existing, as it were, outside of national and even Western experience. His approach to nature is often correspondential, but can also be noncorrespondential, and his view of the natural world is at times essentialist, at times progressivist or vitalist, at times egocentric, at other times more generally anthropocentric, at times nonhumanized. Scholars interested in Thoreau's sexuality have noted how imperious, fearful, and aggressively dismissive his responses are to women. But Journal entries also feature a Thoreau inclined to deify the feminine and idealize women close to him. In more than a few instances he seems to be little more than a custodian of true womanhood and its corollary of a special, narrowly defined woman's sphere centered by the "heart" and expressing itself in the language of "sentiment." In a few of these instances, and in other instances as well, he is much given to a language of sentiment, an expression associated by many of his contemporary male writers with female writing. And, although revealing himself as a priggishly conventional, opinionated New Englander and superior Concordian, the Thoreau of the Journal is also capable of expressing strong sympathy for lower-class groups and individuals and for marginalized people like native North Americans and African-Americans.

In its range of responses to America's aboriginal people, the Journal offers an illuminating exchange between widely representative prejudices in Thoreau's America, the liberal prejudice of idealizing Indians (as totems, unspoiled nobility, or mythic representatives of what Thoreau's essay "Walking" calls the "Wild" and "West"), and his own firsthand, complex, and confusing experience of them. A similarly various treatment is accorded some of Thoreau's closest friends. In the case of Emerson, for instance, the most notable shift is from adulatory references in the early Journal to defensive, self-righteous, and occasionally bitter entries in the 1850s. Yet such opposition to Emerson in the later Journal is a virtue Emerson's personae and their doctrines of repellent orb and independent orbit usually endorsed. Just as Emerson ventriloquized an oppositional Thoreau in his address at Thoreau's funeral, Thoreau's Journal ventriloquizes an oppositional Emerson while expressing both admiration and opposition.

"If I make a huge effort to expose my innermost and richest wares to light," Thoreau noted about his journalizing, "my counter seems cluttered with the meanest homemade stuffs, but after months or years, I may discover the wealth of India . . . in that confused heap, and what perhaps seemed a festoon of dried apple or pumpkin, will prove a string of Brazilian diamonds, or pearls from Corromandel" (*PJ* 1:237). Both "clutter" and "string," one is inclined to say. Here, then, is a metaphor for characterizing the Journal's intratextual heterogeneity, one that has major implications for discussions of text as discourse, ideology, or voice – in short, the Journal as symbolic practice.

(3) For the scholar persuaded of constellated differences in topics, assumptions, rhetorical mode, or style, however, the Journal represents not only a heterogeneous text but also a nest of texts. In this case the task becomes one of describing a multitext and not just mapping what Peck, in referring to *Walden,* has called the "crosscurrents" of a single text.[15] Consider, for example, Thoreau's journalizing about "Nature." His concept of Nature is, in fact, several concepts based on various deductive categories. The same holds true with terms like "soil," "land," "wilderness," "frontier," and "west." Indeed, Peck has proposed that the Journal is "a record of Thoreau's attempt to systematize such views and revise them in accordance with his own perceptions," a proposition prefigured implicitly by Sherman Paul and given pragmatic encouragement by Stanley Cavell.[16] Yet incommensurabilities between Thoreau's different constructions of "Nature" are readily apparent (for example, nature is sometimes feminine, usually capitalized, at times purely mythic in design and meaning, occasionally divine, sometimes the antipode of society or civilization, often the "wild," infrequently the wild as tooth and claw, from time to time mentor in organic form). These differences may be somewhat reconciled by imputing a porousness to the distinctions. If seen as essentially impermeable, such differences tend to yield different species of nature writing. Distinctions between nature writing and other kinds of writing in the Journal are subject to the same principle of differentiation.

The multitextual approach might well depend on the significance given to chronology (author's biography and development). Considered diachronically, some of the distinctions already noted may very well realign themselves in the form of stages of development that indicate a relatively continuous or discontinuous narrative. If the latter is indicated, the scholarly plotting will probably identify early, middle, and late Journal, each of these a text with its own properties. Thoreau's nature writings serve as illustration here as well: the feminine, thoroughly mythic, universal, and salvific "Nature" of Thoreau's meditation titled "Natural History of Massachusetts" might be the most common approach to nature in the early Journal, whereas a different mythologizing of "Nature" in "Walking" might be more characteristic of the Journal of the middle years. The empirically disciplined natural history essay best exemplified by "The Succession of Forest Trees" (Thoreau wrote few such works) might be identified largely with the later Journal. Thus, whether formally or chronologically considered, the Journal might be said to accommodate versions or species of itself, which most broadly classified include daybook, commonplace book, poetic meditations, discrete literary compositions, manifestoes, and *hypomnemata*.[17] Multiple versions also suggest the possibility of multiple passages through the Journal somewhat analogous to the virtually unlimited number of potential paths in a hypertext.

(4) Whether approached intratextually or multitextually, Thoreau's two million words of Journal present difficulties to the reader searching it for the unity and coherence of, say, the "Sounds" chapter of *Walden,* "The Succession of Forest Trees," or the poem on the "Marlborough Road." So receptive and commodious a Journal invites an intertextual approach, first to the Journal itself (understood now in the plural), and second to the Journal's place in relation to the corpus of Thoreau's works. I will briefly comment on the latter before extending the meaning of intertext beyond Thoreau's texts.

Notwithstanding scholarly attempts to distinguish between the Journal and Thoreau's other works generically, structurally, rhetorically, thematically, autographically, and so forth, there are things about the Journal that are characteristic of Thoreau's writing generally. To be sure, Thoreau's non-Journal compositions present tighter structures, less linguistic and thematic vagrance, and less dialectical everydayness than we find in the Journal. Works like *Walden* and "Resistance to Civil Government," Henry Golemba has written, represent Thoreau's "most generous negotiations with reader expectations, cultural myths, and publishers' demands."[18] Yet their difference from the Journal is one of degree. An observation by Buell on the Journal is striking not only because of its appropriateness to Thoreau's journalizing but also for its applicability to works like *A Week* or *Walden:* "the journals of Emerson, Thoreau, and Alcott . . . aspire to an encyclopedic quality, to take in the whole range of human experience, which inevitably they fail to do." Moreover, Walter Benn Michaels might just as well have been describing the Journal when he characterized *Walden* as an open, contradictory form whose several impulses and kinds of writing cannot finally be reconciled but must be accepted at both the literal and figurative level. Barbara Johnson's view that *Walden*'s motif of loss is a form of "transference from traveller to traveller" seems equally as pertinent to *A Week* as to the Journal. And Linck Johnson's examination of the compositional history of *A Week* confirms that, as interrupted as the travel narrative of the first version of *A Week* is by poems, quotations, gazetteer information, short essays, and other so-called digressions, the published text, by contrast, is even more heterogeneous – closer, in this respect, to the Journal. Indeed, Johnson's characterization of *A Week* applies to the Journal: through his cyclopedic form ("poems and translations, essays on writers, and digressions on books and style"), Thoreau "relates his own efforts . . . to the dawning of a new literary era in Concord."[19]

These richly suggestive characterizations apply, furthermore, to much of the new American literary production in Thoreau's time. It is this heterogeneity and irreducibility of Thoreau's writing, and the possibility that a kind of writing like his Journal may be linked to cultural developments, that will frame the rest of my comments on the Journal as intertext.

In a sense Thoreau's Journal could be described as a multitext in search of form. Among the many metaphors he uses to refer to his journalizing are gleaning, harvesting, gathering, collecting, throwing together, storing, preserving, and one that assumes all of these – anthologizing. In speaking of the Journal as anthology I am reaching back, as Thoreau does, to the Greek term *anthologia,* the very term he had in mind when he opined in his 1852 Journal that by journalizing his perceptions and thoughts, "They are now allied to life – & are seen by the reader not to be far fetched. . . . Mere facts & names & dates communicate more than we suspect – Whether the flower looks better in the nosegay – than in the meadow where it grew – & we had to wet our feet to get it!" (*PJ* 4:296). Before *anthologia* came to refer chiefly to a representative collection of the finest lyric poetry, it literally meant a gathering or garland of flowers, usually from the field or garden. Emerson and his brother Charles also refer to their journals as a flower gathering,[20] a figure of speech frequently found in the prospectuses or in editorial apologias in the initial issues of antebellum literary or general cultural journals.

Although early nineteenth-century American lexicons followed Dr. Johnson's lead in defining "anthology" as a collection of the best lyric poetry, obviously the Anthology Club of Boston had a much broader meaning in mind in operating *The Monthly Anthology,* which they founded in 1803 and to which six months later they appointed Emerson's father as editor. Members of this club were also instrumental in establishing the *North American Review.* Their understanding of "anthology" is pretty much summed up by the title of John Frost's 1828 anthology of American literature: *The Class Book of American Literature. Consisting Principally of Selections in the Departments of History, Biography, Prose Fiction, Travels, the Drama, Popular Eloquence, and Poetry; from the Best Writers of Our Own Country.* This usage of "anthology" was finally reflected in the Noah Webster dictionaries of the 1850s but remained absent from British lexicons until the twentieth century. The fact that usage in America was ahead of the lexical record is clear from the titles of American cultural journals in the first half of the nineteenth century, titles that included terms such as journal, museum, magazine, register, repository, miscellany, recorder, port-folio, messenger, world, and, of course, anthology.

Another register of this shift in meaning prompted by cultural activity was the sudden appearance of anthologies of American literature. Anthologies from the late 1820s to the 1850s include collections by William Cullen Bryant, George B. Cheever (at least three), Charles W. Everest, John Frost, William Gallagher, Rufus Griswold (at least five), John Seely Hart (at least three), Samuel Kettell, Henry Wadsworth Longfellow, and George P. Morris. Closely related to these productions was the appearance of encyclopedias. Although the first cultural encyclopedia appeared before the turn of the century, the first national literary encyclopedia was the Duyckinck brothers' two-volume *Cyclopaedia of American Literature* (1855).

In the absence of any culturally contextualized treatise on the merging of republican letters and political economy in Thoreau's lifetime, let me suggest the usefulness of triangulating aesthetics, political economy, and literary production to delineate a cultural anthologizing economy of form. This economy is as discernible in the miscellany form of the first American political economy texts to appear (the earliest is Henry C. Carey's three-volume work in 1840) as it is in the incredible variety of state constitutions, some of them quite experimental, written at this time. The latter were mentored especially by anthological productions like the Federalist Papers, Articles of Confederation, and the federal Constitution, each of which offers its economy of various interests and values. Implicit in these observations is the suggestion of a close connection between anthologizing in the new republic of letters and a mythologizing of the republic. Anthologizing, seen this way, ventures toward a mythologizing of the identity of an imagined American self and of America itself.

A work like Thoreau's Journal strikes me as a remarkably telling entry point into this domain of experiments in anthological form. In literary culture these efforts include sketch book experiments and reworkings of the framed-tale tradition by Washington Irving, Nathaniel Hawthorne, and Herman Melville; new hybrid versions of frontier romance by James Fenimore Cooper and Catharine Maria Sedgwick; more radically experimental romances by Hawthorne and Melville; excursionary narratives by Edgar Allan Poe, Mary Austin Holley, Margaret Fuller, Caroline Kirkland, Melville, and Thoreau; poetic "nonfiction" by Emerson and Thoreau; assays in nature writing by Elizabeth Wright, Susan Cooper, and Thoreau; stockpiling and stocktaking treatises of Lydia Maria Child, Sarah Grimke, Fuller, and Elizabeth Oakes Smith; the multivoiced, stockpiling poetry of Walt Whitman; and the *hortus siccus* dimension and preservationist impulse of

Emily Dickinson's poetry. This preoccupation with form as anthology in Thoreau's era is still a largely unexplored subject, partly because scholars have been inclined to see these formulators (at least those getting attention) as forerunners of modernism. The anthologizing impulse of Thoreau's Journal makes both more and better sense, I suggest, when linked to the literary productions of contemporaries, the new stream of anthologies and encyclopedias, and the literary and cultural journals of the time, virtually all of which presented themselves as anthologies testing ideas of form, selfhood, and national identity.

Whether each flower of the *anthologia* belongs to its own genus is a question inhabiting the Greek term itself, since *legein,* the infinitive form of *logia,* means to gather or collect, yet *logos,* a term that derived from *legein,* can mean a generative or normative word, or principle of relatedness. Which of the two terms is more appropriate for Thoreau's Journal, or for the other works just listed? In the early 1840s Thoreau gave up his projected anthology of English poetry only to turn to the writing of *A Week* and increased journalizing. Like his literary culture, his Journal can be studied as a work of ongoing anthologizing and mythologizing of self and world. At times he presumed to be gleaning many flowers of their own kind; at other times he was willing to consider the possibility that *omne verum veru consonat.* Journal editors and anthologizers and critics have been drawn to the latter in the interest of relation and unity; this essay has emphasized the former while acknowledging both, thereby proposing a *dialogos* between the one and the many. For a long time, the *Walden* narrator notes, he was a reporter to a journal. In Thoreau's case that enterprise and the negotiations it called forth ceased only with his death. He was hardly alone in this work, "this form of our writing," as Emerson put it, "this Journal."[21]

NOTES

1 Buell, *Literary Transcendentalism: Style and Vision in the American Renaissance* (Ithaca, N.Y.: Cornell University Press, 1973), p. 274.
2 The last decade has witnessed a notable increase in criticism on the Journal. The principal studies are, chronologically: William Howarth, *The Book of Concord* (New York: Viking, 1982); Sharon Cameron, *Writing Nature: Henry Thoreau's Journal* (New York: Oxford University Press, 1985); H. Daniel Peck, *Thoreau's Morning Work: Memory and Perception in "A Week on the Concord and Merrimack Rivers," the Journal, and "Walden"* (New Haven: Yale University Press, 1990), pp. 37–114; and Leonard N. Neufeldt, "*Praetextus* as Text: Editor–Critic Responses to Thoreau's Journal," *Arizona Quarterly* 46 (1990): 27–72.

3 Charles Brockden Brown, *The Literary Magazine and American Register* 1 (1803): 305–7.

4 Robert N. Hudspeth, "Margaret Fuller's 1839 Journal: Trip to Bristol," *Harvard Library Bulletin* 27 (1979): 467.

5 Lawrence Rosenwald, *Emerson and the Art of the Diary* (New York: Oxford University Press, 1988), pp. 83–4.

6 Larry A. Carlson, "Bronson Alcott's Journal for 1837 (Part One)," *Studies in the American Renaissance 1981*, ed. Joel Myerson (Charlottesville: University Press of Virginia, 1981), p. 35.

7 For succinct descriptions of Thoreau's changing practice in journal-keeping, see the "Historical Introduction" to each of the published volumes of the Princeton edition of the *Journal (PJ* 1 to *PJ* 4), and Howarth, *Book of Concord,* pp. 5, 9–10, 16, 37–41, and passim.

8 Rosenwald, *Emerson and the Diary,* p. 11.

9 *The Journals of Bronson Alcott,* ed. Odell Shepard (Boston: Little, Brown, 1939), p. 28.

10 Carlson, "Bronson Alcott's Journal," p. 58.

11 Howarth, *Book of Concord,* p. 86.

12 Buell, *Literary Transcendentalism,* p. 279.

13 Brown, *Literary Magazine* 1 (1803): 305–6.

14 Garber, *Thoreau's Fable of Inscribing* (Princeton: Princeton University Press, 1991), passim, and his "Getting the Journal Going" (address at the 1992 Modern Language Association convention – an abbreviated excerpt from his book in progress on the Journal). See also Henry Golemba, *Thoreau's Wild Rhetoric* (New York: New York University Press, 1990), pp. 93–112, and Peck, *Thoreau's Morning Work,* pp. 37–114.

15 See Peck, "The Crosscurrents of *Walden's* Pastoral," in *New Essays on "Walden,"* ed. Robert F. Sayre (New York: Cambridge University Press, 1992), pp. 73–94. Peck's charting of various impulses offers a useful model for mapping the manifold intratextual impulses of Thoreau's Journal.

16 Peck, *Thoreau's Morning Work,* p. 81; Sherman Paul, *The Shores of America: Thoreau's Inward Exploration* (Urbana: University of Illinois Press, 1958); Stanley Cavell, *The Senses of "Walden"* (New York: Viking, 1972), especially pp. 70–93.

17 Neufeldt, *"Praetextus* as Text," pp. 50–1, 54–5, 57–8, 66.

18 Golemba, *Thoreau's Wild Rhetoric,* p. 94.

19 Buell, *Literary Transcendentalism,* p. 279; Michaels, "*Walden's* False Bottoms," *Glyph* 1 (1977): 142–7; Barbara Johnson, *A World of Difference* (Baltimore: Johns Hopkins University Press, 1987), pp. 49–56; Linck C. Johnson, *Thoreau's Complex Weave: The Writing of "A Week on the Concord and Merrimack Rivers"* (Charlottesville: University Press of Virginia, 1986), p. 164.

20 *The Journals and Miscellaneous Notebooks of Ralph Waldo Emerson,* ed. William H. Gilman, Ralph H. Orth, et al., 16 vols. (Cambridge: Harvard University Press, 1960–82), 1:91; Charles Emerson, "Notes from the Journal of a Scholar," *Dial* 4 (1843): 88.

21 *The Letters of Ralph Waldo Emerson,* ed. Ralph L. Rusk and Eleanor M. Tilton, 8 vols. to date (New York: Columbia University Press, 1939; 1990–), 2:286.

9

JOSEPH J. MOLDENHAUER

The Maine Woods

The narrative portion of *The Maine Woods* consists of separate essays based on Thoreau's three trips (1846, 1853, 1857) to the forested mountain and lake country of north-central Maine. This region, physically the most primitive and uninhabited that Thoreau ever visited, was relatively accessible from Concord, and offered the advantages to Thoreau of available companionship, persons knowledgeable about local conditions, and hospitality before and after the wilderness adventure. The Thatchers, relatives by marriage of Thoreau's father, resided in Bangor, the jumping-off point for lumbering operations and for sporting excursions to Moosehead Lake, Chesuncook Lake, the East and West Branches of the Penobscot River, and Mount Ktaadn (Katahdin). Near Bangor, and connected with it by a railroad, was the principal settlement of the Penobscot tribe, on Indian Island at Old Town. Thoreau's cousin George A. Thatcher, a competent merchant, had timber interests on the West Branch, enjoyed the outdoors, and knew many of the Penobscot tribal aristocracy, the pioneer farmers along the rivers, and the lumbering speculators and sawmill owners of Bangor and Orono. He was also an antislavery activist and a pillar of his church. The Thoreaus were welcome in the Thatcher home; Sophia, the last of the family, moved to Bangor in 1873 after her mother's death and died there three years later.

As Thoreau mentions incidentally in *Walden*, he "spent a fortnight in the woods of Maine" (W 172) in September 1846, his second summer of residence at the Pond. Always stimulated imaginatively by mountains (see, for example, "A Walk to Wachusett" and the Saddleback Mountain portion of *A Week*), he knew of Ktaadn, the highest point in Maine, from an account in a Boston newspaper of an ascent the year before by Edward Everett Hale and William Francis Channing (a cousin of Thoreau's boon companion Ellery Channing); and also, presumably, from Dr. Charles T. Jackson, state geologist for Maine and the brother of both Lidian Emerson (Waldo's second wife) and Lucy Brown, a Thoreau household boarder with whom Henry conducted a platonic romance. In any event, Thoreau had absorbed Jackson's book-length report on the geology of the public lands in northern Maine, which described Jackson's ascent of Ktaadn, by the time he published his own narrative. (In subsequent years, he integrated into his *Maine Woods* essays material from Jackson's other books on Maine geology.) After arriving at Thatcher's via rail to Portland and steamboat to Bangor, he set out by buggy with George Thatcher upriver to Mattawamkeag, where they would be joined on the expedition by Charles Lowell, Thatcher's brother-in-law, and Horatio P. Blood, both of Bangor.[1] The plan was to secure native American guides to Ktaadn on one of the islands inhabited by the Penobscots. Near Lincoln, Thoreau and Thatcher found a willing pair of natives, one of whom, Louis Neptune, had guided Jackson on Ktaadn, and made arrangements to meet them and their canoes at a dam forming North Twin Lake on the West Branch, if not on the way. For two days the four excursionists waited at the remote West Branch farmstead of "Uncle George" McCauslin, a former lumberman; and when Neptune and his partner failed to appear they engaged McCauslin and a neighbor, young Tom Fowler, to be their batteau-handlers and guides to the base of the mountain. As revealed in the published essay and in Thoreau's Journal and draft-book for the excursion, it was a congenial company, especially as concerned the friendship that sprang up between Thoreau and Tom.

The mouth of Abol Stream was the closest point to Ktaadn that could be reached by batteau. None of the party had been on the mountain, so Thoreau, experienced in reading landforms as a cross-country hiker, led the way. Evidently he set course for South Peak rather than the mile-high true summit, now called Baxter Peak, which is invisible from the river.[2] Thoreau ascended over loose granite boulders and massed dwarf conifers up to the cloud-line late in the day, while his companions made camp in a ravine, and he climbed alone again in thick clouds the next morning, attaining the great table-land a few hundred vertical feet below Baxter Peak before turning back. The return river journey extended for Thoreau the white-water excitement and the education in small-boat management that the upstream leg had provided. Near Tom Fowler's house at the junction of the Millinocket and Penobscot rivers, the party encountered the Indians from Lincoln, hunting muskrats and still suffering the effects, Thoreau declares, of a drunken debauch near Mattawamkeag.

Not long after he left Walden, in September 1847, Thoreau finished the composition of his Maine narrative. In October he thanked Sophia, then visiting in Bangor, for a long newspaper account of a botanical expedition to the mountain, and on January 12, 1848, he wrote to Emerson in England about the Concord Lyceum lecture he had read to "a large audience of men and boys." It contained, he declared, "many facts and some poetry" (*Corr* 204). Before April he had offered it to Horace Greeley for the *New York Tribune*. Greeley, Thoreau's informal literary agent, thought it both too long and too good for his columns and found a more profitable outlet for it in John Sartain's monthly *Union Magazine of Literature and Art,* where it ran in five installments beginning with the July number. (Greeley contributed free publicity by printing extracts from the magazine text, "Ktaadn, and the Maine Woods," in his newspaper.) Thoreau evidently had no opportunity to read proof; there are some grotesque errors, such as "boys" for "bags," "swallows" for "shallows," and "scows" for "æons." Bayard Taylor, replacing editor Caroline Kirkland of the *Union Magazine* during her half-year in Europe, had to bear responsibility and Thoreau's wrath for these blunders.[3] A copy of the five parts, with misprints corrected in Thoreau's hand, survives, perhaps given by Thoreau to a friend or relative as the installments were printed (he mailed the individual parts to Thatcher) or soon after the serialization was completed. This marked copy, which does not include the footnote references to source material Thoreau read after 1848, references added for the (posthumous) printing in *The Maine Woods,* is now in the Berg Collection at the New York Public Library, together with the 1846 journal notebook.

The following February, having scheduled a lyceum lecture on his Walden experience in Portland for March 21, Thoreau asked Thatcher about the feasibility of a late-winter visit to Chesuncook Lake. He wanted to see the lake while it was still frozen and to witness log-running on the West Branch as the ice broke up. But by mid-March he realized that reading proof-sheets of *A Week,* then in press, would preclude such an excursion and would even prevent him from extending his lecture itinerary beyond Portland to Bangor. His second trip to the Maine wilds took place only in September 1853, with the young Penobscot lumberjack Joe Aitteon as his guide and George Thatcher once more as his companion. This time he took the direct steamer from Boston to Bangor, a voyage of some nineteen hours, and his wilderness destination was Chesuncook, the largest lake on the West Branch, well upstream from the point he reached on his way to Ktaadn. Thoreau's purpose was to learn more about the Maine forest ecology and the ways of the Indian; Thatcher's was to hunt for grouse, ducks, moose, and whatever else might present itself. The route chosen as most fitting for canoe was via Moosehead Lake. Thatcher and Thoreau drove a wagon to Greenville, at the foot of the lake, while Aitteon and his "birch" traveled more rapidly by stagecoach along the same road. On a steamer plying regular routes on Moosehead, chiefly in the service of hunters and explorers for white pine, the three men and their gear were borne to the North East Carry, a cleared lane with a rude wooden railway for the transport of supplies and equipment over the narrow divide between Moosehead (on the Kennebec River drainage) and the West Branch of the Penobscot. They paddled with relative ease downstream to Chesuncook – that stretch of river containing but one major rapid – camping and hunting along the way and investigating tributary watercourses. On one of these, Pine Stream, Thoreau called Joe's attention to a rustling in the alders that turned out to be the sound of a cow moose and her grown calf. Thatcher fired. Aitteon traced, and then lost, the blood trail of the cow, but subsequently found her carcass in a riffle upstream. Thoreau measured the moose and ruefully watched Aitteon skin it and cut off the nose, tongue, and a large roast. Meanwhile, Thatcher hunted unsuccessfully for the calf. The party resumed paddling up Pine Stream to a campsite until another sound in the thicket, made by a black shape, excited Aitteon to whisper successively " 'bear'! ... 'beaver!' ... 'hedgehog'!" – the last identification coming only as Thatcher shot the hedgehog or porcupine (MW 117).

On the shore of Chesuncook the three travelers visited a large pioneer farm and boarding-house for lumbermen, owned by Ansel Smith, where the oxen used for winter log-dragging were summered and where Thoreau had ample opportunity to study backwoods architecture and agriculture. Returning up the West Branch, they camped at the river end of the North East Carry, sharing the spot with a St. Francis tribesman and two of mixed blood, who had killed twenty-two moose for their skins in the past two months. Here Thoreau observed their stretching and curing of moose-hide, the details of their field cookery, and their use of the birch-bark moose call; he interrogated them for moose-lore and for facts, or superstitions, about cougars, beavers, and other large forest mammals; and he conducted a long, nocturnal inquiry into the etymologies of aboriginal place-names. This Indian-camp episode anticipates a visit paid by Thoreau and Thatcher two days later to Old Town. Having studied the native Americans on their hunting ground, Thoreau observed their permanent habitations and their town manners, much influenced by the Roman Catholic church and Yankee modernity. Governor John Neptune, whom Thatcher knew, granted them a long audience, in the course of which Thoreau extracted from the aged chief a creation myth involving moose and whales, and from his son-in-law information about contemporary tribal politics. In a neighboring yard Thoreau watched the construction of a bark canoe (his observations occupy a large stretch of the Journal, but are much abbreviated in the essay). He then visited the largest sawmill in Orono, on the way back to Bangor.

Thoreau's energies as a writer were directed chiefly to the narrative of this excursion between his September 27 return to Concord and December 2, when he sent an unidentified article of fifty-seven manuscript pages, perhaps a version of "Chesuncook," to Francis H. Underwood for a proposed new magazine. (Underwood's scheme was the germ of the *Atlantic Monthly,* which did not begin publication until four years later.) On December 14, 1853, he read a lecture about Moosehead Lake before the Concord Lyceum, and the next November he approached lecture societies in Ohio and Hamilton, Ontario, about readings of "The Wild" (later called "Walking") and a moose-hunting essay. A Maine narrative was solicited for the new *Atlantic Monthly,* in January 1858, by its editor, James Russell Lowell (the author, not insignificantly, of an urbane and humorous backwoods piece, "A Moosehead Journal," in the November 1853 *Putnam's Monthly Magazine*); Lowell was aware that Thoreau had made another long wilderness trip in the summer of 1857. Thoreau declined because his Indian guide, "whose words & deeds I report very faithfully, . . . knows how to read" and might take offense. He offered instead the account of the 1853 journey, which Lowell accepted. Although Thoreau had in hand an early draft of the 1857 excursion narrative in his journal, it was longer than what he knew Lowell wanted for the magazine, and "Chesuncook" was more nearly ready for the printer. He estimated the total length at a hundred manuscript pages, but when he sent Lowell printer's copy of the first half, on March 5, it came to eighty-seven, and the whole must have been between 175 and 200 pages. At this time also he reserved the right to republish "Chesuncook" in another form – an indication that he anticipated a book publication of several Maine woods narratives. "Chesuncook" appeared in three installments, beginning with the June 1858 number. Twice burned by *Putnam's,* whose editors had bowdlerized "An Excursion to Canada" in 1853 and *Cape Cod* in 1855, Thoreau requested proof-sheets of "Chesuncook." Not receiving them for the first part, he complained and was shown proofs of the July installment, where he found an editorial cancellation of a pantheistic sentence about a pine tree: "It is as immortal as I am, and perchance will go to as high a heaven, there to tower above me still." He marked the excised sentence "Stet" to indicate that it should be kept, but was dismayed to discover, when the published issue reached him on June 22, that (as he wrote angrily to Lowell) "that sentence was, in a very mean and cowardly manner, omitted" (*Corr* 515). Lowell ignored Thoreau's demand that he acknowledge the omission in print, and Thoreau had no more correspondence with him than two frosty requests for the $198 due him for his contribution. He submitted nothing else to the *Atlantic* until February 1862, only three months before he died and nine months after James T. Fields assumed the editorship from Lowell.

The 1857 trip was the most ambitious of the three, leading through the wildest country – the headwaters of the Allagash River and almost the entire dangerous East Branch of the Penobscot – and covering much the greatest distance. It would have been longer still, though less wild, had Thoreau followed his initial plan of descending the Allagash to the St. John and following the latter through New Brunswick, either to its mouth on the Bay of Fundy or to a portage point giving access to the Mattawamkeag River drainage. His companion was his Concord neighbor Edward Sherman Hoar, thirty-four years old and recently returned from roughing it in California. Hoar, a member of the town's most distinguished family, had been Thoreau's fishing partner when their campfire set the Concord woods ablaze in 1844; in 1857 and 1858 he often botanized with Thoreau, and they would be companions on a long excursion to the White Mountains in July 1857, after their Maine adventure. Their guide was Joseph Polis of Old Town, aged forty-eight (eight years Thoreau's senior), whom George Thatcher had known since childhood – a master woodsman, a man of property, and a spokesman for the Penobscot tribe. This Maine journey took place almost two months earlier in the year than the previous ones, falling into the midsummer black-fly season. That Polis wanted to kill a moose did not deter Thoreau in negotiations for his services.

The itinerary for the three men from Bangor was via crowded stagecoach to Greenville and thenceforward in Polis's bark canoe up Moosehead Lake to the North East Carry, down the West Branch to Chesuncook, as in 1853, and then up a tributary of the West Branch to Umbazookskus Lake, from which they portaged to Mud Pond in the Allagash watershed. They coasted the shore of Chamberlain Lake and spent a stormy day on the next lake downstream, Heron (or Eagle) Lake, before backtracking to Chamberlain and paddling southeastward into the connecting Telos Lake. Using an artificial channel between Telos and an East Branch Penobscot headwater, a channel created by Yankee lumbermen to avoid New Brunswick log tolls on the St. John, they descended the barely navigable Webster Stream and the turbulent East Branch to its junction with the West Branch and, finally, traveled down the main river to Old Town. There Thoreau and Hoar took leave of Polis, who had killed a moose at Second Lake on the East Branch. The most memorable events of the journey for Thoreau were his discovery of a bright ellipse of phosphorescence in the campfire in the dead of night; his and Hoar's struggle through a swamp between the Mud Pond Carry and Chamberlain Lake (Polis had gone before, shouldering the canoe, and Thoreau and Hoar, with the baggage, missed a sign that Polis left at a branching of the carry path and lost their way); the truly frightening – to Thoreau, not Polis – overnight disappearance of Hoar in craggy, burned-over land along Webster Stream; and Polis's revelations to Thoreau about Indian vocabulary, woodcraft, and a near-fatal winter ordeal in the wilderness he underwent as a boy of ten.

Within five months Thoreau had "written out a long account" for a lyceum lecture (*Corr* 502); then he turned to revising "Chesuncook" for the *Atlantic Monthly*, incorporating some journal passages about the most recent trip or inspired by it. When he reverted to the 1857 journey narrative proper, "The Allegash and East Branch," he included some journal material from the 1853 Chesuncook adventure. Both narratives, in their final form, contain didactic sections about the ecological damage wrought by logging. Some of these passages appear contiguously in draft sheets apparently dating from the spring of 1858, when Thoreau was developing printer's copy for the *Atlantic*. Notwithstanding the reason he had given Lowell for withholding an "Allegash" piece from the *Atlantic* – Thoreau's concern that he "could not face [his guide] again" if Polis should read it – he acknowledged George William Curtis's compliments on the published "Chesuncook" series by remarking, "I am glad if you are not weary of the Maine Woods, partly because I have another and a larger slice to come" (*Corr* 519). "The Allegash and East Branch" did not see separate publication in Thoreau's lifetime, for he was still working on it during his final illness. Some surviving draft pages bear Sophia Thoreau's ink tracings over his own pencil revisions. Thoreau's last discernible words, according to Ellery Channing, who witnessed his friend's death on May 6, 1862, were "moose" and "Indians."

Taking upon herself the care of her brother's reputation and the enormous labor of overseeing the publication of his uncollected papers and unpublished manuscripts, Sophia Thoreau assembled *Excursions* (1863) for Ticknor & Fields and then turned to *The Maine Woods*, with some indeterminate help from Channing. As evidenced by a worksheet in the Houghton Library, at Harvard University, Thoreau had planned the collection of the three narratives, plus an appendix of botanical, zoological, and ethnological data drawn from all three, and had determined the title of the last narrative and the collective title of the book. For "Ktaadn," he left a copy of the *Union Magazine* printing, with misprints marked for correction and additions from his subsequent reading supplied on separate sheets. For "Chesuncook" he annotated a copy of the *Atlantic* installments, restoring the controversial pine tree sentence, omitting a passage based on faulty ornithology, and making other small revisions. Printer's copy for the long Appendix seems to have been an intact fair-copy manuscript by Thoreau. "The Allegash" was apparently a hybrid manuscript, some of the pages (including the first ten or so) being recopyings by Sophia and the remainder being last-draft manuscripts by her brother, with certain clarifications entered in Sophia's hand over Henry's pencil revisions. At some point during her or Channing's or James T. Fields's or the printer's handling of the "Allegash" manuscript, it was shuffled or dropped and reassembled; a passage comprising two-and-a-half pages of printed narrative is out of place in the chronological and geographical sequence, an error not detected for twenty-five years after the first printing of *The Maine Woods* in 1864. And although the Ticknor & Fields cost books record an exceptional hundred hours of labor for plate correction, the first edition and all its reimpressions contain errors in "The Allegash" that reflect the difficulty of Thoreau's penmanship: "Pistigouche" for "Ristigouche" River, "white-beaked" eagle for "white-headed," and "more arable" for "memorable," to name a few. In degree of posthumous popularity among Thoreau's books prior to 1893, when the first uniform edition (the Riverside edition) was issued, *The Maine Woods* fell only slightly short of *Cape Cod* and *Excursions* (which were not far behind *Walden,* as measured by sales). Interest in *The Maine Woods* was doubtless enhanced by the surge of sports hunting and fishing and wilderness vacationing facilities in Maine toward the end of the nineteenth century. In the standard trade format of the Riverside edition, whose volumes could be purchased separately, *The Maine Woods* ranked second only to *Walden* in 1893–1915 sales.[4]

The three journey narratives, whose composition spanned sixteen years (1846–62), predictably vary somewhat in style, thematic emphasis, and authorial attitudes. "Ktaadn" is a youthful, high-spirited, and fast-moving piece, touching on a multitude of topics and exhibiting a large repertoire of literary devices: scraps of verse by Thoreau and of familiar poems such as Gray's churchyard *Elegy* and *Paradise Lost;* whimsical allegories and extended metaphors; comic anecdotes; portentous and sublime descriptions; mythological references, such as those in the remarkable scene of trout-fishing by moonlight; and puns in profusion. In its thematic concern with the return to origins (as embodied physically in upstream voyaging and the ascent of the mountain) it especially resembles *A Week on the Concord and Merrimack Rivers* (1849), on which Thoreau was actively at work in 1846 and 1847. During this period and until 1849, Thoreau was also composing the first two chapters of *Walden,* "Economy" and "Where I Lived, and What I Lived For," and reading these draft versions as lectures on the simplification of life that he practiced at the Pond. "It would be some advantage," he writes early in the former chapter, "to live a primitive and frontier life, though in the midst of an outward civilization, if only to learn what are the gross necessaries of life and what methods have been taken to obtain them" (*W* 11). In "Ktaadn" he attends carefully to the frontier life led by white pioneer farmers, loggers, and watermen: their husbandry, provisions, cookery, domestic architecture, furniture, garb – the topics, in short, of "Economy"; and he even preaches a little sermon to the discontented:

> Let those talk of poverty and hard times who will, in the towns and cities; cannot the emigrant, who can pay his fare to New-York or Boston, pay five dollars more to get here, – I paid three, all told, for my passage from Boston to Bangor, 250 miles, – and be as rich as he pleases, where land virtually costs nothing, and houses only the labor of building, and he may begin life as Adam did? (MW 14)

The topical range of "Chesuncook" is narrower, its episodes fewer, and its narrative rhythms slower. Its subjects, as he summarized them for James Russell Lowell, "are the Moose, the Pine Tree & the Indian" (Corr 504). The represented world that predominates here – and in "The Allegash and East Branch" as well – is neither the cosmic laboratory of rock and cloud of Mount Ktaadn above timberline, nor the glinting panorama viewed from a mountain's slopes in clearing weather, nor the wilderness in process of being redeemed by settlers like McCauslin. It is the Indian's world, the woodlands seen from ground- or water-level in half-light or near darkness, the brooding forest where great trees fall mysteriously on calm midnights. If in "Ktaadn" he idealized the pioneer, in "Chesuncook" the timber-explorers' more rootless life excites Thoreau's admiration: "It is . . . solitary and adventurous . . . and comes nearest to that of the trapper of the west, perhaps. Working ever with a gun as well as an axe, letting their beards grow, without neighbors, . . . far within a wilderness" (MW 101).

But this praise comes with its own deep qualification. The Maine wilderness is not the inexhaustible resource that Thoreau implied it to be in the last paragraph of "Ktaadn"; the timber-hunter foreshadows the logger, a hireling, braggart, and vandal who desecrates the temple of the wilderness and tramples its most delicate growth even as he fells its grandest pines. The frontier economy diminishes in dignity in this essay: it is exemplified in Ansel Smith's Chesuncook farm, a dormitory for lumberjacks, with a vast barn for their beasts. The sport hunter, Thoreau's cousin, shoots an ungainly moose "merely for the satisfaction of killing"; he shoots it without even being certain what creature it is. Killing an animal as inoffensive as one of your neighbor's horses or one of your own oxen is both absurd and wanton. The slaughter of the moose by "Our Nimrod" is analogous to the logger's mercenary destruction of the pine. Thoreau assigns human virtues to both pine tree and moose, and characterizes the felling of both as murder. The three Indian hunters camped at the carry in "Chesuncook" are manifestly superior to Thatcher in hunting skills, but their motive is almost as base: like Joe Aitteon, they take a tidbit or two from the huge carcasses and strip off the hides (which were made to *hide* the shy creatures, as Thoreau puns) for sale to fabricators of moccasins.

Aitteon, son of a tribal governor, is illiterate but not wild enough for Thoreau's taste. He has acquired the habit of swearing from his white logger associates, says "Yes, Sir-ee" and whistles "O, Susanna"; with reckless buffoonery he sounds his moose-call near the timber-explorers' camp the first night of hunting, at the risk of drawing their fire. Unfamiliar with canoe construction and dependent on store-provisions on his camping-trips, he abandons too soon the blood-spoor of the wounded moose, and he denigrates his Abenaki ancestors as "wild fellows, wild as bears."

If there is an implied human norm in the "Chesuncook" narrative, it is the poet and artist of the central meditation upon proper and improper uses of the wilderness (*MW* 118–22), the one who "comes with a pencil to sketch or sing" – as opposed to the thousand who "come with an axe or rifle" – and the poet and philosophic citizen of the closing paragraphs, who recognizes in the wilderness a tonic which he must occasionally consume for his own health, a resource for his "inspiration and . . . true recreation." The figure of the author, the Thoreau persona, approximates this ideal. In a recurrent "Chesuncook" pattern of juxtaposition that extends to "The Allegash and East Branch," particularly its hunting episode, Thoreau depicts himself as absorbed in identifying and admiring flowers while the attention of his companions is engrossed in the chase. This figure has much in common with the persona of the lecture "The Wild," given under that title and that of "Walking" in 1851 and again in the 1856–7 platform season. The *Walden* chapters to which "Chesuncook" seems to me most nearly related in manner and matter are "The Village," "The Ponds," "Higher Laws," and "Spring." To the extent that the contents of *Walden* chapters can be traced to journal drafts, these chapters draw heavily on the 1853–4 Journal, their remaining matter coming almost entirely from the Journal of 1850–2.[5]

Although the shabby and degenerate natives of "Ktaadn" arouse only Thoreau's contempt, and although Joe Aitteon falls well short of his expectations for aboriginal authenticity in "Chesuncook," Thoreau did not despair of seeing those expectations realized in Maine. Beginning in 1849, Thoreau filled a series of blank-books with extracts from his readings in primitive anthropology, principally but not exclusively the ways of the native American. His sources ranged from the *Relations* of the seventeenth-century Jesuits in Canada to the most recent government reports about tribes of the Great Plains, the western mountains, and the Pacific coast. By the end of 1860, or early the following year, he had filled eleven volumes with his notes about primitive cultures, volumes of up to 659 pages and totaling almost three thousand pages! Though very different in nature, it was a project second in extent only to the Journal. Robert F. Sayre, author of the most complete study of the subject, *Thoreau and the American Indians* (Princeton University Press, 1977) – a study that includes one of the few penetrating treatments that *The Maine Woods* has received – questions the assertion of some of Thoreau's earliest biographers that Thoreau seriously intended to write a book on "The Manners & Customs of the Indians of the Algonquin Group previous to contact with the civilized man" (as Thoreau defined his especial interest on December 19, 1853, in response to a questionnaire from the Association for the Advancement of Science [*Corr* 310]). The closest approach Thoreau made to such a book, Sayre implies, is the "Chesuncook" and "Allegash" components of *The Maine Woods*, and Sayre takes at face value Thoreau's excuse to Lowell in 1858 for not publishing a narrative of his most recent wilderness journey: the danger to his friendship with Polis. Indisputably, however, Thoreau's preoccupation with the Indian extract books complements his firsthand observations of and interactions with Aitteon and Polis.

On his return to Concord from the Allagash and East Branch expedition, Thoreau wrote to his Worcester admirer H. G. O. Blake,

> I have made a short excursion into the new world which the Indian dwells in, or is. He begins where we leave off. It is worth the while to detect new faculties in man – he is so much the more divine, – and anything that fairly excites our admiration expands us. The Indian who can find his way so wonderfully in the woods possesses so much intelligence which the white man does not, and it increases my own capacity, as well as faith, to observe it. I rejoice to find that intelligence flows in other channels than I knew – It redeems for me portions of what seemed brutish before.[6]

Joe Polis approached, if he did not wholly realize, the archetypal model suggested by Thoreau's ethnographic studies, and he occupies, or at least shares with Thoreau, the place of protagonist in "The Allegash and East Branch." Having lost little of his ancestral wisdom, he has acquired from civilized society chiefly those skills that enhance personal survival with dignity and that advance the interests of his tribe: reading and writing, careful money management, political know-how. He resembles in this regard the liminal Thoreauvian figure most manifest in *Walden* and "Walking," the man who occupies a midway or "frontier" position between woods and village, radical simplicity and sophisticated culture, who draws from each pole those elements which enrich the mind and spirit, and who recognizes and eschews in each those elements that threaten to exhaust, demoralize, cheapen, and brutalize him. In "The Allegash," the blind and helpless Canadian who lives on the Mud Pond Carry and the Telos Lake dam-keeper who amuses himself by throwing a bullet back and forth between his hands will serve to exemplify "quiet desperation."

Thoreau makes a wise bargain with Polis to "tell him all I knew," in the course of their journey, and he in turn "should tell me all he knew" (*MW* 168) about the Abenaki language and traditions, about Maine woods topography, about the plants, birds, mammals and fishes of the region, about native crafts, about canoeing and cookery and other wilderness skills. On only two occasions does Polis withhold information or find it impossible to communicate. About the techniques of what currently is called "orienteering" from an arbitrary wilderness location, he says, " 'O, I can't tell *you*. . . . Great difference between me and white man' " (185). When Thoreau asks him what native materials he uses to make strong pitch for mending his canoe-seams, Polis asks Thoreau to guess, and finally says "that there were some things which a man did not tell even his wife" (205). Polis's competence in the survival arts is almost universal: he builds his own canoe, steers his way back home from wherever he might be in the forest, reads weather signs, and makes a starchy flour from lily-roots and many herbal teas and medicines from wild plants. When he describes his winter hunting-trips, Thoreau thinks of the Titans and warrior-kings of Homer and Aeschylus:

> Here was travelling of the old heroic kind over the unaltered face of nature. From the Allegash, or Hemlock River, and Pongoquahem Lake, across great Apmoojenegamook, and leaving the Nerlumskeechticook Mountain on his left, he takes his way under the bear-haunted slopes of Souneunk and Ktaadn Mountains to Pamadumcook and Millinocket's inland seas . . . with his load of furs, contending day and night, night and day, with the shaggy demon Vegetation. . . . Or he could go by "that rough tooth of the sea," Kineo, great source of arrows and of spears to the ancients, when weapons of stone were used. . . . Places where he might live and die and . . . never hear of America, so called from the name of a European gentleman. (235–6)

At the same time, Polis owns a home, land, and other property worth $6,000, takes the newspaper, pays a call on Daniel Webster in Boston (the "great lawyer" receives him with bad grace), and represents his tribe in Augusta and Washington. He is more successful than Aitteon in maintaining his native dignity, merely ignoring or deflecting the patronizing or teasing banter of white wiseacres in the stagecoach and in wayside taverns. Respect is paid Polis by Hiram Leonard, a slender young man who looks and acts like a divinity student but is in fact the best white hunter in Maine and a person of remarkable strength and hardihood – a sort of Penobscot County Natty Bumppo. His respect is reciprocated by the Indian, who admires competence and self-discipline whether wrapped in a white skin or a red. Perhaps because Polis satisfies so many of Thoreau's requirements, he inadvertently arouses competitive impulses in his client. Thoreau feels a measure of superiority when Polis, a Protestant Christian, asks whether they will not lie by on Sunday, and when the guide lavishly indulges his sweet tooth, leaves a box of matches out in the rain, trembles with buck fever while reloading for his second shot at a moose, and falls ill of an intestinal disorder toward the end of the journey. Physical contests of speed and strength in portaging and canoe-paddling also take place between Thoreau and Polis, who says, "O, me love to play sometimes" (286). As other commentators on *The Maine Woods* have recognized, Thoreau's desire to match or appropriate his guide's Indian wisdom extends to his preference in the narrative for certain Abenaki terms, like *shecorway* and *Apmoojenegamook,* over their English equivalents.

Of the three essays, "The Allegash and East Branch" is the one most informed by a sense of mystery, myth, blood- or racial knowledge, and the inadequacy of scientific and rational analysis to account for experience. This is, of course, a major issue as well in "Ktaadn," when Thoreau, scrambling up the rocks, feels like Milton's rebellious Satan intruding on regions where he is not welcome, and, descending the mountain the next day, is astonished at the gulf that yawns between self – or consciousness – and pure matter. "I stand in awe of my body," he concludes,

> this matter to which I am bound has become so strange to me. I fear not spirits, ghosts, of which I am one, – *that* my body might, – but I fear bodies, I tremble to meet them. What is this Titan that has possession of me? Talk of mysteries! – Think of our life in nature, – daily to be shown matter, to come in contact with it, – rocks, trees, wind on our cheeks! the *solid* earth! the *actual* world! the *common sense! Contact! Contact! Who* are we? *where* are we? (71)

Those passages in "Ktaadn" about the alienating effect of primeval nature, though they are powerful, stand isolated like set pieces on the Burkean sublime. They do not, in my view, comport perfectly with the joyous sensuousness of the fishing episode (which is also mythic and poetic, but quite reassuringly so) and most of the remaining narrative. In "The Allegash" I find the crepuscular mood and the sense of mystery as pervasive as in Faulkner's "The Bear." The most explicit expression occurs in the midnight scene on the shore of Moosehead Lake; while his companions sleep, Thoreau sees a phosphorescent glow from the sap-wood of a damp and rotting piece of striped maple in the campfire:

> I was exceedingly interested by this phenomenon, and already felt paid for my journey. It could hardly have thrilled me more if it had taken the form of letters, or of the human face. . . . I little thought that there was such a light shining in the darkness of the wilderness for me. . . .
>
> The next day the Indian told me their name for this light, – *Artoosoqu'*, – and on my inquiring concerning the will-o'-the-wisp, and the like phenomena, he said that his "folks" sometimes saw fires passing along at various heights, even as high as the trees, and making a noise. I was prepared after this to hear of the most startling and unimagined phenomena witnessed by "his folks," . . . Nature must have made a thousand revelations to them which are still secrets to us. . . . I was just in the frame of mind to see something wonderful . . . I exulted like "a pagan suckled in a creed" that had never been worn at all, but was bran new, and adequate to the occasion. I let science slide, and rejoiced in that light as if it had been a fellow-creature. . . . A scientific *explanation*, as it is called, would have been altogether out of place there. That is for pale daylight. Science with its *retorts* would have put me to sleep. It was the opportunity to be ignorant that I improved. . . . It made a believer of me more than before. I believed that the woods were not tenantless, but choke-full of honest spirits as good as myself any day, – not an empty chamber, in which chemistry was left to work alone, but an inhabited house, – and for a few moments I enjoyed fellowship with them.   (180–1)

Lest we read this as churlish anti-intellectualism or primitivist posturing, we remember that "The Allegash" contains vastly more botanical and ornithological identification than "Ktaadn." In keeping with the tendencies revealed in his Journal after the 1840s, Thoreau now keeps a steady, watchful eye on the particulars of natural history, carrying in his head Asa Gray's *Manual of the Botany of the Northern United States* and Wilson's *American Ornithology*. But even in the concentrated ecological inventories of plants and trees that Thoreau drew up from his Journal in October 1857 for what would become *The Maine Woods* Appendix, species identifications and listings are not ends in themselves. Thoreau sees them as expressions and evidences of a copious, multiform, and dynamic world, one "choke-full of honest spirits as good as myself." Shallow, classificatory science uninformed by respect for the spirit of life is at issue in the "Allegash" meditation on the glowing ring of moose-wood; so is the typical white man's religion, with its sterile formalities and dogmas. Thoreau declares that the missionaries would have nothing to teach him, and that nothing "would tempt me to teach the Indian my religion [except] his promise to teach me *his*."

Each of the first two Maine narratives, like *Cape Cod* among the other travel pieces, ends with a philosophical coda. That of "Ktaadn" (80–3) concerns the vastness of the northern forest and the relative triviality of civilized settlement and commerce. Thoreau's emphasis in the "Chesuncook" conclusion (151–6) falls on the rapid sacrifice of wilderness to meet the economic, social, and political wants of civilized man. Thoreau laments his countrymen's compulsion to domesticate and subdue nature; although the white man – even the poet – finds the primitive forest unsuitable for permanent residence, Thoreau knows that periodic sojourns in the wild are spiritually, no less than physically, bracing and restorative. He therefore proposes that forest areas be set aside "for inspiration and our own true recreation." The absence of a coda for "The Allegash and East Branch" has been seen as an evidence that Thoreau failed to finish the piece. Another possible sign of its incompleteness is Thoreau's decision to stress, rather than suppress, the diurnal dimension of the narrative, as he introduces the events of each day with the date, like a journal entry. Undeniably, he brought the travel account to an end (the travelers return to Old Town) and refined it through a number of draft stages; and he compiled his Appendix making full use of both his botanical and ethnological observations during the 1857 journey, as recorded in the Journal, and the "Allegash" narrative proper. These considerations suggest that Thoreau himself regarded "The Allegash and East Branch" as a finished work, the culminating one as well as the longest of the three *Maine Woods* papers. It is a matter of speculation whether, had he lived longer, he would have composed a philosophical or didactic ending to his manuscript. However, one need not search far in "The Allegash" for eloquent denunciations of the misuse of wilderness. Near its midpoint Thoreau delivers a jeremiad (228–30) on the despoiling of lakes and forests by vainglorious human vermin: the woodchoppers, the political and commercial boosters for "progress," and the growing, acquisitive, urban Anglo-American population that demands cheap lumber for cheap, mass-produced houses of the sort to which he devotes a disparaging digression in *Cape Cod* (CC 22).

It is Thoreau's persistent concern in *The Maine Woods* with the preservation of the fragile wilderness environment that explains the recent renewal of the book's popularity. Representative of this interest is J. Parker Huber's *The Wildest Country: A Guide to Thoreau's Maine* (Boston: Appalachian Mountain Club, 1981), a handbook for hikers, paddlers, and naturalists who would follow exactly in Thoreau's footsteps and the wake of his batteau and canoe. Yet the history of scholarship and criticism on the book is rather thin. The first extended treatment – and aside from Sherman Paul's dozen pages in *The Shores of America: Thoreau's Inward Exploration* (Urbana: University of Illinois Press, 1958) the only extended treatment in the first century after its publication in 1864 – was in the *Atlantic Monthly* for August 1908, by Fannie Hardy Eckstorm. The author was a third-generation daughter of upper Maine, whose grandparents settled in Brewer about the time the Thatchers established themselves in Bangor, directly across the river, and whose father, Manly Hardy, was an outdoorsman, an intimate friend of George Thatcher, and a confidant of the Penobscot tribe. Eckstorm shaped and retold the historical and folkloric stories passed down to her at the family fireside in such books as *The Penobscot Man* (1904) and *Old John Neptune and Other Maine Indian Shamans* (1945). In the *Atlantic* piece she admires Thoreau's style; but perhaps feeling a proprietary interest in West Branch matters, both human and natural, she quarrels with Thoreau's woodcraft and his command of scientific fact. Of greater scholarly value are Eckstorm's posthumously printed "Notes on Thoreau's 'Maine Woods' " (*Thoreau Society Bulletin* 51 [Spring 1955]), based on her father's annotations in a copy of *The Maine Woods* and her own investigations of Penobscot tribal genealogy.

When Thoreau's 1846 Journal finally emerged from private hands in 1958 and became available to scholars in the Berg Collection, some misconceptions about the excursion could be corrected and the development of the "Ktaadn" essay could be studied, as for example in Robert Cosbey, "Thoreau at Work," *Bulletin of the New York Public Library* 65 (1961). A recurrent issue in the interpretation of "Ktaadn," with larger implications for the understanding of Thoreau's philosophy of nature, had been broached by Paul and was now elaborated by John G. Blair and Augustus Trowbridge in "Thoreau on Katahdin," *American Quarterly* 12 (1960). They see Thoreau's experience on the mountain as a refutation of his confident premise that all nature was organic and analogous to the phenomena of the human spirit. The "*Contact!*" passage expresses emotional trauma and philosophical rupture in a "frantic" outburst; "the mood is one of desperate disturbance." But Ronald Wesley Hoag, in "The Mark on the Wilderness: Thoreau's Contact with Ktaadn," *Texas Studies in Literature and Language* 24 (1982), contests their psychological interpretation, Paul's reading of the passage as a "presentiment of the alien, cold, indifferent nature of naturalism," and related conclusions by James McIntosh, in *Thoreau as Romantic Naturalist* (Ithaca: Cornell University Press, 1974), and Frederick Garber, in *Thoreau's Redemptive Imagination* (New York: New York University Press, 1977). What Thoreau experienced on the mountain and rhetorically constructs for his reader, Hoag maintains, is a transcendental epiphany, an authentic experience of the sublime, of which "an exalted religious awe and holy terror" are appropriate constituents. The mountain is the preeminent sacred space, the "Highest Land," and even naive intrusions like that of Thoreau's pleasure-party are in some measure sacrilegious. In pursuing his thesis, Hoag dwells upon Thoreau's illustrations of and remarks about man's evil in all three of the *Maine Woods* essays, and he finds pertinent a recurrent image in all three: the mark or sign of human passage, occupation, or possession. In contrast to the tracks of animals, these tokens and "graffiti" (such as ring-bolts in the rocks of solitary lakeshores, bricks in thickets, owners' brands in the sap-wood of logs, bootprints, commercial handbills stuck to the resin of blazed pines) are regarded by Hoag as signifying the destructive intrusion of man (Indians included) upon an innocent and spiritually charged natural sphere. For Garber, in *Thoreau's Fable of Inscribing* (Princeton: Princeton University Press, 1991), acts of mark-leaving and sign-reading in Maine are profoundly meaningful ways of adjusting oneself to the wilderness environment, exposing and healing anxieties, and declaring the presence of humanity against great odds, as it were, the deep woods being the scene where the self (individual and social) is at its weakest and where the "alien other" prevails. It is worth observing, in addition, that these processes of marking and deciphering, writing and reading, enact in the field of nature and of labor versions of the author's role with pen and paper, and of the reader's role – our role – with the author's prints before us.[7]

NOTES

1 The identification of these two men, called "Lowel" and "Raish" in the earliest draft, is by Richard S. Sprague, "Companions to Katahdin . . . ," *Thoreau Journal Quarterly* 12, no. 1 (1980): 47–8, 63, n4.

2 See John W. Worthington, "Thoreau's Route to Katahdin," *Appalachia* 26 (1946): 3–14.

3 *Life and Letters of Bayard Taylor,* ed. Marie Hansen-Taylor and Horace E. Scudder (Boston: Houghton Mifflin, 1884), 1:122; Albert H. Smyth, *Bayard Taylor* (Boston: Houghton Mifflin, 1896), p. 74.

4 For details about the printing history of the first edition, the Riverside edition, and the Manuscript Edition of 1906, see Walter Harding, "The Early Printing Records of Thoreau's Books," *American Transcendental Quarterly* 11 (Summer 1971): 45, 50–3; *MW*, pp. 367–76; and Joseph J. Moldenhauer, "Textual Instability in the Riverside Edition of Thoreau," *Papers of the Bibliographical Society of America* 85 (1991): 347–72, 379–81.

5 Stephen Adams and Donald Ross, Jr., *Revising Mythologies: The Composition of Thoreau's Major Works* (Charlottesville: University Press of Virginia, 1988), p. 169.

6 August 28, 1857, in Joseph J. Moldenhauer, "Thoreau to Blake: Four Letters Re-Edited," *Texas Studies in Literature and Language* 8 (1966): 49–50.

7 My introductory essay in *The Illustrated Maine Woods with Photographs from*

the Gleason Collection (Princeton: Princeton University Press, 1974), pp. xi–xxiii, is reprinted as an Afterword in the same publisher's paperback issue of *The Maine Woods* (first paperback printing, 1983), pp. 351–75. While that essay, addressed to a general audience, contains some of the same biographical and bibliographical information as the Textual Introduction to my scholarly edition, published in 1972 (*MW* 355–404), it supplements that information with extensive critical commentary and with observations on the troubled political history of northern Maine forestlands prior to Thoreau's excursions.

IO

PHILIP F. GURA

"A wild, rank place": Thoreau's *Cape Cod*

To most people who recognize the name, Thoreau conjures up his famed *Walden,* but those who appreciate his acute powers of observation and his ability to translate the wonder of what he sees into memorable prose quickly find their way to other of his works. Some become dedicated readers of *A Week on the Concord and Merrimack Rivers,* as meandering a book as the streams it describes, as they seek hints in this early work of how better to understand what came next.[1] But at least as many find their way to *The Maine Woods* and *Cape Cod,* posthumously published "travel" books in whose essays they find the same authority and eloquence as in *Walden,* if not at quite so sustained a level.

Both *The Maine Woods* and *Cape Cod* have at their center Thoreau's encounters with the wilderness he so movingly describes in the penultimate chapter of *Walden,* where he speaks of man's "need to witness [his] own limits transgressed." "Man can never have enough of nature," he observes, and "must be refreshed by the sight of inexhaustible vigor, vast and Titanic features, the seacoast with its wrecks, the wilderness with its living and its decaying trees, the thunder cloud, and the rain which lasts three weeks and produces freshets" (W 318). Thoreau did not like to leave to the imagination what he might experience firsthand: *The Maine Woods* treats one of these wilderness landscapes, *Cape Cod* another.

Thoreau's accounts of his travels to New England's wilderness thus can be read as elaborations – indeed, as further considerations – of the Walden experience.[2] At the pond he found, as Emerson had counseled in his seminal *Nature* (1836), the miraculous in the simple; but Thoreau also yearned for deeper draughts of that "tonic of wilderness" (W 317) he had tasted at different times. Not one given to complacency – by his own admission he worried that he was not "*extra-vagant* enough," that he did "not wander far enough beyond the narrow limits" of his daily experience so as "to be adequate to the truth" (W 324) of which he had been convinced – Thoreau relished the opportunity to front the immense fact of the wilderness and to gauge its effect on him. Moreover, in the 1850s such encounters did not necessarily require elaborate preparation or far-distant travel: in this case, he could take a train from Boston to Sandwich on Cape Cod and meet the wild face to face.

Thoreau visited Cape Cod four times between 1849 and 1857, and as early as 1852 he was shaping his Journal entries about the region into lecture and essay form.[3] Some of this material found its way into print in the mid-1850s, when he placed three installments about Cape Cod in *Putnam's Monthly Magazine*. And while difficulties with *Putnam's* over the editing of his essays sidetracked his plan to submit a book-length manuscript about the region, he thought enough of this project to continue to work on it until his death in 1862, incorporating material from his later visits and from his voluminous reading in the early history of the area. The book that we know as *Cape Cod* finally appeared in 1864, prepared for press by his sister Sophia and Thoreau's friend and walking companion William Ellery Channing.

Having already used a similar format in his *Week*, Thoreau assembled his account of Cape Cod as a travelogue, a popular genre, and grafted material from his various trips onto the original excursion he had taken in 1849 with Channing. The pair of hikers rode the train from Boston to Cohasset and Bridgewater, and then to Sandwich, where they disembarked. From there they traveled by foot along the entire "great beach" (the side of the Cape fronting the Atlantic) to Provincetown, and finally they returned to Boston by steamer across Massachusetts Bay. As one would expect in such a travel book, there is much talk of sand and sea. But what most engages Thoreau's imagination is the way in which the immense fact of the ocean constantly impinges on the lives of the Cape's inhabitants.

His trips to Cape Cod, then, allowed Thoreau further insight into the complex interplay of man and nature that always occupied him; but the reader does well to understand that, unlike what one comes to expect from *Walden*, herein such knowledge often is unsettling. Although early on Thoreau announces that he "did not see why [he] might not make a book on Cape Cod, as well as his neighbor [Bronson Alcott] on 'Human Culture,'" for "it is but another name for the same thing" (CC 3), his grisly first chapter, "The Shipwreck," quickly demonstrates that, if we take him at his word, we have to reconsider man's place in the scheme of nature. Thoreau describes wandering amid the wreckage of a brig bound from Ireland to the New World, most of its passengers drowned within sight of what they believed their land of opportunity.

The sea's indifference to man numbs Thoreau – he describes the "many marbled feet and matted heads, as the cloths were raised, and one livid, swollen and mangled body of a drowned girl" who probably "had intended to go out to service in some American family" (CC 5) – until he learns the lesson he repeats frequently in the course of his narrative: that people who live close to the sea must accept its raw, inhuman power without sentimentality. Watching some townspeople raking and picking the seaweed that the great storm had washed ashore, he marvels at their seeming callousness to the tragedy at arms' length. "Drown who might," he observes, "they did not forget that this weed was a valuable manure." Simply put, the shipwreck "had not produced a visible vibration in the fabric of society" (CC 7), just as it had not affected the majesty of the sea itself. Thoreau quickly draws the lesson: "If this was the law of Nature," he concludes, "why waste any time in awe or pity?" (CC 9).

Amid all the talk of explorers, fishermen, and the harsh, impoverished landscape of the Cape, always we hear this refrain, like the sound of the breakers themselves. For Thoreau, then, the seashore becomes "a sort of neutral ground, a most advantageous place from which to view the world" (CC 147), but a place different from the dreamy, moonlit room his Concord neighbor Hawthorne described in virtually the same words and in which the latter found his purchase on existence.[4] Such internalized realms of the imagination did little for Thoreau. True to his experience at Walden Pond, he sought "to front only the essential facts of life" (W 90), and on the great Atlantic beach front them he did. There "everything" that he encountered, he tersely noted, "told of the sea" (CC 25). And while the landlubber might think that "the ocean is but a larger lake . . . as civil now as a city's harbor, a place for ships and commerce," it was incumbent on him to recognize that it could be "dashed into a sudden fury." "This gentle Ocean will toss and tear the rag of a man's body like the father of mad bulls" (CC 98), Thoreau concluded. It was not simply a larger and deeper Walden Pond.

The people whom he encountered on the Cape, the Wellfleet Oysterman, the keeper of Highland Light, the men and boys who sailed from Provincetown harbor in the mackerel fleet, all could read the immense landscape of the region, a literacy that Thoreau came to admire and, eventually, to emulate. Thus, from an outsider's perspective, the Cape Codders and their compatriots were rough, crude people, and their domiciles, like the "humane" houses built along the beach for the safety of storm-wrecked sailors, were as spartan and salty as the native speech. Yet Thoreau realized that they survived in the sparse and weatherbeaten landscape because they had learned how to make do – to take, as Emerson put it so memorably in his essay "Experience," "the pot-luck of the day" and to make a meal of it.[5] They lived every day by necessity, as Thoreau had voluntarily chosen to live at Walden, and in return they had been given glimpses at least as deep into the world's mysteries. Writing of the "wreck-masters" who sometimes were appointed by a town to oversee the disposition of valuable property washed up after storms, Thoreau wryly, and rightly, made the analogy: "But are we not all wreckers contriving that some treasure may be washed up on our beach, that we may secure it?" (CC 90).

A main thread in this work, then, is that of finding and recognizing treasure, of knowing the difference between appearance and reality, a skill acquired by Cape Cod natives as they acknowledged that over much of life they simply had no control. The shimmering mirages raised by the sun over sand and water, the deception of the senses when confronted with the simplest object on the beach against the vastness of the Atlantic – a few bones in the sand, for example, looking for all the world like bleached spars – such hallucinations figure the larger cipher of the ocean – which skews all attempts to know it – and, by implication, of the universe itself.[6] Thus, looking one day at the numerous vessels of the fishing fleet in open water and realizing that "as far as they were distant from us, so were they from one another," Thoreau and his companion were deeply moved by "a sense of the immensity of the ocean" and "what proportion man and his works bear to the globe." The longer and farther they looked, the water grew "darker and darker and deeper and deeper . . . till it was awful to consider." "Of what use is the bottom" he concluded, "if it is out of sight, if it is two or three miles from the surface, and you are to be drowned so long before you get to it?" (CC 96).

Before we finish *Cape Cod*, we realize that for Thoreau such questions, however unsettling when we first read them, finally have become rhetorical. Such bottoms indeed had their use, if only to teach man to know his place in nature.[7] "I did not intend this for a sentimental journey" (CC 61), Thoreau writes, for he understood his trips to Cape Cod as nothing less than journeys of exploration – in a literal sense, as he linked himself through so many of his asides to those Europeans who had first seen the same shore, and in a metaphorical sense, represented so beautifully in the conclusion to *Walden*, as he meditated on the importance of exploring one's own "higher latitudes" (W 321).[8]

On one level, for example, he delights to think that his experiences are comparable to those of the early explorers, as when he eats a large clam by cooking it in its shell, only to find it a severe emetic. He improves the gastronomic lesson through his discovery of a comparable moment in "Mourt's Relation" of the Plymouth Colony's first years. "It brought me nearer to the Pilgrims," he wryly observed, "to be thus reminded by a similar experience that I was so like them" (CC 74). Yet he also sought to understand what initially had possessed great travelers to take the risks they did, and concluded that it had to do with their willingness to take their own measure as well as that of the world around them. "Be a Columbus," he wrote in the conclusion to *Walden*, "to whole new continents and worlds within you, opening new channels, not of trade, but of thought." "Explore the private sea," he continued, "the Atlantic and Pacific Ocean of one's being alone" (*W* 321), for that is when true discoveries are made. On Cape Cod, he was alone with the immensity of the ocean, just as in the Maine woods he was alone with Mt. Katahdin.[9] And in such places one came face to face with that which made one reconsider the complacency in which most people live. "The ocean is a wilderness reaching around the globe," he told his compatriots, "wilder than a Bengal jungle, and fuller of monsters, washing the very wharves of our cities and the gardens of our seaside residences" (*CC* 148), and too few of them knew it. But just as he had traveled much in Concord, had taken himself, and his readers, to new levels of experience, so on Cape Cod, a mere fifty miles from Concord, he would do it again, in a different but similarly challenging landscape.

The many pages of *Cape Cod* given to discussions of local history, of place – a telling anecdote from his gazetteer about one of Barnstable's first ministers, for example, or extended quotations from Bradford's *Plymouth Plantation* or Champlain's *Voyages* – turn on an individual's having gotten the Cape, so to speak, into him, as Thoreau himself sought to do.[10] Thus, Thoreau wrote, "the heroes and discoverers have found true more than was previously believed, only when they were expecting and dreaming of something more than their contemporaries dreamed of, or even themselves discovered, that is, when they were in a frame of mind fitted to behold the truth." No matter that, "referred to the world's standard," such individuals often seem "insane" (*CC* 95). Like the Artist of Kouroo whom Thoreau invokes in the conclusion to *Walden,* the great explorers "make no compromise with Time" and so "Time keeps out of [their] way" (*W* 326).

Even the pitiful Irish immigrants with whom Thoreau opens his book had conceived of something larger across the Atlantic. "Their owners were coming to the New World," Thoreau writes, "as Columbus and the Pilgrims did" (*CC* 10), searching for a new world. To be sure, like the drowned girl who probably would have become a servant, these travelers had associated America primarily with material opportunity; but however crass their motive, at last they were redeemed by their willingness to dream of something more than what they hitherto had known. Further, the main difference between these unfortunate voyagers and the present-day Cape Codders, themselves frequently as strapped for necessities as the Irish had been, was the former's deeper knowledge that came from taking the ocean as their primer. No matter how many material possessions a person had, in other words, his true goal in life was, as T. S. Eliot so beautifully noted in his own meditations about the sea in "Little Gidding," to arrive where he had started and to know the place for the first time, to recognize, in other words, his fragile mortality.[11]

In *Cape Cod*, then, we learn that the region's first explorers and present inhabitants make Thoreau understand more of the mystery of his own relationship to the world, and, by extension, to the eternity it shadows. Here we might consider how *Cape Cod* fits the contours of those "Higher Laws" that Thoreau had glimpsed in the Walden years. For despite our tendency to associate him with the tenets of Transcendentalism, as enunciated by the "early" Emerson of *Nature* and "Self-Reliance" (1841), in *Walden* and in other works from the 1850s Thoreau moved toward a very different understanding of the universe than that suggested by his contemporaries, even the most radical among them.[12]

I think particularly of the striking passage toward the conclusion of *Walden*'s second chapter, when Thoreau announces that "God himself culminates in the present moment, and will never be more divine in the lapse of all the ages." "And we are enabled to apprehend at all what is sublime and noble," he continues, "only by the perpetual instilling and drenching of the reality which surrounds us" (W 97). At times like this, Thoreau ceases to be a Transcendentalist; that is, he clearly tells us that a desire to *transcend* reality, to move, as Emerson urged, *through* nature *to* the realm of the Spirit, is fatuous. Nature is not to be used, as Emerson in his book by that title suggested, as a ladder on which to move to a higher consciousness. Rather, acceptance of nature, drenching ourselves in the reality around us until we realize that "Shams and delusions are esteemed for soundest truths, while reality is fabulous" (W 95) is the only course for sane people.

Here, then, is a passe-partout to Thoreau's mature writings, for once we recognize the true radicalism of his vision (which we might best call that of a "naturist"), we begin to see how much of what he writes seemingly as figuration he means *literally* – at that moment, for example, in the "Spring" chapter of *Walden* when he peers into the messy railroad cut and observes that he was as "affected as if in a peculiar sense [he] stood in the laboratory of the Artist who made the world and [him], – had come to where he was still at work, sporting on this bank, and with excess of energy strewing his fresh designs about" (W 306).[13] The rawness of Thoreau's sentiment – this view into the earth had suggested, among other things, "at least that Nature had some bowels, and there again is mother of humanity" (W 308) – only increases a few pages later when he notes that we should be "cheered when we observe the vulture feeding on the carrion which disgusts and disheartens us and deriving health and strength from the repast." Even the overpowering stench from a dead horse in his path only serves to remind him "of the strong appetite and inviolable health of Nature." Truly to know the world, then, to know it as a Thoreau rather than as an Emerson would, is to see it red in tooth and claw, and yet to marvel that it "is so rife with life that myriads can be afforded to be sacrificed and suffered to prey on one another" without any harm to its overall health. "The impression made on a wise man," he concludes, "is that of universal innocence" (W 318).

Such passages in Thoreau's great work provide the larger framework for appreciating the achievement of Cape Cod, for therein too we come to learn, albeit in different ways, that "Poison is not poisonous after all, nor are any wounds fatal" (W 318). To speak otherwise is to be merely sentimental. Thus, as Thoreau puts it when he explains why he was so taken with the idea of walking up the Cape, in that way "[he] had got the Cape under [him], as if [he] were riding it bare-backed." "It was not as on the map," he continues, "or seen from the stage-coach; but there I found it all out of doors, huge and real, Cape Cod! as it cannot be represented on a map, color it as you will; the thing itself, than which there is nothing more like it, no truer picture or account; which you cannot go further and see" (CC 50). Of course, those so inclined might observe that, at one level, this passage is "about" the desire for representation and how it is seemingly always doomed to failure.[14] But it also is as much, if not more, about Thoreau's wish to push against the divine envelope in which we live, by "drenching" himself in "the reality that surrounds us."

What, then, did Thoreau go to see? The ocean is "a wild, rank place," he tells us, "and there is no flattery in it." "Strewn with crabs, horse-shoes, and razor-clams, and whatever the sea casts up, – a vast morgue" with "the carcasses of men and beasts together . . . rotting and bleaching in the sun and waves," and each tide turning them "in their beds." An experience as frightening in its way as what he described when he was alone on Mt. Katahdin, but not similarly disorienting – indeed, in its way reassuring. "There [on the great beach] is naked Nature," he concludes, "inhumanly sincere, wasting no thought on man" (CC 147).

Such knowledge and assurance were the choicest fruit of Thoreau's peripatetic exploration of Cape Cod. Amid all the talk of mackerel fishing and hardscrabble farming, the trenchant observations on the Cape Codders' manners and mores, the detailed descriptions of flora and fauna, and the antiquarian lore gathered from the town histories and gazetteers, always there stands out the stark fact of the Atlantic, as profound in its way as

Walden Pond. "The reader must not forget that the dash and roar of the waves were incessant," Thoreau observes, and thus "it would be well if he were to read with a large conch-shell at his ear" (CC 100). Thoreau takes pains to remind us that what we hear therein should be as unsettling as the stench of carrion, yet be, finally, indicative of nature's bounty. In that shell, as in *Cape Cod*, Thoreau wants us to hear nothing less than the sound of our own mortality, and he asks us, first, to accept that knowledge, and then to find joy in it.

Toward such worlds of knowledge, then, Thoreau explored the sands of Cape Cod, and to claim such wisdom he "wished to associate with the Ocean until it lost the pond-like look which it wears to a countryman" (CC 140). In *Walden*, Thoreau had presented his deepest understanding of the natural world through the frequently invoked imagery of the cycle of the seasons. But in *Cape Cod* such imagery is replaced, fittingly, with that of the cyclical tides, their rough patterns affecting us as powerfully as the pulse of our own heartbeats. In *Walden* we learn, as Thoreau did, that nature's variety – indeed, its very vitality – is to be understood through the inevitable return of spring, so beautifully evoked in the chapter of that name. But in *Cape Cod* nature is reduced further, to its lowest terms, so that Thoreau could, as he had famously announced in *Walden*, "front only the essential facts of life, and see if I could not learn what it had to teach, and not, when I came to die, discover that I had not lived" (W 90). "If you stand right fronting and face to face to a fact, you will see the sun glimmer on its surfaces," he continued, "as if it were a cimeter, and feel its sweet edge dividing you through the heart and marrow" (W 98). Such was the painfully sweet knowledge he sought (and found) on Cape Cod as in other places commensurate to his capacity for wonder.

Cape Cod can never replace *Walden*, but it can stand fittingly next to it, alongside *The Maine Woods* and *A Week*, as further testament to Thoreau's commitment to know himself through nature. Always honest, sometimes to a fault, to Emerson's observation that to study nature and to know one's self are the same thing, he took from such scrutiny the hard knowledge that this life is all that we have. That he was able in spite of such knowledge to find the world so filled with beauty and, further, that he was able to convey that beauty so memorably in his prose, marks Thoreau as one of America's treasures. "What are springs and waterfalls?" he asked rhetorically at *Cape Cod*'s conclusion. "Here is the spring of springs, the waterfall of waterfalls." And because "a man may stand there and put all America behind him" (CC 215), it was a place from which one could see one's origins, and thus where he was going, home, to know the place for the first time. Limned in various essays at the height of what historians call the

Transcendentalist period but published at the end of the Civil War, *Cape Cod* offers an important clue as to how Thoreau viewed the carnage perpetrated by his countrymen. Like Whitman's "Drum-Taps," written by another so-called Transcendentalist, *Cape Cod* finally is a book for the realist's shelf.

NOTES

1 For an assessment of *A Week*'s relation to Thoreau's later works, see Stephen Adams and Donald Ross, Jr., *Revising Mythologies: The Composition of Thoreau's Major Works* (Charlottesville: University Press of Virginia, 1988), especially pp. 35–50, 76–103.

2 In many ways, the best account of Thoreau's "project" – economic, moral, and literary – at Walden Pond remains that in Sherman Paul's *The Shores of America: Thoreau's Inward Exploration* (Urbana: University of Illinois Press, 1958); but also see Leonard Neufeldt's *The Economist: Henry Thoreau and Enterprise* (New York: Oxford University Press, 1989).

3 My knowledge of Thoreau's visits to Cape Cod, as well as of their subsequent development from Journal entries to book form, is taken from Joseph J. Moldenhauer's excellent "Historical Introduction" to *CC*, particularly pp. 249–88. Also see Willard H. Bonner's *Harp on the Shore: Thoreau and the Sea* (Albany: State University of New York Press, 1985) for a good general account of Thoreau's interest in the sea.

4 I refer of course to Hawthorne's famous definition of "romance" as elaborated in his "Custom-House" preface to *The Scarlet Letter* (1850), in which he uses the phrase "neutral territory." While I do not apply to *Cape Cod* the word "romance" in the way that Hawthorne and other of Thoreau's contemporaries used it to describe a certain kind of prose fiction, I do think it significant that so many writers, Thoreau among them, sought to describe the most opportune location from which to speak the "truth."

5 Ralph Waldo Emerson, "Experience," in *The Collected Works of Ralph Waldo Emerson*, vol. 3, *Essays: Second Series*, ed. Alfred Ferguson and Jean Ferguson Carr (Cambridge: Harvard University Press, 1983), p. 36. Richard J. Schneider, "*Cape Cod*: Thoreau's Wilderness of Illusion," *ESQ* 26 (1980): 184–96, remarks on the similarity between these two works. It is worth noting that by the mid-1840s Emerson to some degree had moved away from the ebullience of his earliest publications to a vision marked by what he termed the doctrine of compensation. In this view, individual "Power" was locked in perpetual struggle with impersonal "Fate," but Emerson was not as ready as his younger friend to declare the latter's supremacy, nor, by extension, to adopt a similarly "naturist" vision.

6 Schneider, p. 191, observes that in *Cape Cod* "even light, that transcendental symbol of God's presence in the world," sometimes "is illusory or untrustworthy."

7 See Walter Benn Michaels, "*Walden*'s False Bottoms," *Glyph* 1 (1977): 132–49, for a brilliant discussion of Thoreau's interest in the subject of bottomless-

ness; for counterpoint, see Joseph Allen Boone, "Delving and Diving for Truth: Breaking through to the Bottom in *Walden*," *ESQ* 27 (1981): 135–46.

8   In his stimulating essay "Thoreau and the Wrecks on Cape Cod," *Studies in Romanticism* 20 (1981): 3–20, Mitchell Breitwieser notes that *Cape Cod* is "a traversing through symbols of the distance between sentiment and the intuition of the sublime" (10).

9   Literary critics have made much of Thoreau's description of the seeming separation from nature that he experienced on the summit of Mt. Katahdin; see *MW* 69–71. For commentary: Bruce Greenfield, "Thoreau's Discovery of America: A First Contact," *ESQ* 32 (1986): 80–95; John Tallmadge, " 'Ktaadn': Thoreau in the Wilderness of Words," *ESQ* 31 (1985): 137–48; and Stephen Adams and Donald Ross, Jr., "Thoreau's 'Ktaadn': 'The Main Astonishment at Last,' " *English Language Notes* 20 (1983): 39–47.

10 I discuss Thoreau's interest in the early American explorers in "Thoreau and John Josselyn," *New England Quarterly* 48 (1975): 505–18. On his interest in history in general see Joan Burbick, *Thoreau's Alternative History: Changing Perspectives on Nature, Culture, and Language* (Philadelphia: University of Pennsylvania Press, 1987), *passim*.

11 T. S. Eliot, "Little Gidding," in *Collected Poems, 1909–1962* (New York: Harcourt, Brace & World, 1963), p. 208. Also see Sam S. Baskett, "Fronting the Atlantic: *Cape Cod* and 'The Dry Salvages,' " *New England Quarterly* 56 (1983): 200–19, for a suggestive comparison between *Cape Cod* and parts of *Four Quartets*.

12 For a discussion of the differences that emerged between Thoreau and Emerson, see Joel Porte, *Emerson and Thoreau: Transcendentalists in Conflict* (Middletown, Conn.: Wesleyan University Press, 1966). Porte draws the distinction between Emerson's idealism and the reliance by Thoreau on what amounts to a radically empirical understanding of the world, a return, in other words, to the Lockean premises that initially had been contested by the emergent Transcendentalists and the Unitarian group. Porte also has written trenchantly on *Cape Cod*; see his "Henry Thoreau and the Reverend Poluphloisboios Thalassa," in *The Chief Glory of Every People*, ed. Matthew J. Bruccoli (Carbondale: Southern Illinois University Press, 1973).

13 Many literary critics have built arguments around this famous passage. See, for example, Gordon V. Boudreau, *The Roots of "Walden" and the Tree of Life* (Nashville: Vanderbilt University Press, 1990), *passim*; Charles R. Anderson, *The Magic Circle of "Walden"* (New York: Holt, Rinehart, and Winston, 1968), pp. 243ff.; and my own "Farther Afield: Henry Thoreau's Philological Explorations," in *The Wisdom of Words: Language, Theology, and Literature in the New England Renaissance* (Middletown, Conn.: Wesleyan University Press, 1981), pp. 109–46.

14 I have in mind, for example, Naomi Miller, "Aspects of Vision in Thoreau's *Cape Cod*," *ESQ* 29 (1983): 185–95; and Burbick, especially p. 91, where she observes that "In one respect, *Cape Cod* is an exploration of the very possibility of writing an account of the Cape at all."

II

RONALD WESLEY HOAG

Thoreau's later natural history writings

The works considered in this chapter comprise the published late natural history writings of Henry Thoreau, exclusive of material associated with *The Maine Woods*. This sounds simple enough, but explanation is required. Of the eight titles here discussed, six were published posthumously: "Walking," "Autumnal Tints," and "Wild Apples" appeared in the *Atlantic Monthly* in 1862, shortly after Thoreau's death; "Huckleberries" was published in 1970; and not until 1993 were "The Dispersion of Seeds" and a selection from his "Wild Fruits" manuscripts published for the first time in *Faith in a Seed*. Thoreau himself saw in print only a truncated version of "A Yankee in Canada," in *Putnam's Monthly Magazine* in 1853, and "The Succession of Forest Trees," in both the *New York Tribune* and *Transactions of the Middlesex Agricultural Society* in 1860. Because the publication dates do not reflect the order of composition, the latter order is followed here: "Walking" (1851), "A Yankee in Canada" (1851), "Autumnal Tints" (1858–9), "Wild Apples" (1859–60), "Huckleberries" (1860–1), "Wild Fruits" (1860–1), "The Succession of Forest Trees" (1860), and "The Dispersion of Seeds" (1860–1).

While these published titles represent Thoreau's most advanced work with their texts, the published versions of "Night and Moonlight" (1863) and *The Moon* (1927) have been shown to be nonauthorial editions and therefore are not discussed here. However, the surviving manuscripts of what apparently was once an intended book on the moon would be a welcome addition to the Thoreau canon, if someone can assemble and edit them. The same is true for the rest of the "Wild Fruits" manuscripts and for other late writings as well, including "The Fall of the Leaf." We should not, though, expect to read either Thoreau's so-called Indian Book or his so-called Kalendar, because neither of these projects developed beyond the accumulation of raw materials, much of which was shifted to other works.

The natural history writings here discussed have various emphases. Some, for example "The Succession of Forest Trees" and "The Dispersion of

Seeds," are highly scientific; some, such as "Walking" and "Wild Apples," are prophetic; and one, "A Yankee in Canada," seems at first glance to be not so much about nature at all. These works, however, all share two assumptions – that there is more to nature than meets our myopic eye, and that the preservation of both the New World and our best selves depends on learning how to see, and live, more naturally than we do. *Perception* and *relation* are thus passwords for entry into both nature and these texts. A third, related password is *extra-vagance,* coined by Thoreau in *Walden* to indicate the desire and ability to break the physical, mental, and spiritual boundaries that limit our perception of and relation to wild nature. Indeed, extra-vagance and wildness appear to be synonymous in Thoreau's lexicon. In *Walden,* he advocates following dreams past "an invisible boundary," beyond which "new, universal, and more liberal laws" will be established in and around us, or the old laws "interpreted . . . in a more liberal sense" (W 323–4). The works discussed here demonstrate how extra-vagant perception and relation may be employed to that end.

Although Thoreau in the 1850s was concerned with sociopolitical issues such as slavery and American materialism, he devoted the majority of his attention to nature study with an increasingly scientific slant. For much of this century, prevailing critical opinion held that his science and Transcendentalism muddled each other and vitiated his later writings. In recent years, however, his work has been reappraised in light of new information and closer study. One result of this revision is that the later Thoreau emerges as a much more significant naturalist than was previously thought, albeit one whose humanistic science went a different way from the increasing objectivity of the scientific community at large. He still called himself a Transcendentalist, although just what he meant by that term is subject to debate. It should be noted, however, that his shift in emphasis to the physical side of the correspondence between facts and spirit does not of itself compromise his Transcendental standing. To be sure, as he said in *Walden,* one *should* put "foundations" under "castles in the air" (W 324). His later career may be viewed as an attempt to follow his own advice. Finally, as to the artistic merit of these pieces, the passages quoted here are their own defense, even though many of them do not come from finished works.

"Walking" is a union of two lectures, "Walking" and "The Wild," that Thoreau wrote in 1851, soon combined, then revised and separated in 1854, and finally recombined in 1862. Although most of the late natural history essays cluster around the end of the fifties decade and are more informed by history and science, "Walking" nonetheless presages their fundamental concern with mankind's perception of and relation to wildness and with the preservation of that wildness in both nature and humanity. In this essay, *walking* is Thoreau's multiply allusive term for the effort to see and relate to essential nature, an effort that involves both body and spirit, while *the wild* is his name for the boundlessness of nature in all its forms, including the wild speech that suggests nature's ultimate unfathomableness. Connecting the various aspects of both walking and the wild is the concept of *extra-vagance,* the practice of thinking, speaking, and acting "*without* bounds" (W 324). Simply stated, the principal message of "Walking" is that the boundlessness of nature requires an attempt, however necessarily imperfect, at corresponding boundlessness on the part of one who would know it, however necessarily imperfectly.

The first paragraph in the essay establishes the extra-vagant voice of the speaker (whom I will call Thoreau) and conflates this mode of expression with the extra-vagance at the heart of nature. "I wish to speak a word for Nature, for absolute freedom and wildness," he says, thus making unlimited freedom and wildness an appositive to essential nature. "I wish to make an extreme statement," he adds, thereby fitting his tone to his topic.' We recall his fear in *Walden* that "my expression may not be *extra-vagant* enough, may not wander far enough beyond the narrow limits of my daily experience, so as to be adequate to the truth of which I have been convinced" (W 324). In effect, this opening paragraph establishes "Walking," the exercise in rhetorical extra-vagance, as a Transcendental analogue to the saunterer's effort to outwalk the village mindset.

The extra-vagant tone that Thoreau maintains through much, though not all, of the essay is related to mythology and prophecy, which here and elsewhere he regards as expressions of the wild because these "wildest dreams of wild men" transcend the "common sense" (EP 233). Moreover, he proclaims that because the American backwoodsman in our epic landscape is situated as favorably as "Adam in paradise" (EP 233), there may emerge a prophetic "American mythology," not of politics but of nature, to inspire the world's poets (EP 233). Indeed, if our higher than Old World skies do not reflect to us the "immaterial heaven," then "to what end does the world go on, and why was America discovered?" (EP 222–3). This is, in a sense, Thoreau's Transcendentalized version of the New World Eden and manifest destiny concepts, with the West symbolizing the wild in all its forms.

Thoreau here walks as he talks, extra-vagantly; creating his own myth of the saunterer whose inspired walking takes him ever nearer to the essence of the nature through which he travels. Furnishing his own etymology of saunterer as a "*Sainte-Terrer,*" or "Holy-Lander" (EP 205), he identifies the true goal of the nature walk as reconquering the "Holy Land from the hands of the Infidels" (*EP* 206), which is accomplished by realizing, as at the essay's end, that every meadow is a paradise when viewed in the right light. But Thoreau also derives saunterer from "*sans terre,*" which he takes to mean the condition of not being bound to a particular place and therefore at home in all places, a condition that is "the secret of successful sauntering" (*EP* 205). Thus, to saunter successfully is to walk extravagantly; to be "not the Knight, but Walker, Errant" in the crusade to save the holy lands of world and self (*EP* 206). To be sure, one of the definitions of *errant* (all of which enhance Thoreau's meaning) is "wandering outside the established limits" (*American Heritage Dictionary*). For while all land is holy, it is the uncultivated land outside village limits where nature is best displayed to one whose sense has transcended the common.

Commentators have debated whether the shape of Thoreau's walks is, as he claims here, "a parabola . . . like one of those cometary orbits which have been thought to be non-returning curves" (*EP* 217), or simply a circle that returns him every day to Concord and another village deflation. We must note his assurance, however, that every afternoon's excursion can bring the happiness of an "absolutely new prospect" (*EP* 211) – new views and viewpoints which, presumably, are incrementally illuminating rather than redundantly pointless in a Sisyphean way.[2] Given its function as a Transcendental parable, Thoreau's "Walking" itself is indisputably parabolic. "We would fain take that walk, never yet taken by us through this actual world, which is perfectly symbolical" of the ideal, says Thoreau (*EP* 216–17). This is, though, a parable about sauntering "toward the Holy Land" (*EP* 247) rather than relocating there from Concord. "I feel that with regard to Nature I live a sort of border life," he says, "on the confines of a world into which I make occasional and transient forays only" (*EP* 242). Because a final knowledge of nature is too much to expect from even a lifetime of new prospects, he advocates instead an appreciation of "Useful Ignorance," amounting to "a novel and grand surprise on a sudden revelation of the insufficiency of all that we called Knowledge before" (*EP* 239–40). A satisfying epiphany in its own right, this recognition of a nature that will not be impounded inspires further saunterings to the holy land. It also teaches the extra-vagant lesson that wildness preserves both the walker and the world.

"A Yankee in Canada" began as an 1851 lecture account of a train and boat excursion to Montreal and Quebec the preceding fall. It was subsequently twice revised for publication, first by Thoreau in 1853, again by editors after his death. This essay has been regarded, to some extent even by Thoreau himself, as an uninspired anomaly among his later writings, a somewhat cranky, jingoistic critique of another country's people and institutions. Indeed, he frequently scourges present-day French Canadians for a peasantlike subservience to their Old World government, military, and church; and he atypically praises American free-spiritedness and even the beneficently *laissez-faire* American government. Yet however quirky this piece seems, its eccentricities make more sense if we read it as an admittedly failed nature essay. In that light, "A Yankee in Canada" emerges as the record of a flawed trip rather than a flawed place.

The beginning and ending of the essay tell the reader, in effect, that the intervening itinerary should *not* be taken as the way to see Canada. Thoreau confesses at the outset, "I fear that I have not got much to say about Canada, not having seen much." "I wished," he admits, "only to be set down in Canada, and take one honest walk there as I might in Concord woods of an afternoon" (*EP* 3). The Canada he had wished to see and relate to, then, was the saunterer's wild holy land, not the nation as displayed in Canadian cities. The narrative's last sentence confirms both this goal and his failure to achieve it. "I wished to go a little way behind the word *Canadense,* of which naturalists make such frequent use; and I should like still right well to make a longer excursion on foot through the wilder parts of Canada, which perhaps might be called *Iter Canadense*" (*EP* 101). A "march across Canada," with its plethora of natural facts, could not possibly leave him at a loss for words.

The relationship of words to facts is one of Thoreau's touchstones for his trip, a standard by which the name *Canada* itself is problematic. "Though the words Canada East on the map stretch over many rivers and lakes and unexplored wildernesses, the actual Canada, which might be the colored portion of the map, is but a little clearing on the banks of the river, which one of those syllables would more than cover" (*EP* 40). Implied here is the distinction between the sociopolitical Canada that he had seen and the Canadian nature that he had somehow missed. A contrasting example of the attachment of words to natural facts is the geographical name "Pointe aux Trembles," which Thoreau's guidebook tells him is " 'so called from having been originally covered with aspens' " (*EP* 20). He is greatly pleased by this poetic name because it forever reiterates the "slender truth, that aspens once grew there" and, just as important, it implies that "men were there to see them" (*EP* 20). In a testimonial to perception and relation that makes this essay one in spirit with the others considered here, he proclaims, "Inexpressibly beautiful appears the recognition by man of the least natural fact, and the allying his life to it" (*EP* 20).

Another familiar touchstone in "A Yankee in Canada" is extra-vagance, by which Thoreau judges the discoverers and settlers and present occupants of the New World. His supplementary reading about the history of Canada introduced him to the old explorers whose "roving spirit of adventure" led them "not to clear and colonize the wilderness" but "to range over it" (*EP* 43).[3] Paying tribute to such wanderlust, he concedes that "if any people had a right to substitute their own for the Indian names, it was they" (*EP* 56). Just as he admits to having more sympathy for the French and Spanish *explorers* of the continent than for the *settlers* who followed them, in present times he prefers independent-minded Americans to the feudally fettered citizens of all Old World countries, including modern Canada. Whereas Europeans and Canadians can "speculate only within bounds," "Americans have proved that they, in more than one sense, can *speculate* without bounds" (*EP* 83). Thus, the free-spirited American, despite implied materialistic excesses, is "nearer to the primitive and the ultimate condition of man," by which he means the wild (*EP* 83).

At its best, this uncircumscribed speculation relates the perceiver to the answering wildness in nature. We witness a moment of such extra-vagant perception and relation when Thoreau, on the ramparts of the oppressive citadel at Quebec, looks "beyond the frontiers of civilization" to the distant wilderness and experiences a purging "influence from the wilds and from Nature" (*EP* 89). This is the Canada he came to see, and this epiphanic glimpse reassures him, and us, that such a place called Canada exists.

"Autumnal Tints" was written as a lecture in the winter of 1858–9, then combined with other material into a never-finished project called "The Fall of the Leaf," from which Thoreau removed it, in 1862, for revision prior to its posthumous publication. Notable issues here include scientific methodology, aesthetics, spirituality, natural and human history, mythology, the New World and the Old World, and such cultural concerns as economics, patriotism, religion, and education. The principal concern of Thoreau's essay, however, is the perception of nature: what there is to see and how to go about seeing it. In *Walden* Thoreau declared that "The Maker of this earth but patented a leaf" (*W* 308), citing foliation in all its forms as the essential *type* of natural growth. Appropriately, then, he here promotes a true regard for autumn leaves as his paradigm for the proper perception of nature. To encompass their significance, Thoreau describes those leaves literally (from the viewpoints of a close observer, a landscape painter, and a scientist) and figuratively (from the viewpoint of a metaphor-making poetic enthusiast). Most important, he describes them Transcendentally, remarking the physical parallels and moral/spiritual correspondences between their progress and his readers' lives.

With Thoreau as interpreter, the New England foliage teaches, preaches, and inspires with joy. In an allusion to Transcendental correspondence, he affirms that every example of vegetation "stands there to express some thought or mood of ours" (*EP* 257). Citing the maple trees on Concord Common, he states that "by these teachers even the truants are caught and educated the moment they step abroad" (*EP* 272); and extending their influence to adults as well, he terms the village maples "cheap preachers ... ministering to many generations of men" (*EP* 277–8). One lesson taught by New England's trees is that the natural world and, therefore, especially the New World are beautiful and should be celebrated as such. For painters, sculptors, poets, philosophers, and ultimately even mythologizers, the best education is to be gotten at the school of the leaf. More important even than the aesthetics of shape and color, however, are the "joy and exhilaration which these colored leaves excite" (*EP* 274). The riotous colors of autumn's "annual fair" (with a meaningful pun on *fair*) "suggest that man's spirits should rise as high as Nature's" in "an analogous expression of joy and hilarity" (*EP* 275). Thus, even dying leaves underscore Thoreau's longstanding belief, published in his "Natural History of Massachusetts" essay, that "Surely joy is the condition of life" in nature (*EP* 106). Moreover, there is no real death in nature because all true spirits rise.

The color change of the leaf before its fall, says Thoreau, is "the emblem of a successful life concluded by a death not premature, which is an ornament to Nature" (*EP* 254–5). If, as he states, the falling leaves "teach us how to die" (*EP* 270), that lesson is predicated on "answering ripeness" in human life (*EP* 263), a correspondence that would make joy the condition of our deaths too. He offers three consolations – one physical, one mental, and one spiritual – to support this view of death in nature as a joyful harvest. Physically, falling leaves "still live in the soil ... and in the forests that spring from it" (*EP* 269). As long as the biosphere lives, nothing organic dies, not even the dust and ashes of the human race. Moreover, just as the fallen leaves continue to participate in the ecology of nature, so too the harvest of thoughts from one generation, including his own printed leaves, continues to nourish future generations.[4] Finally, the life of the spirit transcends the death of the body – symbolized here by the progress of the scarlet oak leaf from life to death, "Lifted higher and higher, and sublimated more and more" until leaf and light become indistinguishable (*EP* 278).

As a paradigm of perception, "Autumnal Tints" demonstrates at least five different ways of putting leaves and nature in perspective. First, one must extra-vagantly walk through nature to see it best displayed, which involves taking "more elevated and broader views" of the "great garden" of the forest instead of "a few impounded herbs" (*EP* 285). Second, one must regard nature as beauty rather than commodity in order to make a "walker's harvest" (*EP* 253) of the wealth that others overlook. Third, one must "*anticipate*" beauty and significance in nature (*EP* 287), for a "man sees only what concerns him" and finds only what he is "prepared to appreciate" (*EP* 286). Fourth, because "different departments of knowledge" require "different intentions of the eye" (*EP* 286), the naturalist's awareness of species and the artist's eye for color variations are useful even in the field work of a Transcendentalist.[5] Finally, if one is to perceive in these autumnal tints the "burning bushes" of a restored Eden (*EP* 259), one must "observe *faithfully*" and with "*devotion* to these phenomena" (*EP* 289, 281; emphasis added). To witness such "glory" (*EP* 281) is the ultimate goal.

The most polished example of Thoreau's considerable work on wild fruits, "Wild Apples" was written as a lecture in the fall and winter of 1859–60, then lightly revised by Thoreau in 1862 for what became its posthumous publication. Rhetorically complex, the essay makes use of natural history, human history, mythology, autobiography, parable, allegory, prophecy, sermon, primer, and a final ultimatum. From this diversity there emerges a simply stated thesis. Like the Old World apple tree that soon ran wild in the New World, Americans must learn what true nature is and align themselves with it. To do so is to restore and repossess Eden, while the alternative is described in the essay's *or else* conclusion.

Thoreau remarks "how closely the history of the apple tree is connected with that of man" and notes that the name for apple, "traced to its root in many languages signifies fruit in general" or, in Greek, "riches" (*EP* 290–1). Summarizing the apple's natural history, he also reviews the tree and its fruit in various mythologies and says that "Some have thought that the first human pair were tempted" by an apple (*EP* 291). As Kevin Van Anglen has observed, in all these accounts except *Genesis* the apple symbolizes "rejuvenation and immortality," an association that Thoreau appropriates for his revised New World Eden.[6] It should also be noted that in his sacramental tasting of the "frozen-thawed" apple (*EP* 319), resurrected from interment under leaves in a "last gleaning" of the season (*EP* 317), Thoreau revises the New Testament as well. Better than any commercially debased cider, the juice of the frozen-thawed apple has "borrowed a flavor from heaven through the medium of the air" (*EP* 320). Such sublime flavors, however, "are intended for the taste that is up to them" (*EP* 312) and may be appreciated only by the purely sensual appetite.

The recovery of Eden, then, depends on mankind's knowing how to eat an apple with the proper spirit. "Wild Apples" is both a call for Americans to naturalize themselves and a primer on how to do so. The parallel between the apple and humanity becomes autobiographical and extra-vagant when Thoreau asserts that "*our* wild apple is wild only like myself," having "strayed into the woods from the cultivated stock" (*EP* 301). The key to the itinerant apple's success at "making its way amid the aboriginal trees" (*EP* 301) and to the human capacity to be naturalized, as exemplified here by Thoreau, is the same unfettered spirit that causes *Walden*'s extra-vagant cow to jump the fence that yards her. To transform a bordered life into a border-life, one must deliberately transgress its borders, regularly allowing nature to prevail over nurture. "It takes a savage or wild taste to appreciate a wild fruit," says Thoreau, and "a healthy, out-of-door appetite" to enjoy "the apple of life, the apple of the world" (*EP* 313). An *out-of-door* appetite is an *extra-vagant* appetite, which is the only spirit in which wildness may be comprehended.

Like most cows, however, most humans are rarely if ever extra-vagant. Steven Fink convincingly demonstrates that because Thoreau knew this, he developed the necessary trick of writing on two levels at once, one to keep the common herd of readers interested, and another to satisfy the rare extra-vagant reader capable of going out-of-doors for wilder meanings. Fink cites as an example what he terms Thoreau's "metaphorical equation" here, with types of apples representing categories of people in an allegorical contest between wildness and civilization in the New World. "[T]he 'cultivated stock' is the European settler in the civilized communities of the east; the wild apple is the European who, like himself or the backwoodsman, has reattached himself and adapted to the natural environment; and the indigenous crab apple is the native American Indian."[7] The common herd of readers (Thoreau frequently likened the masses to cattle), browsing contentedly on what they took to be a simple essay about apple trees, would not – and could not – penetrate to the prophetic pith.

As prophecy, "Wild Apples" is paradoxical in tone and its ending problematic. The essay addresses the reader, as Fink has noted, from both the prophetic stances of "a Moses catching sight of a new life in the new land" and of "a Jeremiah rebuking the sins and backslidings of the populace."[8] The latter is most apparent in the concluding diatribe from the Book of Joel, with its evocation of a nation that has "come upon my land" and "laid my vine waste" so that "the apple tree, even all the trees of the field, are withered: because joy is withered away from the sons of men" (*EP* 322). The difficulty of squaring this nuclear winter–like ending with the hortatory message of the piece as a whole is reflected in the refusal of some commentators to take it at face value.[9] Another option, however, is to regard it as an ultimatum, with the restoration of Eden made dependent on mankind's realization that joy is the condition of life in a nature that includes the human race. Thoreau's *or else* ending thus signifies that unless and until a properly extra-vagant communion with the apple of the world is achieved, "we occupy the heaven of the gods without knowing it" (*EP* 295), withering ourselves and desecrating the earth.

Thoreau wrote "Huckleberries" as an intended lecture during the fall and winter of 1860–1, extracting it from a book-length manuscript on "Wild Fruits." Although his final illness prevented the completion of either one, the lecture was eventually edited for publication by Leo Stoller. Reminiscent of "Walking," "Autumnal Tints," and "Wild Apples" in its championing of a Transcendentalized perception of and relation to nature as the means for salvaging both Eden and humanity in the New World, "Huckleberries" adds to these themes at least three of its own. First, the essay explores various kinds of accounting with regard to nature, including economic, aesthetic/moral/spiritual, and narrative. Second, "Huckleberries" takes from the concept of democracy its topic, its treatment, its tone, and its intended audience. Finally, combining the need to account with the democratic imperative, Thoreau considers true and false education and then attempts to educate American society on the means for preserving wild nature.

By examining the ways in which American culture accounts for nature, "Huckleberries" reveals the deficiencies in that culture's world view. Society determines worth primarily by size, scarcity, and cost; therefore, the little, the common, and the free are typically overlooked and undervalued. The status of the huckleberry is his representative case. Viewed properly, as by the American Indian who "made a much greater account of wild fruits than we do,"[10] the huckleberry is a kind of *manna*. The earth, accordingly, is a teeming garden, "some up country Eden . . . flowing with milk and huckleberries" (*H* 25). Like wild apples, such berries should be picked and eaten with nature in mind: "It is a sort of sacrament – a communion – the *not* forbidden fruits, which no serpent tempts us to eat"; these are the "innocent savors which relate us to Nature" (*H* 23). However, "we have fallen on evil days," Thoreau says in an echo of the end of "Wild Apples." With the emergence of huckleberries as a cash crop, "The wild fruits of the earth disappear before civilization" (*H* 28).

Related to the accounting of nature in the sense of determining its value is another accounting in narratives ranging from natural and human history to mythology, theology, poetry, and philosophy. Indeed, the way one speaks about something reveals the value one assigns it. Thoreau in "Huckleberries" gives a natural history of wild berries in the Old World and the New, from classical times to the present. By making readers aware of the universality and variety of these "little" berries, especially in America, he indicates their magnitude in nature, underscoring the comment of the classical naturalist Pliny that "Nature excels in the least things" (*H* 3). In the context of human history, Thoreau wonders why the "discoverers and explorers" reported on this fruit but his contemporaries "make comparatively little account of them" (*H* 22). Discoverers and explorers, however, are by definition extra-vagant. Thoreau also demonstrates here that an uninspired account may be as bad as no account, citing a book on huckleberries written by a professor who never left his library. This book, which "should be the ultimate fruit of the huckleberry field," is worthless because it has "none of the spirit of the huckleberry in it" (*H* 29).

Wild without being exotic, ubiquitous yet overlooked and trampled underfoot, the huckleberry, like Whitman's grass, exemplifies American democratic nature. Thoreau identifies this native berry with the aboriginal Americans, a race to whom "the earth and its productions generally were common and free to all" (*H* 30). These were the true democrats, he suggests, not the stinting "fathers who . . . laid out our New England villages" with small yards and undersized commons (*H* 30). Moreover, he portrays the berry as symbolically covering the ground on which American institutions rest, including "the three hills of Boston and no doubt Bunker Hill" and the land "where Dr. Lowell's church now stands" (*H* 14). Even Thoreau's tone in this essay is unusually democratic, as when he assures his readers that "It is my own way of living that I complain of as well as yours" (*H* 30), or speaks companionably of "we dwellers in the huckleberry pastures" (*H* 26). His friendliness is tactical, for in this essay the target of reform is entire communities rather than individuals.

Thoreau redefines for his readers both education and the schoolhouse. He must do so because "almost all that constitutes education" in his view is dismissed by Americans as "a little thing" (*H* 3), while the places in which education occurs are understood in terms of walls rather than extra-vagance. "Liberation and enlargement – such is the fruit which all culture aims to secure," he admonishes (*H* 27); and such is the fruit that children and others may pluck from the huckleberry field, an "expansion" worth "all the learning in the world" (*H* 27). "*There* was the university itself where you could learn the everlasting Laws" (*H* 26) and thus establish the Transcendentalist desideratum of "a simple and wholesome relation to nature" (*H* 29).

Warning against the erosion of wild nature by civilization, Thoreau says, "If we do not look out we shall find our fine schoolhouse standing in a cow yard at last" (*H* 35). To counter this development, he devotes the last pages of his essay to a series of proposals for paradoxically preserving wildness within the boundaries of the community. The centerpiece of his plan calls for each town to have "a primitive forest . . . where a stick should never be cut . . . but stand and decay for higher uses – a common possession forever, for instruction and recreation" (*H* 35). "Let us try to keep the new world new," he says, "and while we make a wary use of the city, preserve as far as possible the advantages of living in the country" (*H* 31). The end of "Huckleberries" is his blueprint for preserving both nature and the border-life in an American democracy.

Thoreau was assembling the "Wild Fruits" book manuscript in 1860–1 before illness caused him to set it aside. The selection considered here was edited by Bradley Dean for *Faith in a Seed* (1993) and comprises the opening section of Thoreau's manuscript. "Wild Fruits" (that is, Dean's so-named selection) begins identically to "Huckleberries," with the same revisionist look at the significance of "little" things. After that identical opening, however, each piece goes its separate but similar way. Minus the essay's democratic emphasis, the book section also attests to the value of wild fruits in relating humanity to nature, contrasting the rewards of gathering from the wild and the vulgar use of fruit as table-fare commodity. New World fruits for New World people is again a theme; and in this piece, too, Thoreau blends citations from natural and human history with his own scientific, poetic, and philosophical observations. Distinctive about "Wild Fruits" is its calendrical organization, indicative of the seasonal averaging that informed Thoreau's nature study and much of his writing in the final decade of his career. Noteworthy too is his repeated use of naturalized descriptions of humanity and humanized descriptions of nature to indicate their essential kinship.

Ever attuned to the literal and imaginative associations of names, Thoreau cites the word *fruit*, "from the Latin *fructus,* meaning 'that which is to be used or enjoyed.' " "The value of these wild fruits," he says, lies "in the sight and enjoyment of them" in the field.'' Here he reminds us that joy is the condition of natural life, in this case the joy, in part, of discovery. Reiterating the promise of "new prospects" in "Walking," he declares that "We can any afternoon discover a new fruit there, which will surprise us by its beauty or sweetness" (*FS* 179). The earlier essay's testimonial to "useful ignorance" is also underscored here in his affirmation that the sight of berries "whose names I did not know" makes "the proportion of the unknown" seem "indefinitely, if not infinitely, great" (*FS* 179). Thus, the joyful discovery of a new natural form brings both the pleasure of knowing and the greater, extra-vagant pleasure of ignorance, which is to say, of knowing there are discoveries yet to come.

In a corollary to his definition of the value of wild fruits, Thoreau says that "the value of any experience is . . . the amount of development we get out of it" (*FS* 181). The wild fruits of New England are thus "far more important to us than any others can be," he says, because "[t]hey educate us and fit us to live here in New England" (*FS* 182–3), thus fulfilling the criterion of "use" in the definition of *fruit*. Wild fruits, when gathered in the wild in a suitably extra-vagant spirit, develop one's relatedness to the place that produced them, to nature as accented in that part of the world. Neither imported fruits "sold in our markets" (*FS* 180), nor native fruits "cornered up by cultivation" (*FS* 192), nor wild fruits narrowly comprehended can bring the joy of discovery and the development of this true relation.

Anticipation, as called for in "Autumnal Tints," is here shown to be based on an acute relatedness to the wild, even when it is manifested in an "apprentice" from the town who annually finds his way to the first ripened strawberries as surely as a bug, while "the rest of mankind have not dreamed of such things as yet" (*FS* 189). To be sure, the season's first strawberry is almost impossible to detect, says Thoreau, "especially if your mind is unprepared for it" (*FS* 188). Repeatedly, he affirms the web of relationships and affinities in all of nature by *likening* people and the natural world, either in people's *liking* of it or their *likeness* to it or, as in the case of the buglike liker of strawberries, both at once. In similar fashion, he discusses spring dandelion greens that feed both the muskrat and people. "He is so much like us; we are so much like him" (*FS* 185). Later, to demonstrate that the equation of nature and humanity works both ways, he compares the young shoots rising from winter-bent blueberry bushes to "erect young men destined to perpetuate the family, by the side of their stooping sires" (*FS* 201). The family that Thoreau would perpetuate includes both blueberries and men.

"The Succession of Forest Trees" was written by Thoreau shortly before its lecture presentation at the Middlesex Cattle Show in September 1860, following which he lightly revised it for an almost immediate publication. The essay operates on two levels, one overtly scientific, the other covertly Transcendental. It is important to note that Thoreau submits questions of doubt and belief in both areas to resolution by evidence based on observation. Ironically, his own Transcendental approach to nature study emerges as more factually oriented than traditional science, at least in its explanation of the succession of trees. However, farmers at a cattle show (not unlike the American herd at large) would be unreceptive to Transcendentalism if they recognized it as such. To appease this audience, Thoreau wryly confesses himself a "Transcendentalist" (*EP* 184) but gives assurance that today's talk has a "purely scientific subject" (*EP* 185). What he does not tell his listeners – and subsequent readers – is that a Transcendentalist's science must have metaphysical significance to be pure. Purposeful Thoreauvian double-speak is just as much in evidence here as in "Wild Apples," entertaining and informing with its text and enlightening with its subtext. If a few farmers are painlessly taught to stop fighting nature in their wood-lots, Thoreau's popular purpose is served. If a few readers get the idea that nature is a manifestation of uninterrupted divine laws and that these laws may be inferred from physical examples, then a higher purpose is fulfilled.

On the scientific level, "Succession" is an account of the manner in which different species of trees – in this case pine and oak – succeed each other in a natural "rotation of crops" (*EP* 190). Indeed, this essay and the larger work that grew out of it, "The Dispersion of Seeds," are both significant documents in the history of science for their pioneering identification of the means by which tree seeds are annually transported to new locales, where they generate under the canopy of different, established species. Thoreau's description of the process of natural succession also comprises an early argument against the prevailing scientific theory of "special creation," or divine intervention, as the means by which new species are introduced. By providing a model of forest succession as an ongoing process with dis-cernible rules upon which reliable predictions may be founded, Thoreau normalized this kind of change in nature. He also demonstrated a grasp of nature as a web of phenomena and processes that made him an ecologist before the word was coined.

Underlying the scientific argument of "Succession" is Thoreau's "purely scientific" subtext, including insults aimed at, but over the heads of, his audience. Early on Thoreau tells the cattle-show crowd that in his "capacity of surveyor," he has often "gone round and round and behind your farm-ing, and ascertained exactly what its limits were" (*EP* 185). His words imply that a Transcendental naturalist has taken the measure of their farm-ing and found it both spiritually and ecologically shortsighted. He subse-quently declares that there is a "patent office" in the "government of the universe" which dispenses seeds with great care and whose "operations are infinitely more extensive and regular" than those of Washington (*EP* 187). His reference to the regular operation of the universe attests to a nature of rules rather than special creations, while his pun on *patent* means that, to the perceptive, these rules are clear enough. "[T]he method of Nature," he says, was "long ago made patent to all" (*EP* 194).

The Transcendentalist message in this essay turns on the difference be-tween a vulgar mystery, or magic, and a spiritual mystery, or wonder. Having begun by announcing that the succession of trees "is no mystery to me" (*EP* 185), Thoreau later attests to his "great faith in a seed." "Con-vince me that you have a seed there," he proclaims, "and I am prepared to expect wonders. I shall even believe that the millennium is at hand . . .

when the Patent Office, or Government, begins to distribute, and the people to plant, the seeds of these things" (*EP* 203). *The seeds of these things* means seeds as sources of wonder, as revealed by his ironic account of six seeds from the Patent Office that yielded him 310 pounds of "large yellow squash," the biggest of which took honors at a local fair (*EP* 203). Typically, mankind pays homage to a large vegetable while failing to wonder at the mysterious little seed that produced it. The millennium is not at hand because "men love darkness rather than light" (*EP* 204), a charge Thoreau supports with a hypothetical example of farmers' sons mesmerized by a magician at a fair. One suspects, though, that his indictment is meant to include so-called scientists who prefer miracles to seeds as the explanation for forest succession. In both cases, the ignorance that shields from his insult also shades from his light.

A message of this essay is that the pursuit of both scientific and Transcendental enlightenment requires an unsparing look at the facts, the purpose of which is to help remove doubt and belief from the realm of conjecture and found them on observation instead. Concerning notions of spontaneous generation, he declares, "I do not believe these *assertions,* and I will state some of the ways in which, according to my *observation,* such forests are planted and raised" (*EP* 187; emphasis added). "[I]f you look through the thickest pine wood," he reports, "you will commonly detect many little oaks" (*EP* 189). *If you look, you will detect* is his "purely scientific" assurance to his audience, warranted by his own observation of nature as the "most extensive and experienced planter of us all" (*EP* 198). A revealing example of Thoreau's reliance on observation is the way he applies it to the question of seed longevity. On the one hand, he "must doubt" the statement in a scientific report that pine seeds "remain for many years unchanged in the ground" because its author "does not tell us on what observation his remark is founded" (*EP* 200). On the other hand, he is "prepared to believe that some seeds . . . may retain their vitality for centuries under favorable circumstances" because he has witnessed an apparent instance with his own eyes (*EP* 201). Pervasively in this essay, Thoreau's faith in seeds is bolstered by strict observance, even when his observations hedge both doubt and belief alike.

"The Dispersion of Seeds," a complete text of which is now available in Bradley Dean's *Faith in a Seed,* includes most of "The Succession of Forest Trees" along with much material added by Thoreau from September 1860 through the following summer, when poor health caused him to stop working on it. Although the bulk of this book-length work is an account of seed dispersion and forest succession, the controlling argument here is that mankind must apply this knowledge to its management of forests and woodlots.

There is no reference to Transcendentalism in "Dispersion," no running subtext intended for the illuminati only. Thoreau's emphasis here is primarily, though not exclusively, secular because his main mission is to preserve nature by convincing the owners of woodlots to work with natural processes instead of ignorantly thwarting them. To succeed, he must convince these people that their financial, as well as their vital, interest is best served by adapting to nature's ways. Thoreau knows that for nature to instruct, either secularly or spiritually, the paradigm it presents must be a true version rather than a perversion of natural law. However, Concordians and most other Americans receive their schooling in nature on the local level, where they witness, to an ever-worsening degree, not nature's purposes but the results of their own cross-purposes. By saving Concord's woodlots now, even if doing so requires an appeal to vulgar economic values, Thoreau preserves an Eden to be recovered when higher considerations prevail.[12]

The broad context of Thoreau's appeal for a naturalized silviculture is not vulgar economy, however, but the ecological economy of nature. He tries to make his readers aware that through the complex processes of seeding and succession, the vitality of all nature is largely maintained. "The consequence of all this activity of the animals and of the elements in transporting seeds is that almost every part of the earth's surface is filled with seeds." Indeed, "The very earth itself is a granary and a seminary, so that to some minds its surface is regarded as the cuticle of one great living creature" (FS 151). The purpose of the earth as granary is to feed the creatures who, in turn, plant the seeds that fulfill the earth's other purpose as seminary, or nursery. This system constitutes a self-sustaining economy in which "the consumer is compelled to be at the same time the dispenser and planter" (FS 114). Among humans, even nonfarmers are enlisted by nature in this process of dissemination and propagation, from children who scatter thistledown to travelers who transport hitchhiking seeds on their clothes. "Thus, the most ragged and idle loafer or beggar may be of some use in the economy of Nature, if he will only keep moving," says Thoreau (FS 97).

By attributing the superficially mysterious alternation of tree species to natural laws, Thoreau brings it too into the ecological economy of nature. Dismissing the "vulgar prejudice that such forests are 'spontaneously generated,'" he also declares confidently that "there has not been a sudden new creation in their case but a steady progress according to existing laws" (FS 36). Early in 1860, he had read On the Origin of Species and found his own thinking confirmed and extended by Charles Darwin. In "Dispersion," he notes that Darwin's "development theory implies a greater vital force in Nature [than does special creation], because it is more flexible and accommodating, and equivalent to a sort of constant new creation" (*FS* 102).[13] To Thoreau, a *constant* – that is, ongoing and unchanging – new creation is better than an *ad hoc* special creation because the inducible laws of the former imply rules for woodlot management and other human conduct. Indeed, for humanity to participate intentionally rather than accidentally in the ecological economy of nature, it must acquire knowledge to take the place of what in other creatures is instinct.[14] Thoreau advocates a close look at both history and natural history as one path to such knowledge. "[I]f we attended more to the history of our woodlots," to the fossil record of nature's purposes and mankind's mistakes, "we should manage them more wisely" (*FS* 164). At present, however, "we hardly associate seeds with trees, and do not anticipate the time when this regular succession will cease" (*FS* 23).

Thoreau demonstrates that by ignoring the economy of nature, mankind ignorantly thwarts dispersion, succession, and its own narrow economic interest. For example, lacking any awareness of the "vast work" of squirrels in reforestation through seed distribution, "The farmer knows only that they get his seed corn occasionally . . . and perchance encourages his boys to shoot them every May" (*FS* 130). The situation is even more dire with regard to the woodlots themselves, where farmers routinely abort the process of succession. The text closes with one such account. Thoreau has gone "to examine the site of a dense white-pine wood which was cut off the previous winter and see how the little oaks, with which I knew the ground must be filled there, looked now." He finds, though, that "the fellow who calls himself its owner" has burned it to get in a crop of winter rye before returning it to woodlot (*FS* 172). By this burning he has cost himself a fine stand of "oaks half a dozen years old . . . only waiting to be touched off by the sun." "A greediness that defeats its own ends," Thoreau calls it. And because oaks must be preceded by pines here, the already "pine-sick" land must await another planting of wind-blown pine seed before beginning again the long, slow succession to oaks. "What a fool!" Thoreau exclaims. "As if oaks would bide his time or come at his bidding!" (*FS* 173).

Despite the emphatically secular orientation of "Dispersion," the Transcendentalist Thoreau has not gone away, if we know him when we see him. For example, in calling the earth a "seminary" (*FS* 151), he signifies not just its biological function as a nursery but also its theological potential as a spiritual training ground. To a Transcendentalist, all natural facts are spiritually significant, and Thoreau makes it possible to read "Dispersion" as a kind of organic gospel, with a seed as its holy child and redeemer.[15] He reports, "When lately the comet was hovering in our northwest horizon, the thistledown received the greater share of my attention," its seedpod "like a silk-lined cradle in which a prince is rocked" (*FS* 87). Such is his biomystical version of the Nativity. And in describing how "Nature sees to it" that lilies are seeded in the freshly dug pond at Concord's new cemetery, he uses an inverted phrase from the burial service, "in the midst of death we are in life" (*FS* 100–01), to testify to a natural life-everlasting. He points out too that even the lilies "which we carry in our hands to church" rose from buried seeds (*FS* 102), a spiritually significant – and spiritually stated – natural fact. Like seeds themselves, "The Dispersion of Seeds" offers "a prophecy . . . of future springs" (*FS* 93). Even in its unfinished state, Thoreau's text upholds its author's reputation as a Transcendentalist poet while advancing his stature as natural historian, scientist, and ecological prophet.

Often-voiced but no longer prevailing, the opinion that Thoreau's late nature writings are too Transcendentally poetic to be good science and too scientific to be good literature rests, as Robert Sattelmeyer suggests, at least partially on a twentieth-century "assumption about the unbridgeable gap between scientific and imaginative truth."[16] John Hildebidle notes that "the sense that observation of nature is inherently a spiritual and moral enterprise seems to have been, at least up to Thoreau's time, a universal assumption, and one seen as in no way in conflict with the necessary tasks of science."[17] This earlier tradition explains Thoreau's attraction to classical naturalists such as Pliny and to classic English natural history writers such as Gilbert White. By the late 1850s, however, as Nina Baym states, "science was coming more and more to eliminate the personality and the capacities of the investigator."[18] A reason for the castigations of science in Thoreau's later Journal, even as his own studies were becoming more scientific, is his awareness that science had turned narrowly specialized, dehumanized, and depersonalized. In his essays, the frequent mingling of human history with natural history underscores his belief that mankind is, and always has been, part and parcel of nature. Moreover, his emphasis on the personality and capacities of the observer – on the human relationship to nature – helped make him a protoecologist, practicing an unborn science that would itself insist on humanity's attitudes as a key to the conservation or degradation of the environment.

NOTES

1 Thoreau, *Excursions and Poems* (Boston: Houghton Mifflin, 1906), p. 205; hereafter referred to as *EP*.
2 See William Rossi, " 'The Limits of an Afternoon Walk': Coleridgean Polarity in Thoreau's 'Walking,' " *ESQ* 33 (1987): 94–109; see also Frederick Garber,

Thoreau's Redemptive Imagination (New York: New York University Press, 1977), pp. 211–20.

3 For discussions of Thoreau's supplementary reading for "Yankee," see the following: Robert D. Richardson, Jr., *Henry Thoreau: A Life of the Mind* (Berkeley: University of California Press, 1986), pp. 216–23; and *Reading*, pp. 92–110.

4 See Willard H. Bonner, "The Harvest of Thought in Thoreau's 'Autumnal Tints,' " *ESQ* 22 (1976): 78–84.

5 See Joan Burbick, *Thoreau's Alternative History* (Philadelphia: University of Pennsylvania Press, 1987), pp. 119–34; see also Richardson, *Henry Thoreau*, pp. 357–62.

6 Kevin P. Van Anglen, "A Paradise Regained: Thoreau's 'Wild Apples' and the Myth of the American Adam," *ESQ* 27 (1981): 31.

7 Steven Fink, "The Language of Prophecy: Thoreau's 'Wild Apples,' " *New England Quarterly* 59 (1986): 219.

8 Fink, "Language of Prophecy," p. 212.

9 See Fink, "Language of Prophecy," pp. 226–8; see also Van Anglen, "Paradise Regained," p. 35.

10 Thoreau, *Huckleberries,* ed. Leo Stoller (Iowa City: Windhover Press, 1970), pp. 15–16; hereafter referred to as *H*.

11 Thoreau, *Faith in a Seed,* ed. Bradley P. Dean (Washington, D.C.: Island Press/ Shearwater Books, 1993), p. 180; hereafter referred to as *FS*.

12 For discussion of the economic implications of Thoreau's silviculture, see Leo Stoller, *After Walden* (Stanford: Stanford University Press, 1957), pp. 77–89.

13 For discussions of Thoreau and Darwin, see Richardson, *Henry Thoreau*, pp. 373–9; see also *Reading*, pp. 78–92.

14 For a discussion of learning vs. instinct and of alleged pitfalls in Thoreau's scientific approach, see Nina Baym, "Thoreau's View of Science," *Journal of the History of Ideas* 26 (1965): 221–34.

15 For discussion of a "vegetable redeemer" in *Walden* and the Journal, see Gordon V. Boudreau, *The Roots of Walden and the Tree of Life* (Nashville: Vanderbilt University Press, 1990), pp. 113–14, 217.

16 Robert Sattelmeyer, "Introduction," in Thoreau, *The Natural History Essays* (Salt Lake City: Peregrine Smith Books, 1984), p. xxvi.

17 John Hildebidle, *Thoreau: A Naturalist's Liberty* (Cambridge: Harvard University Press, 1983), p. 67.

18 Baym, "Thoreau's View of Science," p. 232.

12

LAWRENCE BUELL

Thoreau and the natural environment

Thoreau is today considered the first major interpreter of nature in American literary history, and the first American environmentalist saint. This position did not come easily to him, however. Until almost a half-century after his death, he remained a rather obscure figure; and during his life and career – our main interest here – Thoreau had to struggle to arrive at the deep understanding of nature for which he is remembered today. He started adult life from a less advantageous position than we sometimes realize, as a village businessman's son of classical education rather than as someone versed in nature through systematic botanical study, agriculture, or more than a very ordinary sort of experiential contact with it. Unlike William Bartram, Thoreau had no man of science for a father; unlike Thomas Jefferson, he had no agrarian roots. His first intellectual promptings to study and write about nature were from books, school, and literary mentors like Ralph Waldo Emerson. Though he celebrated wildness, his was not the wildness of the moose but of the imported, cultivated escapee from the orchard that he celebrated in his late essay, "Wild Apples."[1] Thoreau's career in pursuit of nature thus became one of fitful, irregular, experimental, although increasingly purposeful, self-education in reading landscape and pondering the significance of what he found there.

Thoreau is often thought of as Emerson's earthy opposite. But it would be truer to imagine him as moving gradually, partially, and self-conflictedly beyond the program Emerson outlined in *Nature* (1836), which sacralized nature as man's mystic counterpart, arguing (in "Language") that physical nature could be decoded as a spiritually coherent sign-system. Emerson's theory of "correspondence," derived chiefly from the Swedish mystic Emanuel Swedenborg, validated the authority of the inspired creative imagination as the means by which nature's meanings were to be read. The idea that natural phenomena had spiritual as well as material significance had a life-long appeal to Thoreau, although he increasingly took an empirical and "scientific" approach to nature after 1850; indeed, a strong undertone of his growing commitment to exact observation and to keeping tabs on con-temporary scientific thought was a lingering testiness at what he took to be its pedantry and formalism. (Emerson himself was, ironically, less critical of science and technology, although far less knowledgeable.)[2] Hence Tho-reau's famous explanation for his refusal to give a full answer to the As-sociation for the Advancement of Science's query as to what kind of scientist he was ("I am a mystic, a transcendentalist, and a natural philos-opher to boot," he told his *Journal* [*J* 5: 4]). Yet Thoreau became increas-ingly interested in defining nature's structure, both spiritual and material, for its own sake, as against how nature might subserve humanity, which was Emerson's primary consideration. In order to attend as closely to na-ture as he did late in life, Thoreau had to overcome not only the limits of his classical education and his early Transcendentalist idealism, but also of an intense preoccupation with himself, his moods, his identity, his vocation, his relation to other people. This narcissism he surmounted by defining as an essential part of his individuality the intensity of his interest in and caring for physical nature itself.

One of the reasons that *Walden* is Thoreau's greatest book is that the transitional struggles of a lifetime are pulled into it so fully and complexly. In this essay I shall concentrate on it especially, not only because it is Thoreau's most enduring work, but because it embeds much of the history of his relationship with nature, as it unfolded from his apprentice years to his intellectual maturity. This we can see especially well if we think of *Walden* not just as a finished product but also as a work in process, a work that took almost a decade of accumulation and revision to complete: the decade that happened to be the most crucial period of Thoreau's inner life.

To show the promise of this approach, let us start our examination with some passages from "The Ponds." Here we can see Thoreau, as he re-worked and expanded his material from the few simple descriptive para-graphs of his first draft (1846–7), beginning to convert himself from romantic poet to natural historian and environmentalist.

In a previous chapter, the speaker nostalgically remembers having been first taken to the pond at the age of four, so that it became "one of the oldest scenes stamped on my memory" (*W* 155). In "The Ponds," however, early childhood reminiscence seems to produce pain. "When I first paddled a boat on Walden, it was completely surrounded by thick and lofty pine and oak woods" (*W* 191). "But since I left those shores," he goes on, "the woodchoppers have still further laid them waste, and now for many a year there will be no more rambling through the aisles of the woods, with oc-casional vistas through which you see the water. My Muse may be excused if she is silent henceforth. How can you expect the birds to sing when their groves are cut down?" (W 192). This is an arresting sequence for several reasons. First, obviously, because the outburst against woodchoppers abruptly halts the sort of nostalgic fantasy that was indulged earlier. But arresting too because of what it excludes. We are told that the choppers have *still further* laid waste the trees; yet no previous depredations have been mentioned. Perhaps the idyllic mood was so compelling that Thoreau could not bear to discuss them, or (more likely, I think) Thoreau presumed that his nineteenth-century audience – which in the first instance he imagined as his inquisitive Concord neighbors – would take it for granted that the groves of their youth had been steadily thinned. For such was indeed the case; the percentage of woodland in the town of Concord had been steadily declining during Thoreau's lifetime, reaching an all-time low of little more than 10 percent almost at the moment Thoreau penned this sentence.

Even more noteworthy is the transience of the speaker's protest. It does proceed for another paragraph, chiefly devoted to complaints about the "devilish Iron Horse" that has "muddied the Boiling Spring with his foot." The speaker looks for a "champion" that will meet the engine at "the Deep Cut and thrust an avenging lance between the ribs of the bloated pest." But this pugnacity dissipates as the next paragraph assures us that "Nevertheless, of all the characters I have known, perhaps Walden wears best, and best preserves its purity." A little later on, we are further reassured by the fancy that the railroad workers are somehow refreshed by Walden as the train whisks by: "the engineer does not forget at night, or his nature does not, that he has beheld this vision of serenity and purity once at least during the day" (W 192–3). Walden has been transformed back into a pristine sanctuary again.

This sequence dramatizes several important things about Thoreau's naturism. First, it shows that "thinking like a mountain" did not come any more naturally to him than it did to Aldo Leopold, in the famous essay of that title (from *Sand County Almanac*) in which the father of modern environmental ethics confesses his slow awakening to the importance of predators in an ecosystem.[3] Thoreau first wrote *Walden* without even mentioning the history of the abuses suffered by the Concord landscape, even though he was well aware of them. (For example, the Concord and Fitchburg Railroad, laid along the west end of Walden Pond the year before Thoreau moved there, was a significant cause of regional deforestation, for creating roadways and for fuel.) Nor was Thoreau unaware that forest conservation was already a public issue. In the first section of *Report on the Trees and Shrubs Growing Naturally in the Forests of Massachusetts* (1846), which Thoreau read soon after publication and consulted frequently thereafter, George B. Emerson had warned that "the axe has made, and is making, wanton and terrible havoc. The cunning foresight of the Yankee seems to desert him when he takes the axe in hand."[4] Yet even in the finished version of "The Ponds," produced amid recurring Journal complaints at the philistine obtuseness of some of the profit-minded clients for whom he worked as surveyor, Thoreau did not sound the preservationist note loudly. Why? Probably not because he feared readers would disapprove but because his desire to imagine Walden as an unspoiled place overrode his fears about its vulnerability. You cannot argue simultaneously that sylvan utopia can be found within the town limits and that the locale is being devastated at an appalling rate; and the vision of a pristine nature close by appealed irresistibly to Thoreau for personal as well as rhetorical reasons. It was emotionally important to him to believe in Walden as a sanctuary, and it was all the easier for him to do so in the face of contrary evidence given the power that the myth of nature's exhaustlessness continued to hold over many of the astutest minds of his day.

Even if Thoreau had stressed Concord's environmental degradation, he might not have opposed it primarily for nature's sake. In the passages we have reviewed, the denuding of Walden is lamented mainly on grounds of personal taste, as a blow to "My Muse," as ruining the solace of Thoreau's pondside rambles.

Yet the dominance of such aesthetic motives does not imply ethical anaesthesia. As Leopold was later to observe, the cultivation of a noncomplacent bonding to nature at the aesthetic level is one of the paths to environmental concern; so we should not minimize the potential impact of the challenge the speaker throws out at the chapter's end, when he declares of the ponds, "How much more beautiful than our lives, how much more transparent than our characters, are they! . . . Nature has no human inhabitant who appreciates her. . . . She flourishes most alone, far from the towns where they reside. Talk of heaven! ye disgrace earth" (W 199–200). The rhetoric here teeters between the old-fashioned jeremiad's familiar call to spiritual purification and a more pointedly environmental protectionist eviction of humanity fallen from nature. Either way, spiritual renewal is tied more concretely to nature appreciation than in (say) Emerson, who certainly would never have thought of calling Walden a "character." Finally, Thoreau's pleasing dramatization of the nurturing bond to nature, not only for the nostalgic speaker but even for the inattentive brakeman and engineer, is more likely to reinforce in attentive readers a sense of the rightness of an unsullied nature than to reinforce complacency in the railroad system as an unmixed good.

Because Thoreau, when redrafting *Walden*, added much more to the second half of the book than to the first, it is not strange that the sorts of alterations we have been considering reflect the changing ratio of homocentrism to ecocentrism as the book as a whole unfolds. In "Economy," Walden figures chiefly as a good site for an enterprise. Nature is hardly yet present except as a theater for the speaker to exercise his cabin-craft in. Thoreau proceeds for fully one-ninth of the book before providing the merest glimpse of the pond. "Economy" 's message of simplification is certainly consistent with an environmentalist perspective, as it is for James Fenimore Cooper's Leatherstocking, but Thoreau does not as yet advocate it on this ground. Not until the later chapter on "Higher Laws" does Thoreau restate his philosophy of abstemiousness as anything like an environmental ethic, questioning the killing and eating of animals and fish. This slow expansion of the sense of moral accountability toward nonhuman creatures is symptomatic. As *Walden* unfolds, the mock-serious discourse of enterprise, implicit in which is the notion of the speaker as the self-creator of his environment, gives way to a more ruminative prose in which the speaker appears to be finding himself within his environment. The prose begins to turn significantly in this direction as it moves from the heroic classicism of "Reading," with its pedagogical didactics, to "Sounds," where the "language" of "all things and events" impresses itself upon the contemplative. Thoreau's own language helps us to put this directional movement of *Walden* in perspective. Earnest struggle partially gives way to receptivity, self-absorption to extrospection. Thoreau's language helps us to chart this movement. His favorite pronoun, "I," appears in the two opening chapters an average of 6.6 times per page; in the next six (through "The Village"), 5.5 times per page; in the next five ("The Ponds" through "House-Warming" – the last chapter in which the speaker modifies his environment, through plastering), 5.2; in the final five ("Former Inhabitants" through "Conclusion"), 3.6. Roughly inverse to this is his usage of the following cluster: "Walden," "pond(s)," and the various nominal and adjectival forms of "wild": once every 1.8 pages for the first two chapters, 1.1 times per page during the next six (through "Village"), 2.3 times per page during the rest of the book.[5]

These are crude indices. For a more complex understanding of Thoreau's ecocentric revision process, let us go back to the micro-level and examine the use of one small telltale framing device. During the first pondside vignette in "Economy," the speaker devotes a sentence to remembering that "on the 1st of April it rained and melted the ice, and in the early part of the day, which was very foggy, I heard a stray goose groping about over the pond and cackling as if lost, or like the spirit of the fog" (W 42). An emblematic fowl, forsooth: suggesting both the spirit of nature and the uncertain spirit of the speaker, who has already chronicled his losses in symbolic form (hound, bay horse, turtle-dove). The sentence uses the logic of correspondence delicately, evoking it but not depending on it for dogma – true to the uneasy tone of the image. In "Spring," to help draw the year into a symbolic circle Thoreau makes this image return: "some solitary goose in the foggy mornings, seeking its companion, and still peopling the woods with the sound of a larger life than they could sustain" (W 313). This is actually the second of a two-part series of anecdotes, pursued through several paragraphs, the first of which begins: ". . . I was startled by the *honking* of geese flying low over the woods, like weary travelers getting in late from southern lakes, and indulging at last in unrestrained complaint and mutual consolation. Standing at my door, I could hear the rush of their wings; when, driving toward my house, they suddenly spied my light, and with hushed clamor wheeled and settled in the pond. So I came in, and shut the door, and passed my first spring night in the woods" (W 312–13). Thoreau continues by describing the behavior of the "large and tumultuous" flock (he counts them: twenty-nine) the next morning as they disport on the pond, then fly off toward Canada, "trusting to break their fast in muddier pools." Then, after brief mention of a duck flock, comes the solitary goose passage. This sequence is significant in several ways. First, as a formal opening and closing device. Second, as confirmation of the move to a textured and "extrospective" rendering of the natural world, whose particularity is now so cogent that the exact number of the large flock must be reported. One wonders if Thoreau might have been trying to answer Emerson's challenge in "Literary Ethics" to "go into the forest" and describe the undescribed: "The honking of the wild geese flying by night; the thin note of the companionable titmouse in the winter day; the fall of swarms of flies in autumn, from combats high in the air . . . the turpentine exuding from the tree; – and indeed any vegetation, any animation, any and all, are alike unattempted."[6] Third, as a recognition of the delicacy of the complementary project to which *Walden* is committed, namely to turn nature to human uses: nature as a barometer and stimulus to *my* spiritual development. True, the geese are personified; they seem to participate in a logic of natural symbols: geese returning equals spring which equals (we soon find, to no surprise) spiritual renewal. Yet here they are more literalized: when they arrive, the speaker goes indoors so as not to scare them. Though they feel like projections of human desire ("peopling the woods with the sound of a larger life than they could sustain"), the difference between their realm and his is underscored. There is no quick emblematic fix as there was in "Economy" ("like the spirit of the fog"). The correspondence framework remains implicit, but it is complicated by the facticity of the waterfowl and the speaker's respect for their interests. This respect is what begins to modulate Thoreau's romantic enthusiasm toward something like environmental awareness in the modern sense.

But the passage complicates the case I have been building as to the correlation between *Walden*'s unfolding and the biographical unfolding of Thoreau's own environmental consciousness. For these developments do not quite synchronize. It happens, for example, that the earliest surviving Journal entry that Thoreau used in *Walden* (from March 1840, five years before the experience itself: still another comment on wild geese, by the way) was not inserted into the text until the *final* extant manuscript version (1853) (*PJ* 1:119). Again, both geese anecdotes just discussed come from the 1846 Journal, the time of the original Walden experience (*PJ* 2:214, 192–3), and the language used in *Walden* is very close to the original Journal language. On the other hand, although both anecdotes appear as early as the book's first draft (1846–7), it was not until the latest extant manuscript versions that the material became fully elaborated. In version E (1852–3), Thoreau first devised the sentence about shutting his door and passing his first spring night in the woods; and not until version F (1853) did he repeat the stray goose image in "Spring" – before that, it appeared only in "Economy" in phrasing much less faithful to the Journal record than the late addition to "Spring."[7] In his revision, furthermore, Thoreau used the stray goose image at the head of a descriptive paragraph drawing upon his increasingly extensive seasonal observations since 1850, listing sundry other spring signs like pigeons, martins, frogs, tortoises. This strengthens the naturalistic dimension of the image. So Thoreau revised *both* to accentuate schematic design (the circle of the year, the goose as a motif) *and* naturalistic detail more scrupulously respectful of nature's otherness and more "realistic" from the standpoint of the documentary record; and this revision did not simply entail drawing on the more mature findings of the post-Walden years when Thoreau became increasingly the practicing naturalist, but also upon the writings of his "Transcendentalist period."

So Thoreau's biography, the composition of *Walden*, and the "plot" of the published version do not correlate neatly. He began and ended his career fascinated by the vision of the natural realm as correspondent to the human estate. He could not get past the Emersonian axiom that "Nature must be viewed humanly to be viewed at all" (*J* 4:163). No matter how devoted his naturalism became, he continued to want to organize his observations into intellectual, moral, and aesthetic patterns. This at times whetted his appetite for natural history (for instance, his hypothesis of the succession of forest trees, generalizing from some of his observations about the dispersion of seeds) and at other times it reinforced him in the roles of mystic and aesthete, ransacking the local terrain for picturesque views (despite complaining about the bookishness of William Gilpin and other theorists on the subject) and subjecting landscape configurations to symbolic interpretation, like the elaborate conceit about the moral significance of the intersection of lines of greatest length, breadth, and depth, which he half-playfully, half-solemnly infers from his survey of Walden Pond.[8] In the revision of *Walden*, therefore, Thoreau sometimes even seems to move "backward" from his later "naturalist" stage to his earlier "poet" stage, as when he takes his initial (1846–7) straightforward vignette of observing a striped snake arising from its torpid state and turns it into a symbol of regeneration in version C.[9] Yet, overall, Thoreau's revisions show an irregular movement toward discovery, retrieval, and respect for the realm of physical nature whose substantial reality must be honored in the face of the desire to appropriate it for one's own uses.

Indeed, *Walden* reflects Thoreau's pursuit not of one or two but of a cluster of distinct approaches to nature, none of which was wholly original or unique to him. All may be found widely pursued throughout American writing, sometimes indebted to his example. Some of these environmental "projects" were part of the text's original intent, indeed of the original Walden experiment itself. Some developed later, between the two major bursts of compositional activity: 1846–7 and 1852–3. In order to understand fully what nature meant to Thoreau, we need to examine seven of these projects in turn, in the expectation of arriving at an overall picture that is shifting and pluriform, not tidily coherent or reducible to one or two sweeping statements.

One of Thoreau's earliest dreams as a writer and a follower of nature was the pastoral project of recovering for a time, both in experience and in his writing, the feel of a pristine simplicity such as he associated with pre-Columbian America or, more typically, with ancient Greece; in Thoreau's schoolbook version of the Greeks, they symbolize the morning of the human race. (He reminded himself in 1840 that "The Greeks were boys in the sunshine . . . – the Romans were men in the field – the Persians women in the house – the Egyptians old men in the dark" [*PJ* 1:154].) Walden, both the experience and the book, was a pastoral return in two symbolic senses as well as in the literal: a "psychocultural" return, in the spirit of romantic sentimentalism defined by Schiller, to the Homeric world;[10] and a psychobiographical return driven by Wordsworthian reminiscences of former times spent more fully within nature, glimpses of which Thoreau allows us in the boyhood boating memories noted earlier. This nostalgia for youth later became intensified by nostalgia for life at Walden, kept alive by hundreds of additional returns, in body and in recollection, that Thoreau made to the site and in re-examining details of the experiment. So the 1846–7 parable of the author's long-lost hound, bay horse, and turtle-dove, (W 17) came to apply as much to the Walden experience itself as to the past before the experience.[11] There is an exact, though buried, parallel between the vague sadness of that passage in "Economy" and the passage in "Conclusion" (added in 1853) that asserts that "I left the woods for as good a reason as I went there" (W 323), which in the 1852 Journal version reads "I left it as unaccountably as I went to it" (PJ 4:276).

Pastoralism may lead as easily to a bogus as to an actual ruralism. Thoreau was fully aware of the reductions of pastoral art ("the pasture as seen from the hall window"[PJ 1:488]), but he was not above yielding to their blandishments, especially during that first excited summer.

One key sign of this in Thoreau's work that presaged (and, through his influence, helped to shape) the whole course of American literary naturism was the opening up of a split between pastoral and agrarian sensibility that did not originally exist. As Leo Marx has shown, Crèvecoeur and the Virginia planters domesticated the Greco-Roman pastoral ideal in a specifically agrarian context,[12] as did Jefferson's Yankee federalist counterpart, Timothy Dwight. Thoreau, however, satirized ordinary farming as part and parcel of the soul-withering false economy of the work ethic, against which he set his own ethos of contemplative play, which approached farming in a willfully poetic fashion: "Shall I not rejoice also at the abundance of the weeds whose seeds are the granary of the birds?" (W 166). His favorite figure of speech for necessary labor was the myth of Apollo tending the flocks of King Admetus (W 70; cf. J 4:114) – a way of pastoralizing but spurning pasture duty at a single stroke. (It became one of his code phrases for days spent surveying [J 6:185].) Thoreau's desire to imagine an actualization of the pastoral ideal as leisure rather than as work drove him to imagine the rural figure as a Colin Clout rather than as a Lycidas.

Nothing was easier for Milton than to imagine flock-tending as a delightful pursuit precisely because, as Samuel Johnson said, he had no flocks to batten; shepherding was a vicarious activity not expected of him in real life. Thoreau, on the other hand, felt surrounded by townspeople who couldn't understand why he didn't tend his flocks – that is, get ahead in some trade. For them, writing and botanizing were rarefied pursuits of no practical value. Without denying an element of class-based hauteur to Thoreau's intricate allusiveness, his pastoralism was much more a utopian dissent from the economic system than Jefferson's, which was an outright idealization of what he would like to have kept as the status quo. The prominence of stolid agriculturalists among the establishment in Thoreau's district provoked him to a mode of pastoralism condescending to actual farmers. This then became the American literary naturist mainstream, with some partial exceptions like Robert Frost (who is not much of an exception, once one starts noticing the distinctions he draws between self and neighbors in poems like "Mending Wall") and a few clear exceptions like Wendell Berry. In the tradition of Thoreau's not talking much about his social life while at *Walden,* American literary naturists generally underrepresent community. The segmentation of "nature" from "civilization," "country" from "town," already endemic to pastoral, gets even more accentuated.[13]

Also conducive to schematic yet wholeheartedly ruralist vision was Thoreau's correspondence project, religious in character and derived from Emerson, on which I have already commented. Its logic helped undergird Thoreau's romantic Hellenism; it helped him see more than just fancifulness in the proposition that "morning brings back the heroic ages" (W 88), and that in turn opened up the possibility of converting "the faint hum of the mosquito, making its invisible and unimaginable tour" through the dawn into a symbolic "trumpet that recalled what I had read of most ancient history and heroic ages."[14] Thoreau's most extravagant exercise in the metaphysics of correspondences – the moral significance of the pond's dimensions – was probably well worked out by the first draft of *Walden.*[15] In this series of examples – morning, mosquito, pond survey – we see how correspondential vision can lead its devotee to a more textured perception of environmental detail, although these perceptions are also regulated by deductive logic. This was not an inevitable result: as Swedenborg's writing shows, an allegorical vision of nature does not necessarily induce naturism. But in a person like Thoreau, who was attracted to nature to start with, it could have a catalytic effect. The same can be said of the convergence of scientific curiosity and typological vision in the thought of Jonathan Edwards.[16]

A third project of which the same could be said was Thoreau's experiment in frugality. In principle, any habitat might do for this, for economic and moral self-regulation were the keys to its success. In practice, Christian, classical, and romantic precedent all dictated that the best kind of place to conduct such an experiment was rural and the right mode of production was preindustrial and homespun. Hence, Thoreau's droll critique in "The Bean-Field" of the contemporary movement to mechanize and intensify agriculture. Though Thoreau was more interested in the harvest of the spirit than in the hard-earned wisdom he mock-seriously imparts about how to grow beans, it is not wrong to call him "an articulate champion of the preservation of the values of subsistence farming," as environmental historian Carolyn Merchant does. For Thoreau's allegiances, when it came to choosing between options, were all against upscale commercialized farming and on the side of what is now called "sustainable" agriculture: a small-scale, produce-for-needs-rather-than-gain style of husbandry that observed the rhythms he found in the Roman agriculturalists, whose works he read with increasing seriousness in the latter stages of Walden's composition – Cato's *De Re Rustica* (he called it "my 'Cultivator' " [*W* 84]), for example.[17] Turning from that book to present-day Concord, Thoreau was pleased to imagine that "the farmer's was pretty much the same routine then as now." "And Cato but repeated the maxims of a remote antiquity" (*PJ* 4:31). This was wishful thinking, as Thoreau himself knew (cf. *J* 6:108, for instance), but it illustrates his need to resupply a georgic dimension to his pastoral and ascetic commitments. The Journal is studded with unobtrusive references to the rhythms of the agricultural year – planting, manuring, haying, and so on – an attentiveness that stands in contrast to Thoreau's better known scorn of stodgy farmers. This in spite of his even more conspicuous satire of farmers. Thoreau's bucolic data are an important index of just how far he moved, in later life, from his earlier position as the pencil manufacturer's college-educated son, returned home to become village schoolmaster.

This growth of interest in things agricultural, ironically, did not in itself set Thoreau apart from the Brahmin elite whose sons were his Harvard classmates; on the contrary, it was faddish among affluent nineteenth-century Bostonians to take an active interest in farming methods. Thoreau hoeing his beans in ways contrary to ancient wisdom ("Beans so late!" [*W* 157]) was in some ways a writ-small version of contemporary merchant princes' combining of the roles of progressive agrarian and British country squire. But Thoreau's brand of reform, focused upon reform of self, was in opposition to their attempt to play sponsor to new agricultural efficiencies in ways that only the wealthy could afford.[18]

A fourth project, Thoreau's interest in natural history, also came to maturity during the years of composing *Walden* rather than during the experiment itself. During the last dozen years of his life, Thoreau made himself into what we would now call a field biologist of considerable skill: in botany especially, but also in zoology, ornithology, entomology, and ichthyology.[19] The most elaborate of his several aspirations in this line was the plan of devising a comprehensive account of the unfolding of the seasons as physical *and* mental events.[20] The first version of *Walden* does not deal with seasonal change as such until the last tenth of the manuscript. Although Thoreau insisted in that first draft that "I am on the alert for the first signs of spring,"[21] he did not begin a detailed recording of seasonal flora and fauna until 1851, reaching a plateau of minute sophistication in

1852 ("my year of observation" [J 4: 174]), when he made an extraordinarily careful effort to chart seasonal changes through mid-May (J 4:65). By the summer of 1851, Thoreau had begun thinking seriously of this as a major literary venture: "A Book of the seasons – each page of which should be written in its own season & out of doors or in its own locality whatever it be" (PJ 3:253). About this same time, Thoreau becomes irrepressibly eager to identify first appearances of this flower or that bird, to discover foretastes or afterthoughts of one season in another, to identify microseasons – the season of leafing, the season of fogs, the season of fires – and indeed to think of each day as its own possible season sign-system: comprehensive, evanescent, ductile. The final version of *Walden* reflects Thoreau's growing phenological interest by structuring its last major section ("House-Warming" through "Spring") as a seasonal chronicle.

Thoreau's phenological investigations moved his thought toward the kind of multisided inquiry into nature's internal connections that Ernst Haeckel baptized in 1866 as "ecology."[22] Thoreau's late-life studies of plant succession and seed dispersal were a further, more scientifically sophisticated stage.[23] What motivated Thoreau, as he sought to arrange his data, was not the desire for empirical knowledge alone but also the desire for patterns of significance. In this we see the legacy of the old Emersonian correspondence project continuing to affect Thoreau's work even as he became increasingly committed to the scientific study of nature. At all stages of his life, Thoreau had an overriding penchant for conceiving of nature, as H. Daniel Peck puts it, in terms of "frameworks of cognition" that appealed to him for their aesthetic power as much as for their empirical and epistemological solidity. Peck cites Thoreau's preference for finding in seasonal data essential phenomenological designs ("What 'makes' November is not its placement in the year's chronology, but its interrelated properties") and his interest in seeing the visual elements of the Concord environment as coherent arrangements, which Peck rightly says puts Thoreau in the company of landscape aestheticians like Gilpin and John Ruskin, despite his complaints about their bookishness.[24]

This interest in landscape aesthetics can be thought of as a fifth project in itself. Limited though Thoreau's formal knowledge of fine art was, throughout his adult life he liked to see land as landscape, as scene: to relish the elements of composition, self-containment, light, color, texture. It would be instructive to tally up the number of hilltop meditations in Thoreau's Journal, many of which read like eighteenth-century topographical prospect pieces. Thoreau was quite aware of the artificiality of the pleasure he experienced on such occasions, as when he remarks (1850) on the "cheap but pleasant effect" of walking over the hills "ever and anon looking through a gap in the wood, as through the frame of a picture, to a more distant wood or hill side, painted with several more coats of air" (*PJ* 3:105). Indeed it became a kind of game with him to subject mundane objects to aesthetic transformation by using distance and perspective to defamiliarize and then to order them. Filtering his perceptions through the slow dawn following a nighttime walk (one of dozens reported in the Journal), Thoreau experiences "the sound of the [railroad] cars" as "that of a rushing wind" and hears "some far off factory bell" as a "matin bell, sweet & inspiring as if it summoned holy men & maids to worship" (*PJ* 4:65). At first glance, these might seem like classic "machine-in-the-garden" defensive reactions; but this entry registers no discomfort about the baleful effects of industrialization, only a desire to make the ordinary seem poetic.

The Thoreauvian environmental projects I have somewhat artificially isolated so far each required Thoreau to approach nature through a certain kind of schematic, classifying lens, but they also had the effect of thrusting him toward a more multidimensional, particularized immersion in the natural world. As he worked on and beyond *Walden,* therefore, what changed was not so much his commitment to ordering of the environment as the precision of his apparatus for doing so, so as to make his schemes more environmentally sensitive. In the years between the first draft of *Walden* and the last, Thoreau greatly refined his perceptions, or at least his record, of environmental stimuli: his perception of the *variety* of apple blossom odors (*PJ* 3:81), his sense of the felt texture of "the ripple marks on the sandy bottom of Flint's Pond" (3:88), his sense of the likeness between "the quivering of pigeons' wings" and "the tough fibre of the air which they rend" (3:369).

A particularly striking case of this minutely calibrated perception was Thoreau's sensitivity to micro-environments: niches within his township that assumed an integral character as he revisited and contemplated them. "Certain localities only a few rods square in the fields & on the hills," he observed in 1851, "attract me – as if they had been the scene of pleasure in another state of existence" (*PJ* 3:331). One such place was Saw Mill Brook, which he came to think of (November 1851) as "peculiar among our brooks as a mountain brook. . . . It was quite a discovery when I first came upon this brawling mountain stream in Concord woods" (*PJ* 4:161–3). Another sanctuary was Miles' Swamp ("Here is a place, at last, which no woodchopper nor farmer frequents and to which no cows stray, perfectly wild, where the bittern and the hawk are undisturbed" [*J* 4:281]). In the summer of 1853, Thoreau undertook to baptize the various micro-environments of the "great wild tract" he had he decided to call "the Easterbrooks Country" north of Concord village. He spun out a roster of fifteen places, including "the Boulder Field," "the Yellow Birch Swamp," and "the Black Birch Hill" (J 5:239). The later versions of *Walden* reflect this microscopic discovery/invention process recorded in the Journal. Here is an example of such transference (January 5, 1850):

> Discovered a small grove of beeches to day – between Walden & Flints Ponds – standing by a little run which – at length makes its way through Jacob Barker's meadow and a deep broad ditch which he has dug – & emptied it to the River – A tree which has almost disappeared from Conc woods, though once plenty
> It is worth the while to go some mile only to see a single beech tree. So fine a bole it has so perfect in all its details
> – So fair & smo[o]th its bark – as if painted with a brush – and fringed with lichens I could stand an hour and look at one.   (PJ 3:43)

This supplies language for two passages in *Walden* that mention visits to particular groves or trees. The second and more famous depicts the speaker "frequently" tramping "eight or ten miles through the deepest snow to keep an appointment with a beech-tree, or a yellow-birch, or an old acquaintance among the pines" (W 265). The former, part of the exordium to "Baker Farm," praises in a more documentary fashion the virtues of the beech, "which has so neat a bole and beautifully lichen-painted, perfect in all its details, of which, excepting scattered specimens, I know but one small grove of sizeable trees left in the township" (W 201). Both the playful extravagance of the one and the aesthetic fastidiousness of the other arise out of the program of minute scrutiny to which Thoreau was becoming increasingly committed during these years. The culmination in *Walden* is the long sandbank passage in "Spring," wherein Thoreau detects "all the operations of Nature" at work (W 308) and constructs from this a playful, grandiose Goethian allegory of life as metamorphosis.[25] This is both the height of Thoreauvian fancifulness in *Walden* and one of the most rigorously empirical synthesizing observations culled from dozens of visits to the railroad embankment at the west end of the pond. In Thoreau's comparatively de-Transcendentalized later work, the extravagance of Thoreau's metaphysical leaps gets toned down, but the Blakean desire to transfuse minute particulars with cosmic significance stayed with him lifelong.

I have not tried to make an *exhaustive* inventory of Thoreau's range of motives and analytical equipment in approaching nature. A complete survey could take an entire book – and has. Even at that, there is bound to be endless dispute over the priority of one motive or another. Enough has been said to make a couple of complicated fundamental points very clear. First, that the motives that thrust Thoreau toward nature were multiple and shifting, convergent but also at times conflicting. The growing empiricism of his natural history project, for instance, was partially at odds with his pastoral and correspondence projects but was both fueled and regulated by these more long-standing and more poetic interests. And second, the patchwork of convergent and dissonant motives just described, interacting with another dimension of his thought, which I shall get to in a moment, produced both a certain astigmatism and a wondrous acuity of environmental vision: segmentation, disproportion, blurring of focus. One of *Walden*'s more frustrating charms is that it so easily loses the reader in the landscape of the text. The presentation of the Concord environment is deliberately off-center: town cultural geography from the margin. It tells us more than we want to know about some of Thoreau's favorite spots but leaves us with a fragmentary impression of the surroundings compared to what one would find in a more conventional report of traveling in Concord, like Timothy Dwight's.[26] Though *Walden* supplies one or two sketchy panoramas of Thoreau's neighborhood, for the most part it is unclear where anything is located in relation to anything else. Where is the bean-field in relation to the pond? Where are the various ponds in relation to each other? Are the cellar holes of the "former inhabitants" scattered throughout the woods or clustered together? Where is Concord's single grove of "sizeable" beeches to be found? Just how sequestered from the public roads is Thoreau's cabin? All that the noninitiate can bring into focus, if it occurs to him or her to think about such matters, is that Thoreau lives a mile from any neighbor and a mile or so from town on the wooded shore of the pond.

Thoreau's eccentricity as a local guide reflected, in part, his continuing commitment to a subjective, aesthetic vision, in part his practice as a naturalist segmenting the landscape into discrete micro-locales, and in part a final, seventh environmental project, which might loosely be called "political." By terming it "political" (in quotation marks), I mean to suggest Thoreau's interest in provoking social reflection and change rather than participation in the political process as such. This dimension of Thoreau's sensibility is notoriously hard to pin down, for Thoreau's turn toward nature was partly an accommodation to and partly a dissent from nineteenth-century norms of thinking. Insofar as *Walden* caters to romantic armchair fantasies of returning to nature, it can be said to do nothing more than pretend to challenge the status quo. But insofar as Thoreau must be read as seriously proposing the conversion of such fantasies into an actual lifestyle, *Walden* is almost violently anticonventional. From one standpoint, Thoreau stands accused of retreating into privatism, into quietism, after an initial diatribe that appears to attack the forces of capitalism and consumerism head-on. From another standpoint, however, that "retreat" is wholly consistent with Thoreau's initial antisocial thrust: it is as if the author, at some rather early point assuming that the reader (as opposed to the general public) is with him, completes the process of conversion, to which the reader was somewhat disposed anyhow, by immersing him or her so completely in the life according to nature that the reader will be incapable of re-entering civilized life again on the same terms as before.[27] Thoreau's refusal to organize the Walden landscape tidily for his reader may be one sign of his intent to get us irretrievably lost in it.

Thoreau's politics of nature was further complicated by his deepening commitment to nature's interest against the human interest. His frequent insistence that he preferred the companionship of trees and animals was undoubtedly sincere, even if not the whole story. This quickened his search for secluded pockets of wildness that he could savor as unappreciated, unfrequented jewels of the Concord region. From here it was but a short step, in principle, to a self-conscious environmentalist politics: a defense of nature against the human invader. But this step, as we saw when discussing "The Ponds," did not come as readily to Thoreau as a late twentieth-century reader, living in the post–Rachel Carson age of environmental apocalypse, might expect of so environmentally sensitive a person. Thoreau had preservationist leanings before he wrote *Walden;* but his most forthright statements came near the end of his life and were never published. Even at that, he was nowhere near writing an extended treatise on environmental degradation like that of Vermonter polymath George Perkins Marsh, whose *Man and Nature* (1864) was Anglo-America's first major work of environmental history and the first major conservationist manifesto.[28] Thoreau would have seconded Marsh's indictment of man's degradation of nature, though he would probably have disputed that the remedy for human engineering's errors was better human engineering. But the magnum opus Thoreau was drafting at the time Marsh was at work on his was an ecological *summa,* not a book of public policy. As we see from "The Succession of Forest Trees," the one tip of the iceberg to be published during Thoreau's lifetime, this work would have chided the public more for failures of observation and knowledge than for crimes against the land.[29] The circumstances of that lecture-essay's production dramatize Thoreau's political in-betweenness: it was an expository discourse addressed nominally to farmers attending the annual county fair, or "cattle show," and aimed beyond that to announce to the scientific community the discovery of the principle of forest succession, which is Thoreau's main claim to fame as a pioneer of ecological science.[30] Thoreau speaks, as always, in a somewhat oppositional voice, as someone who knows he's considered a crank and is proud of it, as someone looking down on his audience from the height of superior wisdom about seed dispersion ("surely, men love darkness rather than light");[31] but the underlying aim of the address is less to disorder the status quo than to strengthen it, and by implication prove the author's value to society, by contributing useful new information to farmers and naturalists. Thoreau chided his audience on its ignorance of natural systems but did not advocate the radical reorganization of town property into parklands, an idea he broaches in the peroration of the unfinished "Huckleberries." The ecological and environmentalist aspects of Thoreau's thought were symbiotic, but the first matured before the second had time to.[32]

This was predictable. Thoreau felt society's threat to him more keenly than he felt humanity's threat to nature, so it was not surprising that the process of first immersing himself in and then studying nature was more absorbing to him than the cause of defending the environment against its human attackers. Indeed, one could go further than this and say that Thoreau's ability to package nature usefully (as in "Forest Trees") or in an aesthetically pleasing way (as in "Autumnal Tints") served as a more stable bridge between himself and elements of the larger society (local agriculturalists, urban and suburban readers) than did his more explicitly political discourses like "Resistance to Civil Government" or "Slavery in Massachusetts." Even in the Northeast, natural history topics were more widely palatable lyceum fare than abolitionist credos.[33]

So Thoreau was not John Muir. Yet Thoreau leads to Muir; indeed, Thoreau became one of Muir's heroes. For both, a deeply personal love and reverence for the nonhuman led in time to a fiercely protective feeling for nature that later generations have rightly seized upon as a basis for a more enlightened environmental ethic and policy. For both, aesthetics was continuous with environmentalism. Consider these extracts from the "Chesuncook" chapter of *The Maine Woods,* on which Thoreau was probably working at about the same time he was finishing *Walden.* First, from a central section: "Is it the lumberman then who is the friend and lover of the pine – stands nearest to it and understands its nature best? . . . No! no! it is the poet; he it is who makes the truest use of the pine – who does not fondle it with an axe, nor tickle it with a saw. . . ." (*MW* 121). Then, from his final glimpse of the pine forests, the most forthright preservationist statement Thoreau ever published:

> . . . not only for strength, but for beauty, the poet must, from time to time, travel the logger's path and the Indian's trail, to drink at some new and more bracing fountain of the Muses, far in the recesses of the wilderness.
>
> The kings of England formerly had their forests "to hold the king's game,"

for sport or food, sometimes destroying villages to create or extend them; and I think that they were impelled by a true instinct. Why should not we, who have renounced the king's authority, have our national preserves, where no villages need be destroyed. . . .   (MW 156)

From these passages it is easy to see why *The Maine Woods* was the book that first drew Muir to Thoreau, and why Muir marked these passages in his own copy.[34] The progression is clear: from aesthetic pleasure and spiritual commitment to a politics of preservationism. This politics is also wary: Thoreau is careful to dissociate his "program" from the social evils of land sequestration under monarchy and to guard against the kind of abuse that we now call environmental racism.[35]

As we ponder Thoreau's example across a widening historical divide, it is consoling to be able to say, as Auden did of Yeats, "You were silly like us." You were groping toward a vision you never fully achieved; your environmentalism was fitful, your biocentrism sentimental and half-baked. Fine. We mustn't succumb to mindless hero-worship. That would be unjust to the complexity that ought to increase one's interest in cultural heroes, not lessen it. But neither is it productive to "demystify" Thoreau and leave it at that. The onus of fitfulness and inconsistency lies more heavily on us. "After such knowledge, what forgiveness?" says T. S. Eliot's Gerontion, who might have been talking about environmental knowledge.[36] We know much more than Thoreau did about how humans mispossess the environment, but we do less with what we know.

In this light, Thoreau's heterogeneous and somewhat uncoordinated array of nature projects looks admirable, our quibbling shameful; and his fascinating life-work stands not only as a model but also as a resource or laboratory in which we can study what is productive as well as risky about double-edged tools: tools like pastoralism and correspondence and phenology and landscape aesthetics, which can in some contexts (even for Thoreau) become part of the apparatus for exploiting nature, but in other contexts act as transforming agents to quicken or produce an environmentalist commitment.

NOTES

1   "The wild apple," as Steven Fink observes, "is the European who, like himself or the backwoodsman, has reattached himself and adapted to the natural environment" (*Prophet in the Marketplace: Thoreau's Development as a Professional Writer* [Princeton: Princeton University Press, 1992], p. 278).

2   On Emerson's theory of correspondence, see especially Sherman Paul, *Emerson's Angle of Vision* (Cambridge: Harvard University Press, 1952). On the

Emerson–Thoreau relation, the most detailed study is Joel Porte, *Emerson and Thoreau: Transcendentalists in Conflict* (Middletown, Conn.: Wesleyan University Press, 1966), which, however, overstates the contrasts between the two. For a more balanced view see Robert D. Richardson, Jr., *Henry David Thoreau: A Life of the Mind* (Berkeley: University of California Press, 1986). The first chapter of Sherman Paul's *The Shores of America: Thoreau's Inward Exploration* (Urbana: University of Illinois Press, 1958) is very insightful on the subject of how Emerson's ideas and example initially defined the terms of Thoreau's existence, as is Robert Milder, "An 'Errand to Mankind': Thoreau's Problem of Vocation," *ESQ* 37 (1991): 91–105. A searching article on the cooling of the Emerson–Thoreau friendship is Robert Sattelmeyer, " 'When He Became My Enemy': Emerson and Thoreau, 1848–49," *New England Quarterly* 62 (1989): 187–204. For Emerson on science and technology, see Leonard Neufeldt, *The House of Emerson* (Lincoln: University of Nebraska Press, 1982), pp. 75–99; and David M. Robinson, "Fields of Investigation: Emerson and Natural History," in *American Literature and Science*, ed. Robert J. Scholnick (Lexington, Ky.: University Press of Kentucky, 1992), pp. 94–109. On Thoreau, the classic article is Nina Baym, "Thoreau's View of Science," *Journal of the History of Ideas* 26 (1965): 221–34; but see also Walter Harding, "*Walden's* Man of Science," *Virginia Quarterly Review* 57 (1981): 45–61; Robert D. Richardson, Jr., "Thoreau and Science," *American Literature and Science*, pp. 110–27; and the several essays on "Thoreau as Scientist," in *Thoreau's World and Ours*, ed. Edmund A. Schofield and Robert C. Baron (Golden, Colo.: North American Press, 1993), pp. 39–73.

3 Aldo Leopold, *A Sand County Almanac* (New York: Oxford University Press, 1949), pp. 130–3.

4 G. B. Emerson, *Report* (Boston: Dutton and Wentworth, 1846), p. 2; *Reading*, p. 173. For the history of Concord's woods, see Gordon G. Whitney and William C. Davis, "From Primitive Woods to Cultivated Woodlots: Thoreau and the Forest History of Concord, Massachusetts," *Journal of Forest History* 30 (April 1986): 70–81. During the first half of the nineteenth century, the percentage of Concord land tilled also declined steeply as dairy and meat became the town's major agrarian pursuits. On this point, see Carolyn Merchant, *Ecological Revolutions: Nature, Gender, and Science in New England* (Chapel Hill: University of North Carolina Press, 1989), p. 189. Merchant provides the best general ecological history of the larger region during Thoreau's lifetime, but for the Concord area itself, see two valuable essays by Brian Donahue: "The Forests and Fields of Concord: An Ecological History," in *Concord: The Social History of a New England Town, 1750–1850*, ed. David Hackett Fischer (Waltham, Mass.: Brandeis University, 1983), pp. 15–63; and "Henry David Thoreau and the Environment of Concord," in *Thoreau's World and Ours*, ed. Schofield and Baron, pp. 181–9.

5 Tabulations derived from Darlene A. Ogden and Clifton Keller, *"Walden": A Concordance* (New York: Garland, 1985).

6 Ralph Waldo Emerson, "Literary Ethics," *Nature, Addresses, and Lectures*, ed. Robert E. Spiller and Alfred R. Ferguson (Cambridge: Harvard University Press, 1971), p. 106.

7 Ronald Earl Clapper, "The Development of *Walden*: A Genetic Text," Ph.D. diss., University of California, Los Angeles, 1967, pp. 827, 831–2.

8 The best extended studies in print of Thoreau's natural history interests are John Hildebidle, *Thoreau: A Naturalist's Liberty* (Cambridge: Harvard University Press, 1983) and William Howarth's biography, *The Book of Concord: Thoreau's Life as a Writer* (New York: Viking, 1982). For Thoreauvian landscape aesthetics, see especially H. Daniel Peck, *Thoreau's Morning Work: Memory and Perception in "A Week on the Concord and Merrimack Rivers," the Journal, and "Walden"* (New Haven: Yale University Press, 1990). For the development of Thoreau's thinking about nature as concept and as literary image against the background of romantic tradition, see James McIntosh, *Thoreau as Romantic Naturalist: His Shifting Stance Toward Nature* (Ithaca, N.Y.: Cornell University Press, 1974). I have also been much stimulated by Sharon Cameron's *Writing Nature: Henry Thoreau's Journal* (New York: Oxford University Press, 1985), a rigorous, intensive discussion of the Journal as an attempt to work out Thoreau's sense of his relation to nature.

9 Clapper, "The Development of *Walden*," p. 158n.

10 The network of classical pastoral and epic allusions developed in *Walden* was strongly present in the first summer's Journal kept there. See Ethel Seybold, *Thoreau: The Quest and the Classics* (New Haven: Yale University Press, 1951), pp. 48–63. For the romanticist idealization of ancient Greece as (comparatively) a state of nature, see Friedrich von Schiller, *Naive and Sentimental Poetry and On the Sublime*, trans. and ed. Julius A. Elias (New York: Ungar, 1966), pp. 102–6. I simplify somewhat in joining Thoreau's romantic Hellenism with his early idealization of aboriginal culture, which, strictly speaking, was not "pastoral" but hunter-gatherer in its economy. This distinction was less important to Thoreau, however, than the common denominator – or so he took it – of a primordial closeness to nature's rhythms.

11 Stanley Cavell, *The Senses of "Walden"* (1973; rpt. San Francisco: North Point Press, 1981), pp. 51–2 and passim, is particularly sensitive on the general issue of temporal multilayering, as is Barbara Johnson, "A Hound, a Bay Horse, and a Turtle Dove: Obscurity in *Walden*," *A World of Difference* (Baltimore: Johns Hopkins University Press, 1987), pp. 49–56. Johnson concludes "that it is never possible to be sure what the rhetorical status of any given image is . . . because what Thoreau has done in moving to Walden Pond is to move *himself*, literally, into the world of his own figurative language. The literal woods, pond, and bean field still assume the same classical rhetorical guises in which they have always appeared, but they are suddenly readable in addition as the non-figurative ground of a naturalist's account of life in the woods" (pp. 55–6).

12 Leo Marx, *The Machine in the Garden: Technology and the Pastoral Ideal in America* (New York: Oxford University Press, 1964), pp. 73–144.

13 Peter Fritzell, *Nature Writing and America: Essays upon a Cultural Type* (Ames: Iowa State University Press, 1990), pp. 153–71, stresses this point strongly.

14 Thoreau's first draft, printed in J. Lyndon Shanley, *The Making of "Walden"* (Chicago: University of Chicago Press, 1957) p. 139; cf. W 88–9.

15 Cf. Shanley, p. 199, and *PJ* 2:240.

16 Already suggested in the early essay "Of Insects," this linkage is perhaps best illustrated by Edwards' *Images and Shadows of Divine Things*.

17 Merchant, *Ecological Revolutions*, p. 256. For Thoreau's interest in the Roman agriculturalists, see Richardson, *Henry David Thoreau*, pp. 248–52. For Thoreau's bean-farming in the context of Concord's agricultural history, see Robert A. Gross, "The Great Bean-Field Hoax: Agriculture and Society in Thoreau's Concord," *Virginia Quarterly Review* 60 (1984): 361–81.

18 Tamara Thornton, *Cultivating Gentlemen: The Meaning of Country Life among the Boston Elite, 1785–1860* (New Haven: Yale University Press, 1989), especially chapters 1 and 2.

19 On Thoreau's natural history interests, in addition to the work of Baym, Harding, Howarth, Hildebidle, Richardson, and Peck, several more specialized discussions are important: Philip and Kathryn Whitford, "Thoreau: Pioneer Ecologist and Conservationist," *Science Monthly* 73 (1951): 291–6; Kathryn Whitford, "Thoreau and the Woodlots of Concord," *New England Quarterly* 23 (1950): 291–305; Leo Stoller, "A Note on Thoreau's Place in Phenology," *Isis* 47 (1956): 172–81; R. S. McDowell, "The Thoreau–Reynolds Ridge, a Lost and Found Phenomenon," *Science* 172 (1971): 973; Donald G. Quick, "Thoreau as Limnologist," *Thoreau Journal Quarterly* 4, no. 2 (1972): 13–20; Ray Angelo, "Thoreau as Botanist: An Appreciation and a Critique," *Arnoldia* 45 (Summer 1985): 13–23; and parts 2 and 6 of *Thoreau's World and Ours*, ed. Schofield and Baron. This scholarship conclusively establishes three points about Thoreau's prowess and commitment as a naturalist, quite apart from the more ulterior and metaphysical/aesthetic motives that regulated his interest in the "scientific" study of nature. First, that his interest in various branches of natural history became increasingly serious and systematic during the 1850s. Second, that Thoreau's skills as an observer of phenomena were remarkably good, especially in botany. Third, that Thoreau achieved several historic firsts as a naturalist: he was the first to study a body of water systematically, the first to discover the principle of forest succession.

20 See especially Stoller (note 19) and Peck, *Thoreau's Morning Work*, pp. 47–8, 90–106, 163–5.

21 Shanley, *The Making of "Walden,"* p. 202.

22 For Haeckel's significance, see Anna Bramwell, *Ecology in the 20th Century: A History* (New Haven: Yale University Press, 1989), pp. 39–63.

23 "The Dispersion of Seeds" has been published, together with several of Thoreau's other late natural history manuscripts, in *Faith in a Seed* (Washington, D.C.: Island Press Shearwater Books, 1993).

24 Peck, *Thoreau's Morning Work*, pp. 83, 95, 81.

25 For discussions of the verbal, imagistic, and tonal intricacy of this celebrated passage, see Charles R. Anderson, *The Magic Circle of "Walden"* (New York: Holt, Rinehart, and Winston, 1969); Gordon E. Bigelow, "Thoreau's Melting Sandbank: Birth of a Symbol," *International Journal of Symbology* 2 (November 1971): 7–13; Michael West, "Scatology and Eschatology: The Heroic Dimensions of Thoreau's Wordplay," *PMLA* 80 (1974): 1043–64; Philip F. Gura, *The Wisdom of Words: Language, Theology, and Literature in the New England Renaissance* (Middletown, Conn.: Wesleyan University Press, 1981);

and Nicholas Bromell, *By the Sweat of the Brow: Literature and Labor in Antebellum America* (Chicago: University of Chicago Press, 1993), pp. 234–8.

26 See my discussion of "Lococentrism from Dwight to Thoreau," *New England Literary Culture* (Cambridge: Cambridge University Press, 1986), pp. 323–5.

27 Leo Marx thoughtfully appraises this duality from a standpoint slightly, but importantly, different from my own: "As he settles into his life at the pond . . . the problems of ordinary people recede from his consciousness," thereby "dissipating the radical social awareness" generated "at the outset. Considered as a single structure of feeling," however, "Thoreau's masterwork may be described as superbly effective in transmuting incipiently radical impulses into a celebration of what Emerson calls 'the infinitude of the private man' " ("Henry Thoreau: The Two Thoreaus," *The Pilot and the Passenger* [New York: Oxford University Press, 1988], p. 98). Marx's strict notion of what counts as "political" discourse (argument explicitly engaging social issues) leads him, however, to read the discursive shift in *Walden* simply as withdrawal from the political. A looser interpretation of what counts as political would, I think, do more justice to the aims and impact of Thoreau's "celebration" (Marx's equivocal term) of solitary fulfillment within nature, though part of that doing justice must involve recognition of its ideological multivalence.

28 Thoreau could not have been aware of Marsh's environmental researches, nor was Marsh more than idly interested in Thoreau, if that. I have found no substantive references to Thoreau in the Marsh papers at the University of Vermont. As Roderick Nash notes in *Wilderness and the American Mind,* 3rd ed. (New Haven: Yale University Press, 1982), pp. 104–5, Marsh's approach to environmental issues was by and large utilitarian, not romantic.

29 For a discussion of the relation of "Succession" (*Excursions* [Boston: Ticknor & Fields, 1863], pp. 135–60) to the ambitious unfinished project, "The Dispersion of Seeds," of which it was a part, see Howarth, *The Book of Concord,* pp. 192–9, and Robert D. Richardson, Jr.'s "Introduction" to *Faith in a Seed,* pp. 3–17. Another late, unfinished ecological manuscript, excerpted in *Faith in a Seed,* pp. 177–203, was "Wild Fruits" (cf. Howarth, pp. 199–202), from which "Huckleberries" was quarried as a (never-delivered) lecture. Thoreau's last illness cut short these projects.

30 For "Succession" as a contribution to scientific ecology, see Kathryn Whitford, "Thoreau and the Woodlots of Concord" (note 19). The most widely available discussion of Thoreau's overall contribution to modern ecological thought is Donald Worster's discussion of "Thoreau's Romantic Ecology," *Nature's Economy: The Roots of Ecology* (Garden City, N.Y.: Doubleday, 1979), pp. 57–111. Worster paints in broad brushstrokes and accords Thoreau a prominence that is truer to his retrospective canonization than to the facts of the history of ecological theory. For correctives by historians of science, see Frank Egerton, "The History of Ecology: Achievements and Opportunities, Part One," *Journal of the History of Biology* 16 (1983): 259–60; and Hunter Dupree, "Thoreau as Scientist: American Science in the 1850s," *Thoreau's World and Ours,* ed. Schofield and Baron, pp. 42–7. To be fair to Worster, he is less interested in tracking scientific discourse at this point in his study than in the rise of what has come to be called "deep ecology," a commitment to environment based on a holistic affirmation of the symbiosis of all life-forms

(cf. Worster, p. 76). Furthermore, it *is* true that Thoreau's credentials as a pioneer ecological scientist have been sustained by a number of scholars, including practicing scientists. In addition to note 19, see two bibliographical articles both entitled "Thoreau in the Current Scientific Literature" by Robin S. McDowell, *Thoreau Society Bulletin*, no. 143 (1978): 2, and no. 172 (1985): 3–4, calling attention to the frequency of Thoreau citations in the *Science Citation Index*. My check of more recent volumes of the *SCI* bears out McDowell's claim that "real" contemporary scientists take Thoreau seriously.

31   Thoreau, "The Succession of Forest Trees," *Excursions*, p. 160.

32   For Thoreau in the context of the history of environmentalism, see (for example) Worster, *Nature's Economy*; Nash, *Wilderness and the American Mind*, pp. 84–96; and Max Oehlschlaeger, *The Idea of Wilderness* (New Haven: Yale University Press, 1991), pp. 133–71. This subject has been more sketchily explored than the subject of Thoreau's scientific credentials, perhaps because environmentalism in America as an organized movement did not begin until the end of the nineteenth century.

33   For Thoreau's natural history writing as a strategy of audience and marketplace accommodation, see especially Fink, *Prophet in the Marketplace*.

34   From examination of Muir's marginalia in his personal library, Muir Collection, University of the Pacific, Stockton, California.

35   This is not to say that Thoreau was fully aware of the elements of classism and ethnocentricity in his ecological attitudes.

36   Auden, "In Memory of W. B. Yeats," *The Collected Poetry of W. H. Auden* (New York: Random House, 1945), p. 50; T. S. Eliot, "Gerontion," *The Complete Poems and Plays, 1909–1950* (New York: Harcourt, Brace, 1950), p. 22.

13

LEN GOUGEON

Thoreau and reform

Thoreau notes in *Walden* that "moral reform is the effort to throw off sleep" (*W* 90) and there can be no doubt that he himself was deeply involved in that effort throughout his lifetime. Indeed, a concern with reform of all types – personal, social, religious, and so on – permeates his published works, and a comprehensive discussion of the topic would necessarily touch upon all of them. However, this chapter will concentrate primarily on the writings contained in *Reform Papers,* which is based upon, but also adds to, an earlier collection, *A Yankee in Canada, with Anti-Slavery and Reform Papers* (1866). All my page references are to the *Reform Papers* text.

Over the years scholars have argued about the nature and extent of Thoreau's commitment to enterprises for social reform. Some have held that "his first concern was not society; it was man himself," and that because of his nearly exclusive emphasis upon self-reform he tended to ignore the larger, collective social dimension.[1] Others have concluded that "Thoreau was no social reformer," or that, more broadly, "the troubles of mankind caused him no disturbance," or that, if occasionally the press of public events would draw him forth to "deliver jeremiads on the evil of his times," he would soon "draw back and do nothing more, insisting that he had other more important affairs to attend to."[2]

On the other side, some critics have seen him as something of a curmudgeon who was entirely too concerned with the moral rectitude of his neighbors and too willing to offer criticism of them. One such critic insists that Thoreau "believed in inspiration from on high, in his own inspiration, and in the inspiration of whoever agreed with him. . . . Yet there is a suppressed premise in the argument – the premise that this particular human being, Henry David Thoreau, is right, and that anyone who disagrees with him is *ipso facto* wrong." Another observes, along somewhat similar lines, that "if there is a political inconsistency in Thoreau, it lies mainly between his republican sense of American exceptionalism and his sharp antagonism toward so much of his society, a people who, in his view, failed to exemplify the ideals by which he proved America superior to Canada, England, or France."[3]

The notion that Thoreau was only a reluctant participant in the major reform movements of his time is reinforced by his well-known distaste for professional reformers of all types. As Linck Johnson observes, "Thoreau had no more use for organized reform than for organized religion," and he "was particularly hostile to association." Regarding Brook Farm, Fruitlands, and other such utopian social enterprises of the day, Johnson quotes Thoreau's Journal comment: "As for these communities – I think I had rather keep a bachelor's hall in hell than go to board in heaven."[4]

Thoreau's initial antipathy toward most abolitionists was equally strong. Among his early biographers, Henry Seidel Canby believed that he was "never an Abolitionist, although at last, and somewhat reluctantly, he associated himself with the Abolitionist organizations." Similarly, and more recently, Michael Meyer suggests that "Thoreau sensed that there was little room for individuals among the abolitionists. They were, he says in his Journal, unable to 'tolerate a man who stands by a head above them. . . . They require a man who will train well *under* them. Consequently they have not in their employ any but small men, – trainers.' "[5] Overall, Meyer sums up Thoreau's distaste for reformers generally by quoting his pungent statement from *Walden:* "If I knew for a certainty that a man was coming to my house with the conscious design of doing me good, I should run for my life" (W 74). More often than not, in Thoreau's view, such self-proclaimed reformers were individuals who had not yet reformed themselves.

Despite these reservations and criticisms, it is clear that Thoreau did eventually become very much involved in both individual and organized efforts at reform, especially the abolition movement, and made a name for himself in that regard among friends and enemies alike. Mary Chesnut, the Southern Civil War diarist, included Thoreau with Harriet Beecher Stowe, Horace Greeley, Senator Charles Sumner, and Ralph Waldo Emerson as obnoxious New Englanders who, while "shut up in libraries, [write] books which ease their hearts of their bitterness to us."[6] Chesnut may have had in mind the fact that when James Redpath published his *Public Life of Captain John Brown*, in 1860, he dedicated it to Thoreau, Emerson, and Wendell Phillips, "Defenders of the Faithful, who, when the mob shouted, 'Madman!' said, 'Saint!' " Earlier in the same year Redpath had published Thoreau's impassioned address, "A Plea for Captain John Brown" in a volume titled *Echoes of Harper's Ferry*, which eventually sold 33,000 copies. Also, undoubtedly out of respect for one who had rendered noble service in the cause, the *National Anti-Slavery Standard*, one of the most distinguished of the abolitionist journals, published a memorial tribute to Thoreau in 1866; it observed that "the movements of opinion and reform going on around him were reflected in [his] thought and life."[7]

Some scholars note a progression in Thoreau's thinking on reform which reflects a movement from a passive to an active stance, something that would help to explain the broad range of opinion regarding his actual reform philosophy. Walter Harding, for example, insists "there is unquestionably a definite progression in Thoreau's three major statements on the anti-slavery issue, from 'Civil Disobedience,' through 'Slavery in Massachusetts,' to 'A Plea for Captain John Brown.' It is a progression of increased resistance to the state as an institution." Meyer also notes a somewhat similar progression in Thoreau's responses to the various social crises of his time, including the Civil War. Thoreau, he suggests, felt a pronounced ambivalence about his active role as social reformer because "being socially active meant for him being spiritually dormant and yet he could not turn his back on the most important moral and political issues of his time."[8]

Ambivalent or not, an overview of Thoreau's writings that deal specifically with reform in their historical contexts reveals an unmistakable movement from the passive to the active mode. What Thoreau ultimately discovered in his dealings with society is that the reform of individuals, through the development of a virtuous self-culture, can only occur in an environment where personal freedom is guaranteed.[9] Political, spiritual, and physical oppression, especially in the form of the institution of slavery, must be actively opposed.

THE SERVICE (1840)

One of Thoreau's earliest statements on the relation of the individual to society, this essay was submitted to the *Dial* in July 1840. The editor, Margaret Fuller, rejected it for publication.[10] While obviously an early and flawed literary performance, it reveals the polarities of Thoreau's early and late positions on reform. The first part describes the "brave man" as virtuous, self-assured, and removed from the realm of social turmoil. "His bravery," Thoreau notes, "deals not so much in resolute action, as healthy and assured rest; its palmy state is staying at home and compelling allegiance in all directions" (*RP* 3). This stalwart and aloof individual is clearly self-directed and his strength derives from the fact that he was "builded inward and not outward" (4). His spiritual life is personal and derives from "the divinity in man [which] is the true vestal fire of the temple" (5). For this heroic idealist, listening to this inward divinity provides outward guidance, and throughout the essay there is an emphasis upon a rugged moral self-reliance. Thus, in words that would later be echoed in "Resistance to Civil Government," Thoreau here insists that "A man's life should be a stately march to an unheard music, and when to his fellows it seems irregular and inharmonious, he will be stepping to a livelier measure, which only his nicer ear can detect" (11).[11]

Despite this emphasis upon self-culture, social aloofness, and personal independence, all indicative of Thoreau's earliest position on social reform, there is also a decidedly martial strain in the essay that is aggressively active and does not shrink from violence in the name of a cause. This latter element is strongly suggestive of Thoreau's later position on reform, which would culminate in his outspoken support for John Brown following his bloody raid on Harpers Ferry. "War," says the young Thoreau, "is but the compelling of peace. If the soldier marches to the sack of a town, he must be preceded by drum and trumpet, which shall identify his cause with the accordant universe" (9). Virtue must be assertive. "Let not our Peace be proclaimed by the rust on our swords, or our inability to draw them from their scabbards, but let her at least have so much work on her hands, as to keep those swords bright and sharp" (13). Linck Johnson has observed that Thoreau's comments here are reflective of his criticism of the peace and nonresistance movements that became more active following the establishment of the Texas Republic in 1836. However, with the outbreak of the Mexican War in 1846, Thoreau would change his mind about such violent military exploits and would eventually castigate military adventurism in the harshest terms in "Resistance to Civil Government" in 1849.[12] As we shall see, this position, too, would eventually give way to a renewed interest in the need for militant virtue in later addresses like "Slavery in Massachusetts" (1854) and "A Plea for Captain John Brown" (1859).

PARADISE (TO BE) REGAINED (1843)

Thoreau was given the opportunity to express himself explicitly on one area of reform that had generated a great deal of interest at the time, when, in the November 1843 issue of the *United States Magazine and Democratic Review*, he reviewed *The Paradise Within the Reach of All Men, Without Labor, by Powers of Nature and Machinery, An Address to All Intelligent Men* (1842) by J. A. Etzler. As the lengthy title suggests, Etzler's work presents a vision of a futuristic utopia where all humanity's physical needs are met by ingenious mechanical contrivances. As Thoreau puts it, the work "contemplates a time when man's will shall be law to the physical world, ... [and he] shall indeed be the lord of creation" (24). At the outset Thoreau contrasts such mechanistic and materialistic approaches to reform with the Transcendental approach. The difference between the two is striking: "One says he will reform himself, and then nature and circumstances will be right. . . . The other will reform nature and circumstances, and then man will be right" (20). As the review develops there is little doubt as to Thoreau's preference for the former proposition. As a Transcendentalist, he felt that Etzler had, ironically, reversed the natural equation of reform. Later, in *Walden,* Thoreau would define such transitory material gain as an "improved means toward an unimproved end" (*W* 52).

Thoreau also takes exception to Etzler's assertion that "Nothing great, for the improvement of his own condition, or that of his fellow men, can ever be affected by individual enterprise" (41). As a Transcendentalist who was totally committed to the notion of self-culture as the primary element in all social reform, Thoreau found this aspect of Etzler's thought particularly disturbing. As Sherman Paul points out, "self-reform, which was Thoreau's way of reforming the outward life, emphasized what Etzler minimized, that man himself must do the work."[13]

Lastly, Thoreau also objected to the lack of spirituality in Etzler's vision, and this lack explains the absence of inspirational dream power in the work itself. As Thoreau states, "The chief fault of this book is, that it aims to secure the greatest degree of gross comfort and pleasure merely." For Thoreau this is indeed a fatal deficiency: "if we were to reform this outward life truly and thoroughly, we should find no duty of the inner omitted" (45). In an image he would later use in *Walden,* Thoreau observes of Etzler, "His castles in the air fall to the ground, because they are not built lofty enough; they should be secured to heaven's roof" (44–5; cf., *W* 324).

REFORM AND THE REFORMERS (1844)

Thoreau was provided with yet another opportunity to comment on the reform efforts of his time in the spring of 1844, when he was invited to participate in a lecture series on reform at Amory Hall in Boston.[14] His address carries forward many of the issues he had touched upon earlier. Thoreau's general position emphasizes his belief in self-culture as the cornerstone of all social reform. As he notes, "It is not the worst reason why the reform should be a private and individual enterprise, that perchance the evil may be private also" (183). Indeed, it is Thoreau's view that precisely the failure to recognize and rectify such individual deficiencies results in the desire to reform others. If each individual reformer recognized this divine source of inspiration, it would make possible the living of a good, pure, and virtuous life, which, in turn, would contribute essentially and authentically to the reform of all society. Conversely, Thoreau believed that reform cannot be imposed upon society from without even by well-intended zealots. Ironically, for Thoreau, reform associations were a positive hindrance in this enterprise because they were just another kind of institution that, by their very nature, deprive individual members of the freedom necessary to pursue self-culture and personal reform. Because of this, throughout his presentation Thoreau is relentless in his criticism of the many deficiencies of associated reformers. Apparently he and Emerson, who also participated in the series, looked upon this as an opportunity to "reform the reformers." As Linck Johnson observes, "Where the other lecturers at Amory Hall were speaking to the already converted . . . Emerson and Thoreau sought to convert the congregation of reformers yet again, turning their attention from society's ills to the resources of the self, the only realm where true liberation might be gained."[15] Not surprisingly, Thoreau's conclusion exhorts his audience to focus more on their own interior worlds in seeking reform. In words he would later employ in *Walden,* he states, "Is not our own interior white on the chart? Inward is a direction which no traveller has taken. . . . And, O ye Reformers! if the good Gods have given ye any high ray of truth to be wrought into life, here in your own realms without let or hindrance is the application to be made" (193; cf. W 321).

HERALD OF FREEDOM (1844) AND WENDELL PHILLIPS (1845)

Despite such harsh criticism of reformers generally, Thoreau did hold some individual reformers in high regard. Nathaniel P. Rogers, editor of New Hampshire's antislavery journal, the *Herald of Freedom,* was one. Thoreau admired Rogers because his view of social reform did not focus myopically on one particular evil, but instead expressed "hearty indignation at all wrong" (49). Like Thoreau, Rogers also came to believe that all reform must be of an individual nature, and in 1844 he began to call for the dissolution of all antislavery societies because they discouraged such necessary individuality, a position that eventually caused him to be removed from the editorship of the *Herald.*[16] Thoreau apparently felt compelled to express his admiration for Rogers, and the result was his *Herald of Freedom* essay, which appeared in the *Dial* for April 1844. Noting the broadness of Rogers's views on reform, Thoreau sums up his opinion of the man and his work with the statement: "Such timely, pure, and unpremeditated expressions of public sentiment, such publicity of genuine indignation and humanity, as abound every where in this journal, are the most generous gifts which a man can make." Finally, Thoreau paid Rogers the ultimate Transcendentalist compliment: "His was not the wisdom of the head," he notes, "but of the heart" (56).[17]

Not long after the publication of his essay on Rogers, Thoreau was presented with yet another opportunity to defend a noted reformer. When Wendell Phillips, probably the most articulate antislavery orator of his day, was invited to speak before the Concord Lyceum in the spring of 1845, the choice proved to be so controversial that the conservative members of the Lyceum committee resigned in protest. Thoreau, who had vigorously supported the invitation, was one of those appointed to the committee as a replacement. He immediately voted with the new majority in favor of extending the invitation, and the next day he sent to the *Liberator* his first "letter to the editor" defending Phillips's right to speak. In his brief letter, dated March 12, 1845, Thoreau speaks approvingly of Phillips's controversial subject matter and his criticisms of the failures of both church and state. "It was the speaker's aim," he says, "to show what the state, and above all the church, had to do, and now, alas! have done, with Texas and slavery" (59). For Thoreau, Phillips was an exemplary reformer like Rogers, because his concerns were larger than the single issue at hand. He possessed that "freedom and steady wisdom, so rare in the reformer, with which he declared that he was not born to abolish slavery, but to do right" (61).

Thoreau's actions regarding Rogers and Phillips serve to indicate a subtle shift in his reformist thinking at this time. By praising Rogers in the *Dial*, and Phillips in the *Liberator*, Thoreau would be seen by many as aligning himself, at least in these specific instances, with the radical abolitionists and organized reformers whom he had so recently castigated in his Amory Hall address. The most compelling reason for this shift can undoubtedly be found in national developments.

RESISTANCE TO CIVIL GOVERNMENT (1849)

Following its successful fight for independence in 1836, Texas petitioned for admission to the Union. Its admission as a slave state would increase substantially the influence of the South in national politics and, consequently, the measure was hotly opposed by abolitionists throughout the North. Despite this opposition, however, the petition was eventually approved and on December 29, 1845, Texas entered the Union. War with Mexico, which had never accepted Texas's independence, was inevitable, and a declaration of war was made on May 11, 1846. The near certainty of an American victory raised the specter of an exponential increase in slaveholding territory and power.[18] On August 1, 1844, Emerson delivered his first major antislavery address in Concord, in part in response to a recognition that the slave power had now become aggressively active and threatened to dominate the entire Union. Thoreau undoubtedly shared this apprehension. Something more than individual self-culture would be required as a counterforce to such aggressive evil. For Thoreau, this something initially took the form of passive resistance. As a result of his refusal to pay his poll tax, as a protest against slavery and the Mexican War, Thoreau was arrested in July 1846 and spent his now-famous one night in jail. After this awakening experience he began recording a wide range of social, political, and religious commentary in the developing drafts of what would be his first book, *A Week on the Concord and Merrimack Rivers*.[19] In addition to his own recent experience with incarceration, Thoreau was undoubtedly affected three months later by the fate of a fugitive slave who had managed to reach Boston after stowing away on the sailing ship *Ottoman*. Rather than finding freedom, however, the unfortunate fellow was promptly returned to bondage because the ship's owners feared reprisals from the slave's master. The case caused a great furor among abolitionists who held a protest meeting in Boston's Faneuil Hall, where a letter from Emerson was read.[20] For many it was a sign of a growing moral malaise in the society. Mercantile concerns now clearly weighed more than morality in the scale of things, not only in South Carolina, but also Massachusetts.

These new social and moral concerns would eventually find expression in what is undoubtedly Thoreau's most famous protest essay, "Resistance to Civil Government," more popularly known as "Civil Disobedience."[21] This classic document on the individual's relation to the state has been an inspiration to many, from Mahatma Ghandi to Martin Luther King, Jr., and it has been interpreted in a remarkable number of ways.[22] At the outset of the essay, Thoreau indicates his belief in the maxim that "that government governs best which governs least." It is his opinion that, for the most part, government is "an expedient by which men would fain succeed in letting one another alone" (64). William Herr insists that, rather than suggesting a merely negative role for government in this statement, Thoreau uses "expedient" here to mean that government is to function as "a means toward an end," and that end is "to protect the individual's freedom – his right to live in the manner he chooses without interference from others."[23] It would seem clear, given his own one-night incarceration and the recent rendition of a runaway slave from the presumably free soil of Massachusetts, that the present government has failed miserably to meet its obligation to ensure the freedom of its citizens to live virtuous lives. Even the comparative sanctuary of Walden Pond offers no protection from this type of violation. Government, therefore, does indeed have a role to play and, hence, Thoreau's further comment, "I ask for, not at once no government, but *at once* a better government" (64). Such a view also defends Thoreau from the charge that his presumed opposition to government itself leads naturally to anarchy.[24]

Having thus established the obligation of the state to preserve and protect the freedom of individual citizens, Thoreau goes on to describe the obligations of the individual in society. As in his earlier reform writings, Thoreau here insists that "the only obligation which I have a right to assume, is to do at any time what I think right" (65). The perception of right is intuitive, a product of the heart rather than the head, which, in turn, is based upon the existence and efficacy of a "higher law" (81), or the divinity in man. Unfortunately, most people are not inward-looking and therefore do not exercise a proper "moral sense." As a result "the mass of men serve the State thus, not as men mainly, but as machines, with their bodies" (66). The consequence of such mindless and mechanical subservience is the present war with Mexico, the rendition of runaway slaves, and the nearly continuous expansion of the gross institution of slavery. The solution to the problem is obvious to Thoreau. A moral revolution is necessary. This revolution, however, will be wrought primarily through passive resistance and civil disobedience.[25] Reflecting his continuing commitment to independence and self-culture, Thoreau states, "It is not a man's duty . . . to devote himself to the eradication of any, even the most enormous wrong; he may still properly have other concerns to engage him; but it is his duty, at least, to wash his hands of it, and if he gives it no thought longer, not to give it practically his support" (71). This may mean that if the evil one perceives is held in place by the force of law, as in the case of slavery, then one must "break the law" (73). Such lawbreaking may take the form of nonpayment of taxes and, indeed, Thoreau specifically calls upon abolitionists to "at once effectively withdraw their support, both in person and property, from the government of Massachusetts" (74). Such an action would be based, of course, on high principle, and for Thoreau, "action from principle . . . is essentially revolutionary" (72). If these actions result, as in Thoreau's own case, in imprisonment, so be it: "Under a government which imprisons any unjustly, the true place for a just man is also a prison" (76). What if a more violent consequence were to follow? Thoreau is prepared to accept this, too. "But even suppose," he says, "blood should flow. Is there not a sort of blood shed when the conscience is wounded?" It is Thoreau's belief that through the exercise of an active conscience a person maintains a transcendent spiritual life. Any injury to the conscience, therefore, could deprive one of this spiritual life, a much greater loss indeed. "Through this wound," says Thoreau, "a man's real manhood and immortality flow out, and he bleeds to an everlasting death. I see this blood flowing now" (77).

Thoreau continually attacks materialism, reliance on property and the state as the protector of property, and institutionalism as the major deficiencies of society and the major obstacles to moral progress. "Practically speaking," says Thoreau, "the opponents to reform in Massachusetts are . . . a hundred thousand merchants and farmers here, who are more interested in commerce and agriculture than they are in humanity, and are not prepared to do justice to the slave and to Mexico, *cost what it may*" (68).

Thoreau concludes with a recognition that American government can be improved and made acceptable if the people themselves demand it. Individual moral reform, and the influence of reformed individuals, remain key. As he notes, "seen from a lower point of view, the Constitution, with all its faults, is very good; the law and the courts are very respectable; even this State and this American government are, in many respects, very admirable, and rare things, to be thankful for" (86). However, further progress can and must be made, and this "is a progress toward a true respect for the individual." As in his earlier presentations, Thoreau remains convinced of the primacy of the individual in bringing about any real improvement in society. However, here there is a clear recognition that that development is first dependent on the willingness of the state to ensure the freedom of individual citizens to pursue such reforming self-culture. Ultimately, "There will never be a really free and enlightened State," says Thoreau, "until the State comes to recognize the individual as a higher and independent power, from which all its own power and authority are derived, and treats him accordingly" (89).

SLAVERY IN MASSACHUSETTS (1854)

A great many developments would take place on the national scene before Thoreau would be drawn once again into the dusty lists of public controversy and protest. In September 1850, after lengthy and heated debate, Congress passed the Fugitive Slave Law, which mandated the return of all fugitive slaves, even those who had established residence in a free state. Northern abolitionists and others were outraged by this "filthy enactment" and promised to defy it at every opportunity. The first such incident came in February 1851, when a fugitive slave named Shadrach was arrested in Boston. Eventually he was freed by a mob and spirited off to freedom in Canada. His route took him through Concord, a well-established and popular stop on the Underground Railroad where Henry Thoreau frequently served as a "conductor."[26]

Two months later, in April, another fugitive slave, Thomas Sims, was arrested in Boston, then was returned to his master in Savannah and publicly whipped. It undoubtedly seemed to many that Southern political power was becoming more aggressive with each day that passed. Yet another blow came in January 1854, when a bill, known as the Kansas–Nebraska Act, was introduced in Congress. This act would allow these territories to organize into states, and it incorporated the principle of "popular sovereignty," which provided that each state would decide by majority vote for or against slavery. Because of this provision, the measure, in effect, repealed the Missouri Compromise of 1820, which explicitly forbade the expansion of slavery into the territories. The Kansas–Nebraska Act became law in May 1854 as abolitionists sustained yet another major defeat.

Finally, in the same month, Anthony Burns, another fugitive slave, was arrested in Boston. This time abolitionists were determined to use force to free the hapless Burns. Unfortunately, the plan went awry: one man was killed in the abortive attempt, Burns was returned to his owner, and Theodore Parker, Thomas Wentworth Higginson, Wendell Phillips, and others were indicted by a grand jury for their part in the rescue attempt. The fortunes of the abolitionist cause were now at an all-time low. Many felt it was a time for moralists in the North to speak out against these outrageous assaults on freedom and human dignity. Thoreau was one who heard the call.

Thoreau accepted an invitation to speak at a large abolitionist gathering in Framingham, Massachusetts, on July 4, 1854. In what is probably his most acerbic address, Thoreau complains at length that his fellow citizens in Massachusetts are apparently more concerned with events in Kansas than what is happening before their very eyes at home. The state of Massachusetts, in Thoreau's view, is facing a moral crisis. While in "Resistance to Civil Government" he had described the expediency of government as a means of ensuring individual freedom, it is clear now that the governor is "useless, or worse than useless, and permits the laws of the State to go unexecuted" (94). The particular laws to which Thoreau here refers are the Personal Liberty Laws, which were passed in the 1840s precisely to protect runaway slaves. In the light of the 1850 Fugitive Slave Law, however, these laws are now effectively ignored as the state enters into a pernicious partnership with the federal system. As a result, as Thoreau observes, "The whole military force of the State [of Massachusetts] is at the service of a Mr. Suttle, a slaveholder from Virginia, to enable him to catch a man whom he calls his property; but not a soldier is offered to save a citizen of Massachusetts from being kidnapped!" (94).

Thoreau himself is absolutely defiant of the Fugitive Slave Law, which he suggests trampling under foot and "Webster, its maker, with it, like the dirt-bug and its ball" (97).[27] He also attacks those materialists who put physical comfort before justice, citizens who are afraid to oppose the state even when they know they are right, and judges who are more concerned about the constitutionality of a law than its morality. Conversely, he praises those who participated in the recent "heroic attack on the Boston Court-House" as "the champions of liberty" (105). For Thoreau, there is a "higher law than the Constitution," and it is that higher law which must be followed (104).

Clearly, this presentation represents a dramatic evolution from the position developed earlier in "Resistance to Civil Government," and it is a quantum leap from Thoreau's 1844 Amory Hall address, "Reform and the Reformers." The passivist role has now been virtually cast aside in response to the violent aggression of the South. The government of Massachusetts must bring forth sufficient military force to protect its citizens, especially its black citizens, from kidnapping and abuse, even at the risk of confrontation with the federal power. Additionally, individual citizens should follow the example of Parker, Phillips, and Higginson in actively opposing the rendition of slaves, even though, in this case, blood did flow. Clearly, self-culture and private virtue are no longer adequate in dealing with what is fast becoming a national crisis.

It should also be noted that in making his fiery presentation at an abolitionist gathering, Thoreau had apparently put aside his reservations about organized reformers, and one hears in this speech none of his earlier criticism of such individuals and organizations. Also, the speech itself was widely noticed and later published, in whole or in part, in the *Liberator,* the *National Anti-Slavery Standard,* and Horace Greeley's *New York Tribune,* all publications closely associated with, or representative of, the abolitionist cause.

Finally, in the speech Thoreau indicates that even the quiet solitude of Walden Pond and other such natural retreats can no longer effectively insulate him from the evils of the time. Self-culture cannot be practiced in a society where freedom is either denied or actively threatened.[28] Passive resistance is clearly inadequate in the face of overt and violent aggression. Thoreau's conclusion is personally reflective in this regard: "I have lived for the last month . . . with the sense of having suffered a vast and indefinite loss," and what he has lost, he says, is "a country." Previously he had "foolishly thought" that he "might manage to live here, minding my private affairs, and forget it," but that is no longer possible, "since Massachusetts last deliberately sent back an innocent man, Anthony Burns, to slavery." "I dwelt before," he says, "in the illusion that my life passed somewhere *between* heaven and hell, but now I cannot persuade myself that I do not dwell *Wholly within* hell" (106).

It is now clear to Thoreau that "if we would save our lives, we must fight for them" (108). Until the final victory is assured, no peace is possible. Even a walk in the woods brings no relief, because "The remembrance of my country spoils my walk. My thoughts are murder to the State, and involuntarily go plotting against her" (108). Ironically, just ten years earlier, on another Fourth of July, Thoreau celebrated his independence from such tribulation by moving into his cabin on Walden Pond. The times had certainly changed.

LIFE WITHOUT PRINCIPLE (1854)

In December 1854 Thoreau returned to the lectern to offer the first presentation of what would be his most frequently delivered lecture, "Life Without Principle."[29] This lecture, which Thoreau describes as "a strong dose of myself" (155), is a true jeremiad, a sermon indicting the gross moral deficiency of American society, of which slavery is only the most conspicuous aspect. Thoreau's emphasis throughout the piece is on the morally debilitating effects of America's relentless materialism. An earlier title, "What Shall It Profit?," suggests both the moral and economic orientation of the piece.[30]

Thoreau begins bluntly with an indictment of the busyness of American society. "This world is a place of business," he says. "What an infinite bustle! . . . There is no sabbath. . . . It is nothing but work, work, work" (156). The overall effect of this bustle is clearly pernicious. "I think that there is nothing, not even crime," says Thoreau, "more opposed to poetry, to philosophy, ay, to life itself, than this incessant business" (156).[31] As in "Resistance to Civil Government," he observes here that "the ways by which you may get money almost without exception lead downward" (158). Thoreau himself refuses to be drawn into the contest, and suffers public criticism as a result. His fellow townsmen, he says, "look on me as an idler" (156) or "a loafer" (157). So be it. Morality will always have its cost in a corrupt society, and "A man had better starve at once than lose his innocence in the process of getting his bread" (167).

Thoreau goes on to observe here, as he does in *Walden,* that this material corruption infects the entire society. It manifests itself most conspicuously as slavery, not only chattel slavery, but slavery of most individuals to base and superficial values. Such people would rather seek gold in California than "sink a shaft down to the gold within [themselves] and work that mine" (164). Thoreau also indicts the clergy and moral leaders generally, as well as politicians, for their collective failure to condemn this mean corruption. Regarding the latter, instead of legislating to improve society, their commitment to gross material values results in their "legislating to *regulate* the breeding of slaves" (176).

Thoreau concludes with the hope that this social sickness might eventually be cured. "Why should we not meet, not always as dyspeptics, to tell our bad dreams," he asks, "but sometimes as *eu*peptics, to congratulate each other on the ever glorious morning? I do not make an exorbitant demand, surely" (179). Modest as such a demand may seem, however, conditions in American society would suffer continual degeneration in the closing years of the decade as the nation moved ever closer to civil war.

A PLEA FOR CAPTAIN JOHN BROWN (1859)

One of the most provocative events leading up to the Civil War occurred in October 1859, when John Brown, leader of a group of antislavery Kansas partisans and sometime visitor to Concord, attacked the federal arsenal at Harpers Ferry, Virginia, in a desperate effort to precipitate a general slave rebellion. The raid was a failure, and Brown was captured, tried for treason, and hanged on December 2, 1859. The event electrified the North. A few abolitionists declared Brown a martyr to the cause, while most people condemned his wild and bloody attack and the dire tensions which it created between North and South.[32]

Thoreau, who first met John Brown over the breakfast table at his mother's boarding house, came to admire the man deeply, as did Emerson. Thoreau delivered his first address on Brown at the Town Hall in Concord on October 30, 1859. This speech would mark the final and, in some ways, the most dramatic step in the evolution of Thoreau's reformist philosophy.[33] Thoreau here expresses his unqualified admiration for Brown. He recounts Brown's earlier efforts in the Kansas wars and remarks that "it was through his agency, far more than any other's, that Kansas was made free" (112). Thoreau throughout depicts Brown as a man of supreme commitment to moral values; a person who is willing to make any sacrifice for what he believes. Thus he refers to him as a "Puritan," and as "a transcendentalist above all, a man of ideas and principles, – that was what distinguished him" (115). He defends Brown against critics who fail to see the nobility of his act; who claim that " 'he threw his life away,' because he resisted the government"; who ask, "Yankee-like, 'What will he gain by it?' as if he expected to fill his pockets by this enterprise"; and who accuse him of insanity, " 'a dangerous man' " (118–19).

According to Thoreau, those who profess to be active Christians have so far failed to recognize Brown's heroic sacrifice because the contemporary Christian possesses only a sham and hollow faith: "He shows the whites of his eyes on the Sabbath, and the blacks all the rest of the week." For Thoreau, this "evil is not merely a stagnation of blood, but a stagnation of spirit" (121).[34] The newspapers, too, are afraid to do anything other than condemn Brown, because the editors "know very well on which side their bread is buttered" and they fear offending the conservative powers that be (123).

Thoreau's activist view of social reform is further reflected in his condemnation of the politician who recognizes the evil represented in the outrageous growth of slavery, yet "asserts that the only proper way by which deliverance is to be obtained is by 'the quiet diffusion of the sentiments of humanity,' without any 'outbreak'" (124). Thoreau, who was always on the side of *extra*-vagance, in one form or another, is now prepared to take his revolution to its logical conclusion, cost what it may. His new militancy is reflected here in his praise of the "Underground Railroad" and all those who have taken an active, even violent, part in the opposition to slavery. Speaking of Brown and his men, he says, employing his characteristic irony, "These alone were ready to step between the oppressor and the oppressed. Surely they were the very best men you could select to be hung. That was the greatest compliment which this country could pay them" (132). And, lest there be any doubt about where he stands on the use of force, Thoreau goes on to say of Brown: "It was his peculiar doctrine that a man has a perfect right to interfere by force with the slaveholder, in order to rescue the slave. I agree with him" (132). If this brings about bloodshed, so be it. "I speak for the slave," says Thoreau, "when I say, that I prefer the philanthropy of Captain Brown to that philanthropy which neither shoots nor liberates me.... I do not wish to kill nor to be killed, but I can foresee circumstances in which both these things would be by me unavoidable" (133). It is true that there is a great deal of undesirable violence in American society, where Sharp's rifles and revolvers are used to "fight duels ... or to hunt Indians, or shoot fugitive slaves." However, Thoreau notes, "for once the Sharp's rifles and the revolvers were employed in a righteous cause. The tools were in the hands of one who could use them" (133).

Thoreau concludes that Brown "has a spark of divinity in him" (135), and he berates again those so-called Christians who "pretend to care for Christ crucified" and are now preparing to hang one who "offered himself to be the savior of four millions of men" (136). For Thoreau, Brown has reached the point of apotheosis.[35] "I am here to plead his cause with you," he says. "Some eighteen hundred years ago Christ was crucified; this morning, perchance, Captain Brown was hung. These are the two ends of a chain which is not without its links. He is not Old Brown any longer; he is an Angel of Light" (137).

Thoreau would express public support of Brown on two more occasions. On December 2, 1859, the day of Brown's execution, Thoreau participated, with Emerson and others, in "Exercises at Town Hall, Concord," which consisted of a series of readings to memorialize the fallen hero. Thoreau translated a brief passage from the Roman poet Tacitus, and included excerpts from poems by Andrew Marvell and Sir Walter Raleigh, for his presentation, which he appropriately titled "Martyrdom of John Brown." He observes at the outset that "So universal and widely related is any transcendent moral greatness," that it is not difficult to find lines in any collection of great poetry applicable especially to the case of Captain Brown, whom he classes with "heroes and martyrs" (139).

Thoreau's final comments on John Brown were prepared for a John Brown celebration in North Elba, New York, on the Fourth of July, 1860. Brown's body had been buried in North Elba, and his widow continued to live there on the family farm. "The Last Days of John Brown" was read for Thoreau, who had not been able to make the trip. Here Thoreau indicates once again how contemporary events, and in this case John Brown himself, took him away from his previously tranquil study of nature: "I commonly attend more to nature than to man," he says, "but any affecting human event may blind our eyes to natural objects. I was so absorbed in him as to be surprised whenever I detected the routine of the natural world surviving still" (145). Thoreau goes on to note that in the six months from Brown's execution the general opinion of the man has begun to change. Many critics have heard Brown's words read and now see him as a spiritual hero who "with the Bible in his life and in his acts . . . actually carried out the golden rule" (146). In short, he was a Transcendentalist who put his creed into his deed, a man who demonstrated compellingly Thoreau's notion that action from principle is revolutionary. The newspaper editors and politicians have come around somewhat, but still have a long way to go, because "They seem to [know] nothing about living or dying for a principle" (149). Ultimately, John Brown's life will go on in the memory of his heroic actions. For Thoreau, this fact is an undeniable, personal truth. "I meet him at every turn. He is more alive than ever he was. He has earned immortality" (153).

By the spring of 1861 it was clear to many that civil war was unavoidable. Initially, Thoreau was an enthusiastic supporter of the cause and looked forward impatiently to dramatic reform. In the early spring he wrote his cousin George Thatcher, of Bangor, Maine, to suggest that the sooner the

Southern states leave the Union the better. A great moral improvement then would be possible, at least in the North. As he notes: "if the people of the North thus come to see clearly that there can be no *Union* between freemen & slave-holders, & vote & act accordingly, I shall think that we have purchased that progress cheaply by this revolution. A nation of 20 million freemen will be far more respectable & powerful, than if 10 millions of slaves & slave holders were added to them."[36]

Despite the enthusiasm of this letter, less than two weeks later, with his health failing and his death only weeks away, Thoreau strikes a more negative tone, and one that is reminiscent of his view of social reform almost twenty years earlier, in a letter to Parker Pillsbury: "I do not so much regret the present condition of things in this country . . . as I do that I ever heard of it. . . . As for my prospective reader, I hope that he *ignores* Fort Sumter, old Abe, & all that, for that is just the most fatal and indeed the only fatal weapon you can direct against evil ever."[37] Given the lengthy record of active crusading that he had compiled at this point in his life, it is clear that this could only have been a passing mood.[38] For Henry David Thoreau, the struggle for reform endured as long as life itself.

NOTES

1 *Thoreau: People, Principles, and Politics,* ed. Milton Meltzer (New York: Hill and Wang, 1963), p. xi.

2 See James Goodwin, "Thoreau and John Brown: Transcendental Politics," *ESQ* 25 (1979): 157; Mark Van Doren, *Henry David Thoreau: A Critical Study* (Boston: Houghton Mifflin, 1916), p. 44. Taylor Stoehr, in *Nay-Saying in Concord: Emerson, Alcott, and Thoreau* (Hamden, Conn.: Archon Books, 1979), implies a similar kind of reserve when he says of all three, regarding their attitude toward the social problems of their day, that they were "more likely to abstain entirely. Theirs was the most conservative attitude of all, neither approving nor rejecting but simply awaiting the outcome – as their Eastern philosophers would say it, standing back out of the way. The Universe could be trusted to unfold without taking a vote" (p. 20). See also Barry Kritzberg, "Thoreau, Slavery, and 'Resistance to Civil Government,' " *Massachusetts Review* 30 (1989): 537.

3 Vincent Buranelli, "The Case Against Thoreau," *Ethics* 67 (1957): 263; Leonard Neufeldt, "Henry David Thoreau's Political Economy," *New England Quarterly* 57 (1984): 363.

4 Linck C. Johnson, "Reforming the Reformers: Emerson, Thoreau, and the Sunday Lectures at Amory Hall, Boston," *ESQ* 37 (1991): 265 (quoting *PJ* 1:277).

5 Henry Seidel Canby, *Thoreau* (Boston: Houghton Mifflin, 1939), p. 383; Michael Meyer, "Thoreau, Abolitionists, and Reformers," in *Thoreau Among Others: Essays in Honor of Walter Harding,* ed. Rita K. Gollin and James B. Scholes (Geneseo: State University of New York, College at Geneseo, 1983), p. 23.

6 *Mary Chesnut's Civil War,* ed. C. Vann Woodward (New Haven: Yale University Press, 1981), p. 245.

7 *National Anti-Slavery Standard,* 23 June 1866, p. 4.

8 Walter Harding. *The Days of Henry Thoreau: A Biography* (New York: Alfred A. Knopf, 1965), p. 418; Meyer, "Thoreau, Abolitionists, and Reformers," pp. 25–6.

9 David Robinson, in "Margaret Fuller and the Transcendental Ethos: *Woman in the Nineteenth Century*" (*PMLA* 97 [1982]), quotes William Ellery Channing by way of providing an excellent working definition of the important Transcendental concept of "self-culture": "Like 'a plant [or] animal' the 'nobler' qualities of any individual can also grow, and if that individual 'does what he can to unfold all his powers and capacities, especially his nobler ones . . . [he] practices self-culture' " (84–5).

10 The essay was first published in 1902 (ed. F. B. Sanborn [Boston: Charles E. Goodspeed]). Page references are to *Reform Papers*.

11 The title of Thoreau's famous essay on civil disobedience has been controversial since Wendell P. Glick opted to employ "Resistance to Civil Government" (the title used in the essay's original publication) in *RP*. Glick sees the more familiar title, "Civil Disobedience," as lacking authority. I have opted to use the earlier title only because it is employed in *RP*, which is my textual source throughout. For an excellent overview of the controversy, and a persuasive argument for the authority of the title "Civil Disobedience," see Fritz Oehlschlaeger, "Another Look at the Text and Title of Thoreau's 'Civil Disobedience,' " *ESQ* 36 (1990): 239–54.

12 See Linck C. Johnson, "Contexts for Bravery: Thoreau's Revisions of 'The Service' for *A Week,*" in *Studies in the American Renaissance 1983,* ed. Joel Myerson (Charlottesville: University Press of Virginia, 1983), pp. 281–96. Johnson also observes in *Thoreau's Complex Weave: The Writing of "A Week on the Concord and Merrimack Rivers"* (Charlottesville: University Press of Virginia, 1986) that "The Service" was written at a time when Thoreau "believed in individual rather than group reform. He was therefore highly critical of organized reformers and avoided direct involvement in their activities" (p. 85). Leonard Neufeldt has observed that in "The Service" Thoreau displays a strong interest in "*vir* (manhood marked by noble strength), [and] *virtus* (manhood marked by noble sentiments and allegiances, particularly devotion to the republic), and virtue (intellectual, moral, and imaginative nobility expressing itself in those values that will best promote self-culture and a sound American culture)" ("Henry David Thoreau's Political Economy," *NEQ* 57 [1984]: 367). All these values would remain with Thoreau, but their application to specific social reform efforts would vary over the years.

13 Sherman Paul, *The Shores of America: Thoreau's Inward Exploration* (Urbana: University of Illinois Press, 1958), p. 153. See also Robin Linstromberg and James Ballowe, "Thoreau and Etzler: Alternative Views of Economic Reform," *Midcontinent American Studies Journal* 11 (1970): 20–9, for an interesting and informative discussion of the Fourierist element in Etzler's work.

14 For an excellent detailed and comprehensive discussion of this series and Thoreau's address, see Johnson, "Reforming the Reformers," pp. 235–89. Johnson points out that the essay that appears as "Reform and the Reformers" in *RP*

actually consists of extracts from the lecture and that the complete lecture has never been published.

15 Johnson, "Reforming the Reformers," p. 237.

16 For the *Herald of Freedom* controversy, see Len Gougeon, *Virtue's Hero: Emerson, Antislavery, and Reform* (Athens: University of Georgia Press, 1990), pp. 96–7.

17 For a discussion of Thoreau's view of Rogers as an ideal "man of principle," see Wendell P. Glick, "Thoreau and the 'Herald of Freedom,' " *New England Quarterly* 22 (1949): 193–204. For information on Thoreau's revisions of "Herald of Freedom," and an informative and cautionary note on Glick's editing of the essay for *RP*, see Linck C. Johnson, " 'Native to New England,' Thoreau, 'Herald of Freedom,' and *A Week*," *Studies in Bibliography* 36 (1983): 213–20.

18 For a discussion of the significance of Texas to Transcendentalists generally, see John Warren Smith, " 'The Texas Question' – Big Burr Under Transcendentalist Blanket," *Journal of the American Studies Association of Texas* 18 (1987): 24–30.

19 Johnson, *Thoreau's Complex Weave*, p. 86.

20 For a complete account of the incident, see Gougeon, *Virtue's Hero*, pp. 127–9.

21 For the controversy concerning the title of the essay, see note 11. Thoreau's first public statement on "the relation of the individual to the State" was a lecture delivered at the Concord Lyceum on January 26, 1848. The essay, "Resistance to Civil Government," was published by Elizabeth Peabody in her *Aesthetic Papers* on May 14, 1849, and was, with some changes, published as "Civil Disobedience" in *A Yankee in Canada* in 1866.

22 For background on this influence, see Walter Harding's introduction to *The Variorum Civil Disobedience* (New York: Twayne, 1967), pp. 11–28. Those interested in Thoreau's political reputation, much of which derives from that essay, should consult Michael Meyer's *Several More Lives to Live: Thoreau's Political Reputation in America* (Westport, Conn.: Greenwood, 1977).

23 "A More Perfect State: Thoreau's Concept of Civil Government," *Massachusetts Review* 16 (1975): 470–87. Wendell P. Glick, in " 'Civil Disobedience': Thoreau's Attack Upon Relativism" (*Western Humanities Review* 8 [1952–53]: 35–42), presents the essay as a deliberate repudiation of William Paley's "philosophy of expediency" in dealing with established governments. While Paley judges the expediency of rebelling against governments by calculating the relative cost of such an endeavor, Thoreau insists on doing what is right, "cost what it may," and thereby follows the dictates of a "higher law" rather than mere expediency.

24 Myron Simon argues persuasively against this charge in "Thoreau and Anarchism," *Michigan Quarterly Review* 23 (1984): 360–84.

25 William Herr argues in "Thoreau: A Civil Disobedient?" (*Ethics* 85 [1974–5]: 87–91) that, according to contemporary definitions of the term, Thoreau was not an advocate of civil disobedience, and he suggests an alternative term, "civil resistance." James Duban, in "Thoreau, Garrison, and Dymond: Unbending Firmness of the Mind" (*American Literature* 57 [1985]: 309–17), locates some of Thoreau's thoughts on "non-violent resistance to civil authority" in the

writings of Jonathan Dymond, who influenced William Lloyd Garrison in the formation of the Non-Resistance Society in 1838. If this is so, given Linck Johnson's suggestion that some of Thoreau's comments in "The Service" were intended as specific criticism of the Non-Resistance Society, then Thoreau's turnabout on the subject between 1840 and 1849 was dramatic indeed.

26 For a well-informed discussion of Concord's and Thoreau's experience with the Underground Railroad, see Gary L. Collison, "Shadrach in Concord," *Concord Saunterer*, 19, no. 2 (1988): 1–12.

27 Leonard Neufeldt, in "Emerson, Thoreau, and Daniel Webster" (*ESQ* 26 [1980]: 26–37), points out that Thoreau held a consistently negative opinion of Webster, whom he criticizes in "Resistance to Civil Government" also.

28 Barry Kritzberg, in "Thoreau, Slavery, and Resistance to Civil Government," argues that Thoreau was especially concerned about the Burns case in part because of the overwhelming force used by the state to return the fugitive. "The collaboration of his native state in perpetuating this wrong convinced Thoreau that something more vital than the rights of black men was now at stake. His own freedom – of which he was more than usually jealous – was threatened as well. A philosophic individualism, such as he practiced, was only possible in a state where moral principles had some claim over political expediency. The rendition of Burns was a denial of that transcendental belief, and ultimately, a challenge to his own freedom" (p. 548).

29 *RP*, p. 369. For an important and detailed study of the evolution of the essay and its textural history, see Bradley P. Dean, "Reconstructions of Thoreau's Early 'Life Without Principle' Lecture," in *Studies in the American Renaissance 1987*, ed. Joel Myerson (Charlottesville: University Press of Virginia, 1987), pp. 285–364.

30 For a detailed and insightful analysis of Thoreau's economic rhetoric in this piece, see Leonard Neufeldt, *The Economist: Henry Thoreau and Enterprise* (New York: Oxford University Press, 1989), pp. 79–95. Robert D. Richardson, Jr., in *Henry Thoreau: A Life of the Mind* (Berkeley: University of California Press, 1986), pp. 332–3, sees the address as an attack on the "Protestant ethic and the spirit of capitalism." For the opposite argument, which holds that Thoreau was actually compromised by the very economic system which he here condemns, see Jesse Bier, "Weberism, Franklin, and the Transcendental Style," *New England Quarterly* 43 (1970): 179–92. For a discussion of the relationship between morality and economics in the essay, see William Stull, " 'Action from Principle': Thoreau's Transcendental Economics," *English Language Notes* 22 (1984): 58–62.

31 For an excellent discussion of Thoreau's criticisms of his own home town, a place he both admired and at times disparaged, see Robert A. Gross, " 'The Most Estimable Place in All the World': A Debate on Progress in Nineteenth-Century Concord," in *Studies in the American Renaissance 1978*, ed. Joel Myerson (Charlottesville: University Press of Virginia, 1978), pp. 1–15.

32 For a discussion of Brown and his influence in Concord, see Gougeon, *Virtue's Hero*, pp. 238–49.

33 James Duban, in "Conscience and Consciousness: The Liberal Christian Context of Thoreau's Political Ethics" (*New England Quarterly* 60 [1987]: 208–22), attempts to resolve the apparent contradiction between the passivity of

"Resistance to Civil Government" and the radical, even violent, activism of "A Plea for Captain John Brown." He suggests that liberal Unitarian theology, which had a substantial influence on Thoreau, equated the terms *conscience* and *consciousness* and that humanity's "common moral nature becomes *conscience,* as the very name imports, only in so far as it is put forth into consciousness and activity" (217). The form of the activity can vary from passive resistance, to active, even violent, resistance depending upon circumstances. The important thing is to incorporate into one's actions the content of one's conscience.

34 Despite such harsh criticisms, Robert Albrecht, in "Thoreau and His Audience: 'A Plea for Captain John Brown' " (*American Literature* 32 [1961]: 393–402), argues, through rhetorical analysis of earlier Journal entries and the finished speech, that Thoreau adjusted his rhetoric to avoid offending his Concord audience and to win them over to his view of Brown.

35 Vincent Buranelli, in "The Case Against Thoreau," criticizes Thoreau extensively for "pledging his allegiance to inspiration rather than to ratiocination and factual evidence," which, he says, helps explain Thoreau's admiration for Brown. "The lunatic of Harper's Ferry possessed the two necessary qualifications [for Thoreau's admiration] – he claimed divine inspiration to violate the law in the name of righteousness, and his delusion took an antislavery turn" (262, 263). Michael Meyer, in "Thoreau's Rescue of John Brown from History" (*Studies in the American Renaissance 1980,* ed. Joel Myerson [Charlottesville: University Press of Virginia, 1980], pp. 301–16), suggests that Thoreau probably knew about John Brown's participation in the massacre at Pottawatomie, Kansas, where five unarmed proslavery men were murdered, before he delivered his eulogy, but he either discounted the reports as untrue fabrications of a hostile press, or he simply ignored the reports because "he wanted to see Brown as a 'Transcendentalist above all' " (310). Leonard Neufeldt, in "Thoreau's Political Economy," also accepts the idea that Thoreau was more interested in a "John Brown ideal" than the actual person. He sees in Brown a manifestation of Thoreau's concept of the Transcendental hero: "An individual of high 'ideas and principles' who, with 'rare common sense and directness of speech, as of action,' carried out 'the purpose of a life' " (380).

36 This letter is in the *Concord Saunterer,* 12, no. 3 (1977): 20–1.

37 Boston Public Library, April 10, 1861; quoted by permission.

38 Michael Meyer, in "Thoreau, Abolitionists, and Reformers," quotes this letter and also Thoreau's views of black emigration as a solution to the slavery problem, as indications of his "inconsistency in his attitudes toward reform" (26). For a more detailed discussion of Thoreau's views of slaves, see Meyer, "Thoreau and Black Emigration," *American Literature* 53 (1981): 380–96.

FURTHER READING

TEXTS

The Correspondence of Henry David Thoreau, ed. Walter Harding and Carl Bode.
New York: New York University Press, 1958.

The Writings of Henry D. Thoreau, ed. Walter Harding, Elizabeth Hall Witherell,
et al., 11 vols. to date. Princeton: Princeton University Press, 1971– . Published
so far are *Walden* (1971), ed. J. Lyndon Shanley; *The Maine Woods* (1972), ed.
Joseph J. Moldenhauer; *Reform Papers* (1973), ed. Wendell Glick; *Early Essays
and Miscellanies* (1975), ed. Moldenhauer and Edwin Moser; *A Week on the
Concord and Merrimack Rivers* (1980), ed. Carl Hovde, et al.; *Translations*
(1986), ed. K. P. Van Anglen; *Cape Cod* (1988), ed. Moldenhauer; and *Journal*
(1981–), ed. John C. Broderick, Robert Sattelmeyer, et al., 4 vols. to date.

Faith in a Seed: The Dispersion of Seeds and Other Late Natural History Writings,
ed. Bradley P. Dean. Washington, D.C., and Covelo, Calif.: Island Press/Shear-
water Books, 1993.

BIBLIOGRAPHIES

Borst, Raymond R. *Henry David Thoreau: A Descriptive Bibliography.* Pittsburgh:
University of Pittsburgh Press, 1982.

Harding, Walter. *A Thoreau Handbook.* New York: New York University Press,
1959.

Harding, Walter, and Michael Meyer, *A New Thoreau Handbook.* New York: New
York University Press, 1980.

Scharnhorst, Gary. *Henry David Thoreau: An Annotated Bibliography of Comment
and Criticism Before 1900.* New York: Garland, 1992.

BIOGRAPHIES

Borst, Raymond R. *A Thoreau Log: A Documentary Life of Henry David Thoreau
1817–1862.* New York: G. K. Hall, 1992.

Canby, Henry Seidel. *Thoreau.* Boston: Houghton Mifflin, 1939.

Channing, William Ellery. *Thoreau: The Poet-Naturalist.* Boston: Roberts Brothers, 1873; rev. ed., ed. F. B. Sanborn, Boston: Charles E. Goodspeed, 1902.

Harding, Walter. *The Days of Henry Thoreau.* New York: Alfred A. Knopf, 1965; enl. and corr. ed., New York: Dover, 1982; rpt. with new afterword, Princeton: Princeton University Press, 1992.

Lebeaux, Richard. *Thoreau's Seasons.* Amherst: University of Massachusetts Press, 1984.

Lebeaux, Richard. *Young Man Thoreau.* Amherst: University of Massachusetts Press, 1977.

Meltzer, Milton, and Walter Harding. *A Thoreau Profile.* New York: Thomas Y. Crowell, 1962.

Richardson, Robert D., Jr. *Henry David Thoreau: A Life of the Mind.* Berkeley: University of California Press, 1986.

Salt, H. S. *The Life of Henry David Thoreau.* London: Bentley, 1890; rev. ed., London: Walter Scott, 1896.

Sanborn, F. B. *Henry D. Thoreau.* Boston: Houghton, Mifflin, 1882.

Sanborn, F. B. *The Life of Henry David Thoreau.* Boston: Houghton, Mifflin, 1917.

Schneider, Richard J. *Henry David Thoreau.* Boston: Twayne, 1987.

CRITICISM

Adams, Stephen, and Donald Ross, Jr. *Revising Mythologies: The Composition of Thoreau's Major Works.* Charlottesville: University Press of Virginia, 1988.

Anderson, Charles R. *The Magic Circle of Walden.* New York: Holt, Rinehart, and Winston, 1968.

Bickman, Martin. *Walden: Volatile Truths.* New York: Twayne, 1992.

Boudreau, Gordon V. *The Roots of Walden and the Tree of Life.* Nashville: Vanderbilt University Press, 1990.

Bridgman, Richard. *Dark Thoreau.* Lincoln: University of Nebraska Press, 1982.

Burbick, Joan. *Thoreau's Alternative History: Changing Perspectives on Nature, Culture, and Language.* Philadelphia: University of Pennsylvania Press, 1987.

Cameron, Sharon. *Writing Nature: Henry Thoreau's "Journal."* New York: Oxford University Press, 1985.

Cavell, Stanley. *The Senses of Walden.* New York: Viking, 1972.

Christie, John Aldrich. *Thoreau as World Traveler.* New York: Columbia University Press, 1955.

Fink, Steven. *Prophet in the Marketplace: Thoreau's Development as a Professional Writer.* Princeton: Princeton University Press, 1992.

Friesen, Victor Carl. *The Spirit of the Huckleberry: Sensuousness in Henry Thoreau.* Edmonton: University of Alberta Press, 1984.

Garber, Frederick. *Thoreau's Fable of Inscribing.* Princeton: Princeton University Press, 1991.

Garber, Frederick. *Thoreau's Redemptive Imagination.* New York: New York University Press, 1977.

Golemba, Henry. *Thoreau's Wild Rhetoric.* New York: New York University Press, 1990.

Hildebidle, John. *Thoreau: A Naturalist's Liberty.* Cambridge: Harvard University Press, 1983.

Howarth, William L. *The Book of Concord: Thoreau's Life as a Writer.* New York: Viking, 1982.

Johnson, Linck C. *The Complex Weave: The Writing of "A Week on the Concord and Merrimack Rivers," with the Text of the First Draft.* Charlottesville: University Press of Virginia, 1986.

Johnson, William C., Jr. *What Thoreau Said: Walden and the Unsayable.* Moscow, Idaho: University of Idaho Press, 1991.

Krutch, Joseph Wood. *Henry David Thoreau.* New York: William Sloane, 1948.

McIntosh, James. *Thoreau as Romantic Naturalist.* Ithaca, N.Y.: Cornell University Press, 1974.

Meyer, Michael. *Several More Lives to Live: Thoreau's Political Reputation in America.* Westport, Conn.: Greenwood, 1977.

Moller, Mary Elkins. *Thoreau in the Human Community.* Amherst: University of Massachusetts Press, 1980.

Neufeldt, Leonard N. *The Economist: Henry Thoreau and Enterprise.* New York: Oxford University Press, 1989.

Paul, Sherman. *The Shores of America: Thoreau's Inward Exploration.* Urbana: University of Illinois Press, 1958.

Peck, H. Daniel. *Thoreau's Morning Work: Memory and Perception in "A Week on the Concord and Merrimack Rivers," the Journal, and "Walden."* New Haven: Yale University Press, 1990.

Porte, Joel. *Emerson and Thoreau: Transcendentalists in Conflict.* Middletown, Conn.: Wesleyan University Press, 1966.

Sattelmeyer, Robert. *Thoreau's Reading: A Study in Intellectual History, with a Bibliographical Catalog.* Princeton: Princeton University Press, 1988.

Sayre, Robert F. *Thoreau and the American Indian.* Princeton: Princeton University Press, 1977.

Seybold, Ethel. *Thoreau: The Quest and the Classics.* New Haven: Yale University Press, 1951.

Shanley, J. Lyndon. *The Making of Walden.* Chicago: University of Chicago Press, 1957.

Stoller, Leo. *After Walden: Thoreau's Changing Views on Economic Man.* Stanford, Calif.: Stanford University Press, 1957.

Taylor, J. Golden. *Neighbor Thoreau's Critical Humor.* Logan: Utah State University Press, 1958.

Wagenknecht, Edward. *Henry David Thoreau: What Manner of Man?* Amherst: University of Massachusetts Press, 1981.

COLLECTIONS

Critical Essays on Henry David Thoreau's "Walden," ed. Joel Myerson. Boston: G. K. Hall, 1988.

Emerson and Thoreau: The Contemporary Reviews, ed. Joel Myerson. New York: Cambridge University Press, 1992.

New Essays on "Walden," ed. Robert F. Sayre. New York: Cambridge University Press, 1992.

The Recognition of Henry David Thoreau, ed. Wendell Glick. Ann Arbor: University of Michigan Press, 1969.

Thoreau as Seen by His Contemporaries, ed. Walter Harding. New York: Dover, 1989.

The Thoreau Centennial, ed. Walter Harding. Albany: State University of New York Press, 1964.

Thoreau in Our Season, ed. John H. Hicks. Amherst: University of Massachusetts Press, 1966.

INDEX

Cambridge Companions to Literature

Printed in the United States
56602LVS00005B/142-150

9 780521 445948